Also by Harry Rolnick::

A Samlor Named Desire
Asian Portfolio
Chinese Gourmet
Complete Book of Coffee
Eating Out in China
Eating Out in Hong Kong
Flavors: Thailand's 100 Most Interesting Restaurants
Feng Shui
Macao: A Glimpse of Glory
The Sun-Blessed Land: Thailand's East Coast
Fodor's, Lonely Planet, Travelers' Tales, Scribner
Encyclopedia of Food and Culture, Australian Opera Guide (contrib.)
Wagner's Bagels/ The Chinese-Jewish Lexicon (in preparation)

SPICE CHRONICLES
Exotic Tales of a Hungry Traveler

Harry Rolnick

SEVEN LOCKS PRESS

Copyright © 2006 Harry Rolnick. All rights reserved.

No part of this publication may be reproduced, distributed, or transmitted in any form or by any means, including photocopying, recording, or other electronic or mechanical methods, or by any information storage and retrieval system, without prior written permission from the publisher, except for brief quotations embodied in critical reviews and certain other noncommercial uses permitted by copyright law. For permission requests, write to the publisher, addressed "Attention: Permissions Coordinator," at the address below:

Seven Locks Press
P.O. Box 25689
Santa Ana, CA 92799
(800) 354-5348

Individual sales: This book is available through most bookstores or can be ordered directly from Seven Locks Press at the address above.

Quantity Sales: Special discounts are available on quantity purchases by corporations, associations and others. For details, contact the "Special Sales Department" at the publisher's address above.

Cover and Interior Design by Kira Fulks   www.kirafulks.com

Printed in the United States of America

Library of Congress Cataloging-in-Publication Data is available from the publisher

ISBN: 1-931643-90-3

To S.D. and C.T.D

"It is difficult to argue with the belly, since the belly has no ears."
—Marcus Portius Cato (200 B.C.)

Acknowledgements

Many stories here were originally written for other publications. Appreciation to The Christian Science Monitor, Wall Street Journal, Asian Wall Street Journal, Diversion, Travel and Leisure, International Herald Tribune, Travelers' Tales Publishing San Francisco, Thai International, Cathay Pacific, Bangkok Post, South China Morning Post, and Weldon Russell Publishing Company (Australia).

CONTENTS

1. Exploring the Alimentary Canal . . . 1
    Recipe: Thai Hill Tribe Jungle Curry . . . 8
2. The Enchanted Fish of Albania . . . 11
    Recipe: Patellxhane . . . 22
3. An Ex-Zorba-tant Reprobate . . . 23
    Recipes: Selinosalata/Kotopoulo Me Damaskina . . . 31
4. Plato's "Slimposium" . . . 34
    Recipe: Cassata Gelata alla Siciliana . . . 42
5. Cannibalism I: The Religious Experience . . . 44
    Recipe: Baklava for Bedu . . . 54
6. Vatican Archives: "Suddenly Last Supper" . . . 56
    Recipe: Farouk's Bamia . . . 61
7. Mysteries of the Bottomless Pit . . . 62
    Recipe: Coffee Glazed Peaches . . . 73
8. Odes to a Large Fish: "Caviars Longa, Pita Brevis" . . . 74
    Recipe: Caviar . . . 79
9. The Veal of Turin: A Miraculous Tail . . . 80
    Recipe: Peppers Stuffed with Pasta . . . 85
10. One Octopus Sandwich, and Hold the Dodo! . . . 87
    Recipes: Octopus Vindaye/Fried Wasp Grub and Onions . . . 96
11. Federico Garcia Lorca: The Gravy of Redemption . . . 99
    Recipe: Tortilla à la Española . . . 102
12. The Great Durian Airline Disaster . . . 103
    Recipe: Terengganu Laksa . . . 113
13. In Darkest Borneo, with Andy and Mayonnaise Jar . . . 115
    Recipe: Spicy Stuffed Eggplant . . . 123

14. From Soup to Notes: Two Musical Musings . . . 125
        a.Richard Wagner: "The Ring of the Nibbling" . . . 129
        Recipe: Medieval Venison Stew . . . 129
        b.Antonio Vivaldi: "Le Quattro Gelati" . . . 131
        Recipe: Cikolata Tatlisi . . . 135
15. Crazy Rhythms in the Sultan's Kitchen . . . 137
        Recipe: The Omnipresent Satay . . . 142
16. The Spirit Is Willing, but the Flesh Is Inedible . . . 145
        Recipe: Tom Kha Thalay (Seafood Soup) . . . 151
17. The Pizza Papers . . . 153
        a. Ernest Hemingway: "The Dough Also Rises" . . . 153
        Recipe: Blasted Brownies . . . 156
        b.Shakespeare: "Hamlet: The Trattoria Scene" . . . 158
        Recipe: Pizza Rustica . . . 161
        c.The Egyptian Book of the Dead . . . 163
        Recipe: Labna . . . 165
18. Travels with My Ants . . . 166
        Recipe: Mee Grob . . . 173
19. Picnic on the Grass: A Laotian Memory . . . 175
        Recipe: Kai Yang – Laotian Grilled Chicken . . . 184
20. Snacking Away in Downtown Mandalay . . . 186
        Recipe: Ginthoke (The Ginger Mix) . . . 191
21. The Day of Swine and Hoses . . . 193
        Recipes: Ayam Rica Rica (Spicy Chicken)/Rendang Beef . . . 203
22. The Monastic Tryptych . . . 207
        a.St. Francis at Eventide . . . 208
        Recipe: Greens and Beans . . . 209
        b.Pére Gorgonzola Blesses a Lobster . . . 210
        Recipe: Lobster Salad with Grilled Vidalia Onions . . . 213
        c.Jesuits in the New World . . . 214
        Recipe: Sweet Potato Buns . . .217
23. The Ten Commandments of Chinese Restaurants . . . 218
        Recipe: Almond-Flavored "Bean Curd" . . . 226

24. The French, Hong Kong, and Chinese Banquet Roadshow . . . 227
    Recipe: Hou Tin Ngarp with Pancakes . . .244
25. "MacBeth: The Chinese Restaurant Scene" . . . 247
    Recipe: Scottish Honey Mead . . . 251
26. The Dog Who Cried "Woof"! . . . 253
    Recipes: Howl Wheat/Smaller Collar Diet Bone . . . 258
27. Graham Greene: "Our Man in Macao" . . . 260
  Recipe: Suspiros (Sighs) . . . 266
28. Yangtze Noodle's Dandy (But Enough's Enough Already!) . . . 267
    Recipe: Congee with Dried Beef . . . 275
29. Where Shepherds Yell by Night . . . 277
    Recipe: Lamb from the Forbidden City . . . 284
30. Of Cabbages and Kims:
    An Epic Romance of Korea's National Vegetable . . . 285
    Recipe: Pukpuui T'ongbaech'u Kimch'I . . . 295
31. A Buffet of Haiku . . . 297
    Recipe: Raw Japanese Eggplant Salad . . . 304
32. Rhapsody in Balut . . . 305
    Recipe: Pearl's Affritrada . . . 311
33. "Malone Dines" by Samuel Bake-It . . . 312
    Recipe: Mocha Tart . . . 319
34. Cannibalism II: The Secular Experience . . .321
    Recipe: Kokoda . . . 329
35. Miss Emily Dickinson: "The KFC Poems" . . . 330
    Recipe: Fruit Compote . . . 334
36. Babani's Pants and the Conversion of Saint Paul . . . 335
    Recipe: The Trousers of the Sheikh . . . 343
37. Mozart and "The Magic Fruit" . . . 345
    Recipe: Turkish Keshkul . . . 352
38. L'envoi: "How Do I Love Thee?". . . 354
    Recipe: Tea with Lavender . . . 355

Recipe Index . . . 356

"…we talked about eating, and she said she would like an orange, and I said how about a banana do you know what a banana is oh yes she said I used to eat them, but my younger brothers and sisters they never saw a banana and some of them cannot remember an orange, well she said sighing, the time will come yes it will of course. One does not need bread, but one does need oranges and lemons and bananas too."

—Gertrude Stein

CHAPTER ONE

Exploring the Alimentary Canal
Recipe:
Thai Hill Tribe Jungle Curry

This is not your last-night-oh-man-I-got-stoned-and-now-my-head-feels-like-a-tunnel-full-of-Indonesian-gongs-while-the-Balinese-sun-comes-up-over-my-rattan-hammock kind of book. My hammocks have been blanketed, my head is blessed with firm Thai papaya, and my Balinese sun radiates crayfish and hearts of palm sizzling on a grill. The hash is the corned-beef kind.

Actually, I've never eaten corned beef hash. The closest recipe to hash in this book is rendang, the explosive beef from Sumatra. I have nothing against ordinary food or ordinary recipes. But since my travels have taken me to exotic ports of call, I see no reason not to indulge in an exotic life with exotic fodder.

But here be a second caveat. And for this, I must paraphrase from Richard M. Nixon, who stared with slit-eyed vengeance at a spluttering stove in the Oval Office. In each hand, he held a raw egg. His feet and his dark eyebrows sputtered in apprehensive defiance as he rose to his full height of five-feet- nine-and-a-half inches. Abruptly, the President lifted his arms, threw back his hands, and hurled the eggs directly at chicken legs sizzling on a burner.

The eggs found their mark, splattered, and the yolks dripped to the floor. Nixon stared, turned around to the empty chambers, and whispered those five words that would later turn his administration into charcoal.

"I," he had whispered with the softness of a quail egg quivering in a Chinese saucer, "am not a cook!"

Whatever we may think of Mr. Nixon (e.g., demons churning his emotions like fires under a pan of sizzling Thai peppers), his confession of an inability to poach eggs, mince mushrooms, or skin Peking ducks is an inspiration to those, including the author of these tales, who would rather consume than cook.

And in that Immaculate Consumption, I have dedicated part of my travels and my life.

True, food as an international indulgence was never part of my family. Outside of pot roast and potato pancakes, our ethnic adventures were confined to "eating Chinese" on Sundays. Only later did I realize "Yonkers egg roll" has as much in common with "Chinese egg roll" as a double cheeseburger has to do with Mignon de boeuf en croûte Lutèce.

Inevitably, though, I learned bits of kitchen crafts and lore, having enjoyed the pleasures of the professional kitchen in my early years. As a merchant marine on an American super-tanker, I was assigned to the galley, indoctrinated into a Leviticus-like codex of plate-scrubbing, followed by the myths of Ancient Grease. Later, I mastered the arts of tomato-slashing, onion-mincing, and heedlessly cleaving the core from helpless lettuce heads for myriad salads.

That was my professional cooking career. Years later, I learned to cook Laotian curries so scorching that dinner guests would run screaming from my dining room. On a Sri Lankan beach, I could toss freshly-caught squid into ghee-sizzling eggs for a vibrant seafood omelet. And while editing a magazine in Budapest, my midnight snacks of tuna fish salad, vitalized by a ragout of green olives, pimentos, chopped fresh paprika, and capers, mollified by a covering of light mayonnaise, snacked while strolling along the Danube, offered a texture akin to sturgeon skin gleaming under the Caspian Sea moonlight.

Still, I cannot call myself a cook. I call myself an eater. Not gourmand or gourmet or gastronome or bon vivant. I eat. So this book is dedicated to eating, not dining. The eating, however, has possessed a singularity affiliated with my occupation as a writer/journalist in countries where few writers/journalists prefer to live. Having resided in lands devoid of great libraries, museums, or concert halls, I have enjoyed what they enjoyed: turning the fauna and flora of their countries into often-delicious delicacies.

After wandering heedlessly around the mainly Asian world, with occasional jobs (selling cod liver oil in Sarawak, teaching in Teheran, playing the accordion in Damascus, picking pomegranates in Israel), I was tossed up in Bangkok during the heady 1960s, and didn't move out for many years because it was so easy—and because I became the first English-language food writer in the city, on the venerable Bangkok Post.

The first restaurant I reviewed was Bangkok's Pizza House. I was doing a stint as proofreader on the paper when the editor decided he needed a restaurant column. With three years of hitchhiking experience behind me, I volunteered for the job. While the original column has long deteriorated into history, I remember the Pizza House owner galloping to the newspaper office on the day of his favorable review and thrusting an envelope bursting with money into my hands. When I refused his lagniappe, he seemed on the verge of tears, hurling himself into the editor's office, explaining that I didn't understand Thai gratitude. I was called in to explain myself, and after some negotiation, I agreed (a) not to take the money, but (b) to be given a twenty percent discount on each pizza I would purchase in the future.

And while I never again entered that restaurant, it was obvious that I had been selected for a potentially profitable (and peripherally prurient) profession.

I was equally fortunate that Bangkok was an eclectic bouillabaisse of nationalities, all of whom were willing to go to their favorite ethnic hash joints (frequently accompanied by other hash joints) to teach me the mysterious ways of their kitchens. Thus, over the next few years, I learned the secret of a famous Sri Lankan dessert (a good dosing of dry opium amid the cream), creating lump-free humus, and once learning the subtleties of fish-head soup.

"We shall, Harry," said a Hakka publisher, "do a comparative tasting of fish-head soup."

"Well, Khun Suk" (for that was his name), "two fish-heads are better than one."

"You may laugh," he said. "But we shall have at least eight heads of fish tonight." Which we did. And countless bottles of Mekhong, the Thai whiskey. The winning broth, I remember, was chowder in a restaurant so renowned for the dish that the window was filled with hanging fish-heads, like a maharajah's trophy room or the denouement of a Carl Hiaasen novel.

During those years in Thailand, I sampled bee-grub and live lobster, quail egg in sweet sauce, sour mud clam, and the now extinct Phuket sea-grasshopper pie. The latter dish is, alas, a sad memory. We can't always have archaic and eat it too.

At times, I had to sample European food as well. Bangkok's famed Two Vikings Danish restaurant spread out a herring buffet in which I indulged, and a Hungarian named Nick Gero had his own inn with goulash galore (much better than the gulyas soup I had to eat when later living in Hungary). This all resulted in a few locally published books of which first editions are rare treasures. (Er…no second editions were published.)

When transposed to Hong Kong, the world of Chinese food was surveyed with the same delight. I learned the intimate details of Hangzhou slippery-smooth shuen chai, and its snow-shrimp lightly fried with tea leaves, along with countless Peking duck dishes and sauces of Mongolian barbecues which, placed on the table, had the colors of a Tintoretto palette. And while I do not love porcine products, I indulged once in a three-hundred-year-old all-pork restaurant in Canton, and lapped up the almost liquid pork named after the poet Su Tung Po.

Not that other parts of Asia were ignored. The official tour leaders of North Korea tried to impress me with their poached ginseng chicken (not a good choice). Singapore outdoor restaurants would offer a world of Asian dishes over many evenings in what had to be called "Satay Night Fever." Macao women would unveil their home-cooked recipes each Wednesday in a tiny Macanese palace. And I was one of the few foreigners who actually relished Filipino balut.

Later, as editor of Budapest's first English-language weekly magazine, I had a chance to sample Hungary's sadder gourmet hangouts, where smoke, slow music, and twenty-watt light bulbs illuminating la vie triste were more memorable than the heavy dishes, heavy sauces, heavy ancient waiters, and cumbrous atmosphere. Trips to surrounding countries in Eastern Europe brought forth more disappointments.

A junket to East Africa provided the two most memorable

aromas, the extremes of evil and poetic. Evil was my trip into Addis Ababa, where the rank odor of putrefying meat filled the whole center of the city. (It all came from the Mercato, Ethiopia's central market.)

The most poetic scent was in Zanzibar. The city was crumbling, the Omani-Arabic architecture decaying…but the aroma of cloves floated over the hot tranquil Indian Ocean like Chagall's seraphim. On the island of slaves arose the incense of saints. And also the best lobster I have ever experienced.

In this infinity of foods, drinks, stories (heard and written), I have tried to harvest an Oxford English Dictionary of aromas, a Larousse Gastronomique of tastes, but most of all, a Rand McNally Atlas of memories. A few of my favorites are recounted here.

As for Mr. Nixon, he was not only "not a cook" but not much of a diner, either. When writing Eating Out in China, I had been sitting on the balcony of Beijing's Kao Ro Je Restaurant, and was told that President Nixon himself had been a private guest after his state banquet with Chairman Mao Tse-tung.

"It was not such a great occasion," said the manager of the restaurant, "so I offered him our specialty. Fresh north China scallops, Yunnan forest mushrooms, and sturgeon eggs from Mongolia, baked together with scrambled eggs. Mr. Nixon said that the seventy-five yuan price (about eight dollars) was far too much."

Instinctively, I ordered two plates of that dish. When they say in China that "the mouth is a limitless measure," they must be referring to this dish, which embraced earth, sea, and the blossoming harvest of the Elysian fields.

Finally, a note on the form of this book. The adventures begin in the Mediterranean, continue in the Middle East, go on to Asia, a sojourn in the Pacific, and finally home to America, where my adventures continue in that restaurant-buffet of New York's Greenwich Village East.

After each story is one or two recipes picked up for testing and memories. Since they almost all have their original rare ingredients, they could be made for "armchair chefs." Others might want to experiment with substitute ingredients. Most can be reproduced in any enterprising household, give or take a few shopping trips to nearby oases, jungles, or anthills.

Finally, while waiting for meals, I would doodle fantasies about food, also reproduced here under the subtitles, "Napkin musings."

Summing up, we know that the world is comprised of readers and writers, eaters and chefs. But we also know, as the great eighteenth-century poet Yuan Mei said, that "people and recipes are both comprised of unique ingredients."

A salut to us all.

Recipe:
Thai Hill Tribe Jungle Curry

Nobody has yet written "The Thai Hill Tribe Cookbook." But Mr. Sunthorn Sonakul has made a concerted effort to find the rarest dishes of Mae Hong Son, a true jungle province on the Thai-Burmese border. The tribal people here, the Thai Yai, have a real jungle curry, which he assures me is printed here for the first time. Three lists of ingredients are given: for curry, wafer, and fish paste. They are all as different from Thai restaurant curries as shishkebab is from Irish stew.

Curry

Ingredients:
>
> Any leafy vegetable (like spinach), with any other vegetable
> Shoots of pumpkin vine (available at any pumpkin farm)
> Dry salt fish
> Fresh chilies
> Tiny pea eggplants
> Fermented soya sauce (see below)

A. Curry Preparation
1. First, roast the dried fish on an open fire.
2. When roasted, pound this fish in a mortar and pestle to a coarse consistency.

3. Now, put this coarse paste into a pot of water with fresh chilies, tiny pea eggplants, and all the fresh vegetables.
4. Boil until tender, and spoon out onto rice.
5. Cover with fish sauce to taste (see below).

B. Fermented Soya Sauce
Ingredients:
Fermented soya beans
Water
Sunshine
Fire

1. Take soya bean cakes (found in any grocery) and ferment them in water for two nights until they are soft and almost rotten-smelling.
2. Finely chop the cakes.
3. Press the cakes into thin round wafers and set them in the sun until almost completely dry.
4. When ready for eating with the curry, roast the wafers over the fire until they turn dark yellow.

C. Nam Phrik Oob: Thai Yai Fish Sauce
Ingredients:
Chilies
Salt
Fresh turmeric
Shallots
Minced pork
Fermented soy sauce
Forest olives
Tomatoes

1. Pound together in a mortar and pestle chilies, salt, and fresh turmeric. Make sure it is of very fine consistency, almost a paste.
2. Cut the shallots into thin slices and fry until fragrant.

3. Mix in with the pounded chilies, salt, and turmeric.
4. Fry this until it gives off an appetizing aroma. The soya sauce wafers (see above) had been roasted and pounded to powder. This is added to minced pork and added to the mixture above.
5. Finally, add tomatoes (the Thais use coconut, which is abhorred by hill tribes) and hard olives.

A variation is called Nam Phrik Nock, which comes from the English word "knockout." Very fitting, since it is made by pounding dried chilies, salt, and roasted soya wafer, then mixing in dried fish and tomatoes that had been cooked on a grill. It is all pounded together with a little water.

Chapter Two

The Enchanted Fish of Albania
Recipe:
Patellxhane

The journey began when the only strange woman on our commonplace street in Yonkers, New York, gave this ten-year-old child a book of Albanian fairy tales. She wore unfashionable black ankle-length sack-dresses, spat, muttered and mumbled, and once handed me the Albanian book, which I read and re-read. So I began this voyage of discovery where nobody should begin, in Albania.

Granted, Shqipërisë (Albania's official name; the "u's" were deleted as a cost-cutting measure) is hardly the first goal of group travelers, its famous denizens notwithstanding. Mother Theresa was obsessed with seeing dead people. King Farouk drank and ate himself to death before she got a chance to meet him. John Belushi died long before his time.

On the other hand, looking at Albania as the European equivalent of North Korea was rewarding enough. Albania is actually only a few miles away from nowhere else. But in the late 1990s, while editing a magazine in Budapest, I was relatively close, so on a whim, I bought a plane ticket, flew into Tirana, and had a week filled more with revelations than repasts.

Tirana was dull, muddy, soggy, rainy. The food was fatty, the cigarette smoke was carcinogenic, the zoo-cages were empty, the men walked around until way past midnight, simply because walking around was the major amusement, the Albanian equivalent of "South Park" and La Scala. Oh, I did go to the potshelled concert hall: The forty-five-piece orchestra outnumbered the audience by two to one.

Although I was anxious to leave Tirana, an official at the Ministry of Foreign Affairs had explained that there were certain rules about traveling in Albania.

"Do not go to the south of the country," he said. "We still have shootings there. The north is usually safe. Until sundown. Then you must stay in your room. Because of the shootings."

That was the diplomatic way of saying: "What possible reason would anybody want to come to this place for?"

Two examples indicate the traveler's opportunities and obstacles.

I had been staying at an inn in what the Albanians affectionately call the Desolate Mountains. Since this is where smugglers take their arms to Kosovo, and a few of the more rambunctious gents had indeed shot up the inn the night before I arrived, neither water nor warmth was available.

Still, that evening I had been entertained around the sparse and smoky lobby by traveling minstrels who sang a traditional fourteenth-century Homeric epic about killing infidel Serbians. They strummed their lute-like bouzoukia and whistled, chanted, and shouted with traditional excitement. Outside the inn were caves, where shepherds and their flocks wandered about, oblivious to the bellows of executions and slaughter. Like this part of Albania, oblivious to all history.

A few nights later, sheltered in the Hotel Korçé, a virtual crater in the town of Korçé near the Macedonian border, machinegun fire continued for hours. It reminded me of a Saturday night in Houston. But at 6:00 A.M., just as I was nodding off, there were loud knocks at my lockless door and a trio of Albanian teenagers pushed in.

I thought I was a goner (as Gabby Hayes would have said), but the gallants brusquely laid their shotguns by the door. Then they started crying. The three, whom I had seen the previous night manning the wooden boards that served as a reception desk, had important news for me:

"You ... you Frank," they said. "You Sinatra, music man been take to hospital. He sick, okay, dead."

I thanked them for their kindness and they picked up their flintlock rifles and rushed downstairs, presumably to tell other Albanians the big news.

Such unexpected courtesies were a daily occurrence, and I thanked Albanians ceaselessly during my whole week in the country. For this tiny Balkan state, with its burned-out buildings, endless miles of cannibalized cars and trucks, with an unemployment rate, according to one British expert, of "ninety-nine percent give or take a few points" is, within its misery, almost gratuitously amiable.

People are genuinely affable, sometimes embarrassingly so. Sitting at bar-cafés in five different towns for a refreshing anise-tasting Albanian arak, I was unable to pay for a single glass. Strangers watching me from the side would shout "No!" when I was ready to pay the bill. If customers hadn't noted the foreigner, then the manager would adamantly refuse payment. In Berat, way up in the mountaintop fortress, an old man and a young girl spent hours looking for keys to different old churches, explaining tutti tutti in Italian. They were bewildered that I would offer them any lek for their kindness.

Food is adequate throughout the country. Lamb and biftek were tough but tasty, fresh salata and yogurt were light, made with Mediterranean delicacy. Some day, Albania probably hopes to join civilization by bringing in fast-food franchises, but for the moment one survives on local produce and ingredients smuggled in from Italy or Greece.

But I didn't go to Albania in search of fun. I went to search for a fish.

Perhaps I was the only person to go to Albania for a fish. It was a selfish and a stupid choice, since most restaurants had been burned down during the 1996 riots, which turned the entire country into one big Jonestown. But hope springs eternal, and since childhood, I knew that some day I would find this famous legendary fish, the kóran.

Albania is fifty percent Muslim (its official atheistic policies during Communism were largely ignored), but this kóran was not the holy book of Islam. It was a fish that swam through my mind ever since reading about it as an eleven-year-old child. For reasons unknown, I had been given a gift, a book called Wonder Tales of Albania. These were children's stories about minstrels, magic cows, a boy who sells his name, and other outrageous tales for any age from this most remote land.

One of these fantasies dealt with somebody selling his palace, treasures, and gold, all for a taste of the "wondrous delicious fish of the world," the kóran. I had completely forgotten about this fish, but the first night in Tirana I dreamed about that book (the mind being a greater treasure house than the British Museum), and asked at the hotel desk about its existence.

"Of course," said a charming lady. "But we do not have the kóran in Tirana. For that, you must go to Ohrid Lake, which is a long distance from here. Far into the mountains."

Her eyes looked beyond the hotel, past the street into a fairyland of her own imagining. And I knew that the kóran was the Holy Grail (or the holy mackerel) of my journey.

Now, getting to the Albanian main bus terminal is not the same as getting to Grand Central Station. You begin early in the morning, jumping over bodies that are asleep or dead, then gingerly stepping through the potholes on the main street until reaching a river of mud. This leads for a mile to a field of overturned tanks, burned-out trucks, and rusty cattle cars. This is the main bus terminal.

Should you wish to leave Tirana, you climb aboard the nearest shuddering, heaving, giant, rusted tin can that has the word "Bus" scrawled somewhere on its thorax. You recognize its imminent departure since gray cigarette smoke hovers like a topcoat over the waiting passengers and black smoke pours out of a hole in the bottom of the bus. Within an hour, the bus makes noises like the death throes of an Edgar Allan Poe victim, wheezes up, and chugs over the grass to the rocks that serve as the municipal road. It stops. You want to hold your breath hoping that it will start again, but that would only increase the risk of instant lung cancer.

Relief. The bus coughs again, then chugs down a highway with potholes like caves, past endless cannibalized, scorched vehicles on the roadside. The passengers have given up the faintest hope of actually arriving anywhere (an obvious metaphor for the entire country), but hopefully the driver has some idea where he is going. When we reach the destination, or the gasoline has given out, we debark and pray that the guns will be silent.

It was not easy going to Ohrid Lake. The lake itself separates Albania from Macedonia, and the journey entails two bus changes and the long struggle of those ancient engines over the ancient mountains. Even worse was that at the top of the mountains, it started to snow. Yet, the bus chugged on, stalling or stopping completely every three minutes or so. We somehow rolled down the mountains to the lakeside, turning right at the Macedonian customs post. I disembarked (a polite Albanian euphemism meaning, "jumping off") in the tiny lakeside town that was famed for its kóran.

Not that I could see Ohrid. Through the dirty-white clouds, the snow and the slush, I could barely make out the silhouettes of black buildings. The town was now virtually a lake in itself, the lack of anything even remotely like a sewer creating a dim demographic entity of water and mud. The snow became rain, and with no eaves or marquees under which to take shelter, the fatalistic Albanians trudged on. Looking neither up nor down, they simply slogged, plodded, staring ahead into the mist.

Speaking no Shqipe, the language of the officially named Republika e Shqipërisë (a destitute country, I reasoned, that was unable to afford the "u" after the "q"), I could usually get along with English and Italian. But here, only Shqipe and Macedonian were spoken. But the rain had become a torrent, so I stepped into a sweets shop where the owner spoke a torrent of his own English. We chatted for a few moments, and then I asked about finding the legendary kóran.

"Ah, the kóran," he mused. And I took it for granted that the kóran was a myth of the past. That would be just my luck. But he continued: "You are lucky. Today is Sunday," he said. "They will serve kóran today only. You walk down the street...."

"Street?" I looked at the lake outside his door.

"Please walk through left-side puddle and walk then through puddle toward lake. Before you reach shore, you find restaurant with kóran fish."

I bought some crumbly chocolate from the old man, thanked him, pushed aside the soggy beaded curtain that served as a door, and sloshed my way down to the lake. A tiny sign on a wooden building read "Peshk Restorant": Fish Restaurant. And even before I had time to knock, the tiny door was opened. But not for me. It was for a boy in a black jacket sweeping water from the floor of the establishment out to the street.

Could this, I thought, be the restaurant of my childhood reveries? I spoke to him with the eloquence of Horatio:

"Kóran?" I shouted. "Fishy? Fishes?? Pesci??? Yum-yum-yum????"

The boy ran back to the room screaming. In a second his father, foot-long moustache quivering, came out with an angry look. When he saw me standing in the puddle, bedraggled, hungry, and possibly with money, he smiled and bade me enter.

Inside was a wooden room, linoleum floor with a fireplace, three tables, one occupied by a young pretty woman and, obviously, her parents. Again luck had triumphed, for the girl spoke English. She looked at me at first with suspicion, then, as if in the recitative of a minor eighteenth-century Italian opera, she offered information.

"I," she proclaimed, "am Pano. I am Pano Sylvia. Who are you? And what do you want?"

If this was the beginning of a Mozart singspiel, I was ready to oblige. Almost chanting out the refrain.

"I am Rolnick. Rolnick Harry," I said hopelessly, soggily trying to imitate Placido Domingo in a recitative. "And I am hungry. And I want a fish. A plate of kóran fish."

There was a moment's silence, during which I imagined four staccato chords played on a jewel-embossed harpsichord. It was Pano Sylvia's turn. And she didn't flinch.

"How?" she asked. "How you want your kóran fish? You want plain? You want with sauce?"

The offer caught me off-guard. She had come to the point so quickly that I shrank back, a virgin ready to make love without the foreplay. An explanation of choices, and a question. No emotion. No feeling. I decided to supply the feeling.

"Please, Sylvia. This is too soon. Please be kind. This is my first time."

Sylvia, part holy inquisitor, part dominatrix, was not to be placated.

"So," she said. "How you know about kóran fish? Where you learn? How much knowledge you got?"

Now, I felt, was time for the Aria of the Grand Flounder. I was to provide both music and words, and the lyric background had to be worthy of the sacred Wolfgang Amadeus himself. In my mind, I dredged up the original joy I had experienced as a child in bed, reading from my Wonder Tales of Albania. Then, like an Actors Studio neophyte, I attempted to duplicate the flowery language devoured in those more innocent days.

"Many years ago," I said, warming to the subject, "the repute of the kóran fish reached my father's dwelling place in Yonkers, a poor but humble hamlet near the mighty metropolis of New York."

"What you mean, Hamlet?" asked Sylvia. "I talk fish, you talk Shakespeare?"

I explained the difference, and then, bowing to my listeners, the rainwater softly dripping to the floor, like pizzicato notes from the cellos, I proceeded.

"Since that time, I have traveled across desert, mountain, and sea to find this remarkable denizen of the deep. That has been my pilgrimage, my hallowed journey, my culinary hajj.

"For in my land of Yonkers, we had marveled about the meat of the kóran fish, soft as the footstep of an ant, pure as a child's dream. We had longed to behold the colors of the kóran, as white as the Himalayan snows, as pink as orchids in the Borneo jungles. We longed for its scent, wafting over my Yonkers bedroom reverie like the incensed oases of Araby..."

Finishing with the eloquence of a Yeats, the elocution of a Gielgud, the lyricism of a medieval mastersinger, I gazed at Sylvia, who shook her head.

"What? You crazy? Why you speak that way about a fish? Sit down. I order you fish."

Sylvia, like most Albanians, had no frills. She got straight to the point. My epic suddenly halted. I told her that I would eat the kóran any way the chef wanted to prepare it. Sylvia called over the publican, who had been listening, and gave the order. He strolled back to his kitchen and pulled a bucket from under the sink. From the bucket he pulled two bottles of Albanian wine for me to enjoy while waiting.

Should you be interested, the Riesling was pallid, the merlot was tangy, and the bread that came with it was black and rough as a cassoulet terrine. Into what soggy Elysium had I wandered?
Sylvia and I talked for a while. She was an engineer, in charge of an Italian-financed shoe factory that was not making shoes anymore. It didn't make anything anymore. But she had enough money to take her parents to lunch in the town each Sunday. Her history was recounted in twenty minutes, after which two platters of whole fish were placed on the table. Both had a masculine (okay, tough) texture, with tastes to match.

The kóran, as I later discovered, is something like the sturgeon, being a primitive beast, now confined to Lake Ohrid, living in its deepest channels. The fish blends two tastes, one a kind of woody/salty trout flavor. But this was enveloped by a smoother salmon delicacy. The two tastes, like a prince and a pauper, played in perfect harmony in my mouth, marred only faintly by the crunchy profusion of bones on one of the platters.

The fish had been prepared in two styles. One was plain with butter sauce, filleted, quite moist. The other had a pungent sauce of tomato and garlic punctuated by crumbled pistachio nuts (and a few shells). Under other circumstances, with stiff napery, pristine wine glasses and gravity-laden Wedgwood crockery, it would do well in Le Cirque or La Côte Basque. Here, it was a dish of scrumptious fish consumed in the center of an East European boggy swamp.

Equally unexpected was that Sylvia, despite the evaporation of her job, wouldn't allow me to pay. Like those drinkers in the dark Tirana bars, she shook her hand at me and took the bills from her beaded pocketbook. There could be no argument.

But Sylvia was ready to show me another surprise. Although the shops of Ohrid were closed, she, her mother and father and I walked through the slush and snow back to the main street, then to the metal-barred windows of a near-empty jewelry shop. She took her hands from her pockets, removed her mittens, and pointed through a window to a heap of tiny, glistening white balls.

Two words she uttered. And in this, the poorest country of Europe, I thought I had heard wrong.

"Like…pearls," Sylvia said. "Albania pearls," she repeated.

Then Sylvia laughed – and I would have eloped with her that instant if only to hear that throaty, full-bodied laugh.

"But they are not pearls," she laughed. "No, they are from the fish you were eating."

While her parents took shelter in a doorway, Sylvia and I stood in the rain and she explained about the scales of the kóran fish. How for six hundred years (at least) two families had the monopoly on the scales of the fish. They took the scales – probably the very bones I had carefully placed on my plate – and they had crushed them and made a paste of them. That paste was made into pearl shapes, which were somehow cooked until they indeed became pearls.

Revelations, I guess, are where you find them. In people, in love, in music...and in a fish from a remote lake.

Sylvia had a Fiat, and she and her family drove me from the rain up to the hills, through the snowstorm to a hotel in a nearby town where they lived. Snowed in, I stayed there for two days of utter boredom, relieved only by the memory of the most holy kóran. I never saw Sylvia again, and hope that she is fine. And while not religious, I still pray for the people of those god-forgotten, human-forsaken lands.

Postscript: My final day in Tirana was underwater, the torrent of rain creating a sea of mud. So I took refuge in the public library, one of the few buildings that hadn't been burned into a junk-heap from the riots of the previous year. In the library, I met the chief librarian, who descended to the archives and retrieved for me–yes, yes! – my childhood dream, the Wonder Tales of Albania. The Beautiful-of-the-Earth, the magical cows, and yes, again, the miraculous kóran.

Miracles, like prehistoric subterranean fish, do exist...

Recipe:
Patellxhane

No recipe for kóran fish is available, but one would suppose that any salmon-like fish cooked with a marinade including pistachio meat, minced onions, and parsley would do the trick. The following is an Albanian dip (the word patellxhane means eggplant) used extensively. It is provided by the Albanian American Foundation.

> 3 large eggplants, unpeeled
> 2-3 peppers (bell peppers for mild, paprika for hot)
> Parsley
> Pepper
> Garlic
> Salt

1. Wrap the eggplants in tinfoil and cook them in the oven over low heat for about 45 minutes. Drain for as long as possible.

2. Chop up peppers, garlic; mix with the eggplant mixture, adding parsley.

3. Now serve as a dip, preferably with Turkish-style pita bread.

CHAPTER THREE

AN EX-ZORBA-TANT REPROBATE
Recipes:
Selinosalata/Kotopoulo Me Damaskina

T he journey from Albania to Greece is easy enough if you are a murderer, smuggler, if you carry grenades and guns and take the kind of boat that makes Haitian refugee craft look like the QE II. That, I was not ready to do. Fortunately, I had been to the Aegean islands several times before. As they are too beautiful for words, I would wander the hills, visit the occasional church, and shamelessly sit on the beaches doing nothing.

But on my first visit, Homer's "wine-dark sea" was transformed into one "wine-sloshed writer."

First, a confessional footnote: My feet are for walking, not dancing. I never dance. And unlike the old song, they can't make me. Never could, would, did dance. Nothing, in fact, could make me dance except Greece. And a Greek night. Greece was the exception.

The exception to my decidedly un-Fred-and-Gingerishness wasn't on the dance floor. It was over the port of Souvala on the island of Ægina, where each joyful, awkward, sometimes hysterical endless step was begot from a joyful, hysterical endless Olympian dinner of food and wine. It was a half-mooned May night, and a night when, when, like Alan Bates in the breathtaking final scene of Zorba the Greek on a deserted beach in Crete, I danced until the sun rose over the Saronic Gulf.

This mini-epic started more than three decades before, at another revel, a May Day nocturnal street fair merry-making in Yugoslavia, with a morning after when I had apparently lost my travelers' checks. Later, I would find them in the bottom of my bottomless rucksack. But on May 2, when Belgrade streets were filled with sleeping bodies and all was hushed, I was bereft and penniless. Worse, my own consular officials had been of no help at all. The marine guard had motioned me off the diplomatic premises, refusing to allow me to contact a consular official on this holiday. I was obviously in financial and psychological pain.

By chance, wandering through the deserted streets of Belgrade, I passed the Greek chancery, where the door was unaccountably open. I entered, saw a middle-aged woman behind a reception desk, and inquired, doubtfully, whether her country would allow me entrance. With doleful countenance, I explained that for the moment I had not a single drachma to my name. In Athens, I told her, my money would probably be refunded by American Express.

The Greek consular official looked straight at this Chaucerian tale of woe, and her eyes turned black with annoyance. At first, I thought she was annoyed by my story. But it was soon clear that she believed it. What she couldn't believe was the reaction of my consulate, and she let me know her annoyance in no uncertain terms. "What?" this Greek official asked incredulously. "Your own embassy won't help you? You are a young fool. You are nothing except foolish. If I were you," she scornfully lectured me, "I would go in there and demand that your ambassador – not your lowly consul – loan you the money."

And then, with the wrath of a Medea, she threatened: "If your ambassador doesn't give you the money, then I will give you the money. And I will come to that embassy of yours myself and tell them what I think of them."

Aeschylus couldn't have put it more dramatically. Then, with the warmth of a Theocritus ode, she lowered her voice: "As for Greece, you will be given entrance. We do not turn people away."

Yes, this was a more idyllic time, but she (whose name I forget, but who gave this bedraggled stranger courage, guts, welcome, and joy in a few sentences) became the spirit of Greece. I obeyed her Delphic oracular instructions, got a pittance of help, found my travelers' checks, and bought a third-class ticket to the Greek border. The train was so slow that it made the epic of Odysseus seem like a walk in the woods. But the spirit of this kind lady was that of a compassionate Minerva.

Starting to hitchhike south, I realized that the glory that was Greece is embodied every day for the young traveler. Town agoras would produce, for a few cents, bagsful of sour olives, some packets of crumbly goat's cheese, perhaps a flaky spanakopitta spinach pie and a few loaves of black bread, and I would tramp through the roads full and happy. And yes, Greece still had Greek shepherds, and women with sparkling skirts. Some huts could have been built at the time of Homer; some distant mountains could have been built for the gods. Grape leaves might be so tough they would lodge in the teeth, but the olive-oiled splendors of domades were delicious. I could finally even accept eggplant, a vegetable once scorned.

Camping down on the plains of Sparta, I could open a can of gigantes and spoon out the butter beans and eat them raw. Sitting outside in Rhodes's central square one night, I could feast like Agamemnon on roast lamb and baby okra, and drink ouzo. The next days, I could hike over the hills to Lindos, carrying only some Kaseri cheese and bread and wondering why Saint Paul – who wrote one of his endless letters from that dazzling port – could be such a dark-browed grouch in such a sunny country.

But my main memory was of dancing on the island of Ægina. Ægina was chosen because it was the closest island to Piraeus port. Hydra was too trendy, Poros too far away. Ægina was close, few visitors went there in late spring, Kazantzakis apparently loved the place, and I would feel ... well, away from it all.

The island itself had a feeling of timelessness. I took a little room, went on a bus, saw a few remnants of temples, and walked over to some old ruins about five kilometers from the main town. While walking back around 4:00 P.M., an old pickup truck came rumbling down, stopped, and picked me up. I sat between Nicholas and his wife. Nicholas had some relatives in North Carolina, and was initially a little offended that I didn't know them. Still, in Greek fashion, he told me that I would still be welcome that night for "a few drinks," which he would be enjoying with his friends.

"I will put down my wife," he said, "and walking the baby. And feeding the dog. And then we will go to bar and enjoy Retsina. At eight-thirty on dot."

The traditional naif at that time, I had never encountered the word "Retsina" before, but was ready for yet another wine. At "eight-thirty on dot," I was prepared, but no Nicholas. Nor at 9:00 or 10:00. So, I went out to the port, joined a group of sponge fishermen eating at a table, but without much Greek and them with no English, we were at a loss.

At 10:30 "on dot," Nicholas showed up at the table. No apologies for tardiness, just joy in seeing me, greetings to the fisherfolk, and dragging me out to another table, where I was baptized into the ritual of Retsina.

Certain comestibles stand out in the memory for their very ghastliness upon first consumption. Thailand's durian, of course. And Chinese sea cucumber. And Japanese natto. And the Retsina of Ægina. Not, I must add, the Retsina so nicely bottled and exported to trendy Upper East Side New Yorkers who love the pleasant taste with a soupçon of pine fragrance.

No, I speak of the resin peeled off of pine trees, smashed into alcohol, left to vegetate for a few weeks like an errant child standing in a corner, and finally served in great grayish glasses to men of the sea and farmers who hoe the rocks of Sparta.

I speak of the Retsina served on Ægina, poured from bottles with no labels, not poured smoothly but in chunky amber-brown globules, one of which was served to me.

No liquor this, but a torture of fermented tar, the alcohol biting the tongue, the resin sticking to the upper mouth, the odorous brew, rather than being swallowed, clinging to the throat like a leech from the Malaysian jungles or the talons of a West Australian koala bear, before sliding down into the screaming gullet.

"Well?" asked Nicholas, my host, waiting for my reaction.

"Delicious," I said, "absolutely scrumptious." And then I gagged – not for telling a lie, but because the Retsina had made a sudden jump back into the throat as if to escape, an alcoholic incubus ready for a night out.

I swallowed again, and again expressed my appreciation. But no further words were needed. Already, another unlabelled carafe was pulled from the shelf, a large dusty rag was slapped against the glass, and the dust flew out like angry sprites. Then the cork was pulled away.

"Another," said Nicholas. It was a command. The brownish liquor glared at me. Nicholas glared at me.

"To your health," he said.

"Thanks for the blessing," I said. And down went the Retsina. With the second gulp, my inhibitions gave out, and I asked the inevitable.

"Who the hell...?"

Nicholas gazed at me and poured out another glass. He was waiting for the sentence to be finished, but I had forgotten the question. Then it came.

"Who on earth invented this thing?"

Nicholas translated for the others now gathering around and filling up from the carafe. Nicholas had no answer, but one fisherman rattled away in some ancient Attic language, and it came out that Retsina was (in Nicholas's words) "a mistake. An accident."

The explanation was a good one. The original wine from the ancient Greek vines, which still cover southern Italy, was simply a grape wine. But the barrels were sealed with pine tar; the pine tar seeped into the wine, and the Greeks decided that they liked it.

"As you like it," said Nicholas with Shakespearean eloquence. At this point, I couldn't help but like it. Especially since a plate of goodies came with the next carafe. These were Greek mezdes, probably a Levant transplant like Lebanese mezze. The cheese wasn't feta but something called galotira. Like the Retsina, it tasted awful: sour, mushy. I had more. The cucumbers were bitten down, the octopus tentacles dangled off the plate.

And with the fourth carafe of Retsina, I found my own legs pushing off the floor, and my own body lying on the floor. Others in the taverna laughed at my discomfort (I was laughing, too, of course), and my legs and body, disembodied, were put together, and I faced the Retsina again. Along with a different kind of cheese and some kind of sweets. Nuts and honey and a paper-thin pastry, which was pushed into my mouth.

Vaguely, I heard an unknown word—now I know it as Rembetika – and next thing, I was hoisted upon various shoulders, thrown into the back of a truck, and landed (God knows how many minutes later) in an old barn where music was playing. The barn was at another port, with no lights. Just a few candles burning.

And the music? Rembetika was like Retsina: sour, loud, unpalatable, jumpy in rhythm. Obviously, they were wailing about something. Days later, I realized that Rembetika was the 1960's version of gangsta rap, criminal songs about cocaine and heroin. That night, though, I felt anything but Greek. The fierce drink, the grating music, the whining words became a whirl unto themselves. And I began to whirl with the music.

First, a slow stepping, then I fell and was helped up, and then, with men holding up both arms, a dosing of Retsina to keep me awake, and at this time the brew resembled jellied vodka spiked with razor blades. No carafe this time, either. The Retsina was wheeled over in an old oak barrel, and ladles-full were poured into my glass.

Perhaps fifty or sixty men were here, with a few women in the corners. The smoke was everywhere, both from harsh cigarettes and the smoke of endless candles, as if this were some kind of exorcism. Soon, even the candles went out, and in the shadows some of the men seemed to be doing mime tricks, and the music became even louder and more mournful.

Some of the older men simply went to sleep, but others insisted on dancing; and, of course, I danced with them. I suppose I danced with them. It all became a clamorous dream in the darkness as my arms were held up, as one slow foot went in front of the other. I must have fallen a dozen times, but soon a group of us were dancing out on to the port, looking at the boats bobbing in the sea under the half-moon. Dancing on the pier, walking nowhere, with shouts and music. I was the young zombie wandering soulless, with a concertina player following me along the quayside, his notes as disembodied as my legs.

And that (as they used to say in the 1940's films noir) was all I remembered. For the next morning, I woke up in a little bare room. In a bed. I looked in my pocket, and not a single banknote had been removed. I had been treated, apparently. My own clownish excesses were an entertainment to people who loved to be entertained.

The room had no windows, so I walked out and saw the sun and the boats along the quay. It was like the set for an Agnes DeMille ballet, until some men sitting at a table shouted out, "Hey! Kalimeera."

It was a good morning, indeed. The air sparkled azure, the coffee was muddy and black, the sea was blue, and the bakery offered a supply of pastries with honey and cheese and – oh, how well I remember – those bittersweet Ægina pistachios, crumbled and crunched.

And still today, remembering the night they made me dance, and now so far from the sea, I (in the words of another Grecophile, D.H. Lawrence) "…weep like a child for the past."

Recipe:
Selinosalata (Parsley Salad)

This story was originally printed in Lonely Planet's World Food: Greece, written by one of the world's greatest foodies, Richard Sterling. He has volunteered this recipe, a salubrious contrast to the unhealthy ingredients above.

- 4 oz. parsley, leaves only
- 3 cloves garlic, minced
- ¼ c. olive oil
- 1 hard-boiled egg
- Salt and pepper to taste
- 1 small onion, minced
- 1 tbsp. lemon juice
- 8 Kalamata olives
- 1 tbsp. Greek or balsamic vinegar

1. Toss together all ingredients except egg and olives.
2. Chop the egg and olives and sprinkle over the mix. Serve immediately with bread, cheese and wine, ouzo or Retsina.

As an appetizer, this will serve four.

Recipe:
Kotopoulo Me Damaskina
(Chicken with Prunes)

This dates back a hundred and fifty years, to the Thessalonika family of the late Sophie Cavacos, one of the earthy Grande Dames of the Baltimore Greek community. Plums, you see, were originally from Egypt and Asia, since the Greeks and Romans loved the fruit. Aristotle's friend, the great botanist-philosopher, Theophrast insisted that the goddess Athena loved the fruit above all others. So, plums had to be shipped by sea. There were two ways to keep the fruit edible on its long journey up the Nile through the Mediterranean. The most luscious-sounding was to put the plums in barrels of honey and sweet wine. The more pedestrian was to dry them and send them in (what we now know as) prune form.

- 1 whole chicken fryer, cut into serving pieces
- 1 onion, diced
- 2 tbsp. olive oil
- 1 small can tomato sauce
- 1 bay leaf
- Cinnamon, to taste
- Pepper, to taste
- 1 box prunes, with pits intact
- 2 tbsp. butter

1. Sauté chicken parts with onion in olive oil. Brown lightly until onions are transclucent.

2. Add tomato sauce and rinse can with one can of water, or more, to barely cover.
3. Add bay leaf, cinnamon, and pepper.
4. Cook for about 45 mintues.
5. In separate pan, sauté prunes in butter.
6. Before chicken is done, add prune mixture. If liquid measure doesn't cover chicken, add a little of the sauteed water to the mixture and add to chicken.
7. Cook for another 15 miinutes.
8. Prunes may be removed before serving, leaving only the nice flavor to the sauce.

Chapter Four

Plato's "Slimposium"
Recipe:
Cassata Gelata alla Siciliana

Sicily's "Italianness" is a fairly recent phenomenon, this wonderful island having been inhabited and conquered by Lombards, Germans, Phoenicians, Saracens, Arabs, and—of course—the Greeks. In fact, this was the place where Plato was apparently arrested and spent some time under house arrest. The reasons have never been clear, but it had something to do with corruption. I don't believe it. If ya can't trust a philosopher, who can ya trust? Anyhow, while dining on the lovely "Greek" island off of Syracusa, I literally did scribble this Platonic piece on a napkin. The napkin was thrown away, but (in Platonic terms) the idea lingered on.

CHARACTERS:

>Socrates: Socratic philosopher
>Archimedes: Peloponessian polymath
>Moussaka: Graphic graffitiist
>Baklava: Sushi sous-chef
>Figleeves: Fabulous fabulist

The fabulist Figleeves related that he met Socrates and Moussaka, fresh from a picnic on the Greek theatre near the Sicilian colony of Syracusa. Socrates was carrying a spoon and a fork, with a napkin folded in his toga. Moussaka was drinking from a bottle of Marsala wine as they strolled along the harbor. Figleeves asked whither those two were heading, and Moussaka blurted out that they were going to the home of Archimedes, who had prepared a buffet dinner.

"Well, then," said Figleeves, "I am also hungry, so perhaps I will join you."

"But," asked Moussaka, "are you invited to the banquet?"

Socrates laughed. "It is not a banquet but a buffet, so of course Figleeves is invited. Had Archimedes prepared a banquet, then each dish would be equally apportioned to please each guest, and nothing would be left over. Not a shrivel, not an ort…"

"Pray tell," said Moussaka, "but what is an ort?"

"It is," said Socrates, "a crumb, a scrap left over from the dinner table. Do you not know this word from the crossword puzzles?"

Moussaka frowned. "No, I do not. For it was said by Dolmas, the son of Kalamatas, that a crossword turneth away kindness. But continue, Socrates."

"Okay," continued Socrates, "anyhow, a banquet is for a specified number of guests, while a buffet is laid out so that each guest can partake of what he wishes with no need to eat what displeases him. So, should more than the officially invited guests be allowed to join, each person can consume to his stomach's pleasure."

"But what," asked Moussaka, having finished his carafe, "if a single dish, say a plate of tripe bathed in olive oil, is of particular attraction? What then, if we all wished to eat this tripe? Why, then, an extra guest would be an impediment!"

Socrates was prepared to answer, but by this time the three friends had reached the house of Archimedes, who stood outside and welcomed each of them in turn. He especially welcomed Figleeves, who had not been at his home for many years, and who would make a fitting partner for his other guest, Baklava. Archimedes, however, had not even a toga on his body, but stood as natural as Venus coming from her bath.

Glancing at his body (which resembled more a Gorgon than the Goddess of Beauty), he blushed slightly but made no excuses.

"You must not glance at this…well, this lack of attire. I had been in my bath when suddenly a thought had come to me and I said 'Eureka!' and ran out, and that was when I saw you three coming to my home. Now I will don my toga."

Socrates laughed and said, "Forget the toga, Archimedes, but tell us what thought had come to you that you yelled 'Eureka!' and ran out the door."

"It was a simple thought," said Archimedes, tying his robe in the form of a Euclidian equation. "Hardly one for the generous mind of yourself, Socrates."

"But I am a simple graffiti-ist," said Moussaka. "Certainly, you will not be ashamed to tell me."

"That is true. My thought was, of course, about food. And it was actually a question. Since the gods and goddesses were bountiful enough to give us the gifts of food, why, then, when we dine too much on their bounties, do we suffer from it, with our stomach resembling hippos of the Nile and our necks like the columns of the Parthenon, with feet like Nubian camels, with…"

"Enough," said Baklava, who, until this moment had been silent. "I believe you mean that your idea was that delicious food gives delight to the eye, the nose, and the tongue, but it gives wretchedness to the body."

"Exactly," said Archimedes. "Socrates, you are judged a gourmet of types, always noshing in the agora. What say you?"

"What I say is that I can't stand my wife's cooking. Ergo the agora. Or argo the egora. But before we start the discussion, what may be proclaimed the Slimposium, let us go to your dining room, Archimedes, and see what has been prepared."

They entered the room where a simple wood table groaned with all manner of delicacies. So, this hungry quintet fingered delicacies from both Sicily and Athens. Appetizers included baby eggplants stuffed with minced lamb and parsley; sea snails shaken with salt, lemon juice, and oregano, then stewed with black pepper; fresh mussels with onions and white wine, with a side dish of razor clams; pickled capers; red peppers, roasted, skinned, and drizzled with oil and vinegar. Main platters included chunks of veal with cinnamon and paprika; rice with prawns and onions; squid stewed with water and cinnamon; cheeses, not only Feta but Sicilian sharp sheep cheese, and Sicilian cassata, dazzling with sugary fruits and macaroons. Wines included Bartolo from Syracusa itself, Marsala from the east, and Greek vines growing in southern Italy, from Salerno.

While the guests applauded Archimedes, he but shrugged his shoulders and introduced his chef, a measly little man who had somehow juggled the pots and pans to produce this buffet.

And that was when our polymath began again to ask how the gods could bestow such treasures of the forest, sea, farm, vineyard, and sky, yet by consuming, did we become as fat as the swine simmering in wine with orange peel and cinnamon.

The usually silent Baklava, who himself had worked in kitchens from far-off Edo (later known as Tokyo), declared that this was the practical joke of the gods.

"It is," he said, gulping down a slice of cornbread dotted with cinnamon and raisins and orange juice, "like the seductions of Zeus. How fearlessly he prepares his bait, how conspicuously he consumes, and afterwards, when chided by his wife, how he regrets his gluttenous glutinous act. So it is in eating these dishes, how we revel in their tastes, and how we rue each grain as we perform our ablutions."

"No, no," retorted Moussaka, tugging at a swordfish nugget on the skewer, the lemon and oregano mixture spattering on his tunic. "This is no practical joke at all. Great recipes are our gift from the gods. We live and live well, we die and we die well. Hopefully our last gesture on earth, in fact, is patting our stomachs in joy."

The diners looked at Socrates, but he was busy with his own thoughts. Figleeves, though, was holding in his hand the regal mustalevaria, a pudding of boiled grape juice with flour and cinnamon.

"It was said," he hummed with the modality of an epic from the blessed Homer himself, "that when Bacchus wished to elevate himself from a mortal to a god, he tried everything to impress the inhabitants of Mount Parnassus. He made love with the sharp precision that Baklava wields the sushi-dagger. He ran the Marathon with the speed that the cooks of Cathay quick-fry oysters. He drew mosaics with the invention that a grand baker draws intricate filigrees upon a cake for the Tyrant of Syracusa himself.

"Nothing impressed the gods until…"

The other guests waited.

"Until," hummed Figleeves, "he inspired the fig to make a perfume of its pulp…"

("Ah," said the guests.)

"…and drew sweet wine from the grape."

("Ohhh," said the guests.)

There was silence, as more tumblers of ouzo, frozen between licoriced ice, were brought to the table. It was at that point that Socrates spoke. The others listened.

"Little do I say to you, my friends, tonight," said Socrates, "since I am feeling tired. Perhaps it was something that I ate." They all smiled.

"And yet, we are generalizing on great recipes and dishes. I believe, like my colleague in far-off China, that whether dishes are simple or complex, each ingredient holds within it a truth. That whether we fast or diet or eat until we burst, each element has its own truth. We adore, my friends, the mushroom, and yet this is a voluptuous poison, as the Romans will call it. Like life itself, the mushroom calls upon us to eat it again and again … and like life, too, when we have too much, we will fall and die.

"You have here in your hand an egg," said Socrates, looking at a small omelet filled with wild greens. "Some would say it is a sin to eat this, which is destined to create chickens. For myself, I see the egg as the emblem of the world and its four elements. The shell is the earth; the white, water; the yolk, fire; and the air is found within the shell.

"And now we come to the cow. Not the meat, which is of little importance. But the milk is of divine origin. Free from passions and fears, our first men and women surrounded by streams of milk and nectar from which they drew health and life, and later presented to Minerva herself."

Archimedes held up a milk vessel, decorated with crowns of flowers, but the others said, "Shhh."

"Cheese? It was invented by a bastard son of Apollo, who by his creation finally gained honor by the people of Greece. Nestor, wise and aged, in the middle of the Trojan War, brought wine to Machaeon, who had been wounded in the right arm. Machaeon refused to drink, so Nestor gave him goat's cheese as well, which with the wine remedied him so he could fight another day.

"Nor did Homer forget the thrush, to which he wrote a poem so beautiful that the people of Athens forbade their children to eat of this beautiful bird (though as a mark of manhood, they were allowed to partake).

"And even the lowly mussel…well, at the wedding feast of Hebe, Jupiter took the ambrosial wine and insisted that it be discarded for the mussel (though we know not its dressing).

"All at the table is for our satisfaction. Even the salutation. For wine is intended to satisfy all the senses: the tongue, the eye, the nose, and now let us clink together our glasses…"

The resonances were light and cheery.

"…and now the ear."

It was at this point that Socrates stopped. He felt drowsy, he said. He wished only to sleep. Perhaps, he said, it was something he ate.

"That antediluvian waiter at the banquet," Socrates said, "could not hear even with his ear-horn. I had a longing, outrageous as it was, for a part of the pig. The hock, I believe. I ordered ham hock. 'What?' said the waiter. 'I want ham hock,' I shouted. 'Coming right up,' he said.

"But the plate was not ham hock at all. He had heard me to say 'hemlock'.' Being a philosopher and a fatalist, and being courteous to my underlings, I took the hemlock and swallowed it with joy. The same joy I feel when I dine with such fine companions as yourselves."

Socrates closed his eyes and whispered. He owed some money for a chicken he had bought, and wished to return it. Then he re-closed his eyes, and at that moment the blessed Socrates discovered the Wisdom of Eternity, which no living being is allowed to know.

Three of the friends looked on, but Archimedes repaired to his kitchen to prepare the Greek dish, which even to this day is served on the day of death. The koliva is made with soft-boiled wheat kernels, dried fruit, pomegranate seeds, sugar, and nuts. Archimedes served it at once.

"The fruit is the sweetness of our friend, the pomegranate seed is fertility. And the wheat, forever sprouting, is that of eternal life, eternal memories, and the joy of life itself."

"Socrates," said Figleeves, "now knows the secret of eternal life. But what, my friends, is the secret of earthly life?"

Archimedes smiled, even as a tear coursed down his cheek.

"The secret is less spinach, less water, more cinnamon, more wine."

The friends cried and laughed together, sucked on cinnamon sticks, and drank their wine until the chariot of the sun seemed to rise in the west.

Recipe:
Cassata Gelata alla Siciliana

(This dish comes from the Lonely Planet Guide to Greece, with much thanks.)

The dolce desserts of Sicily have the most decadent eclecticism in the kingdom of sweets, since their texture and taste come from Italy, Greece, North Africa, and Spain. The original cassatas, with almond paste, sugar icing, candied fruits, vanilla, and chocolate are difficult to duplicate, but most recipe books can give some kind of indication. But this is a different dessert, an iced cake taken from one of the only two recipes codified in the 1963 Venetian Culinary Congress. (The other was Saltimbocca alla Romana.) Chef Paolo Cascino was inspired to make this rather complicated dessert.

He offers no recipe for the original pastry filling, but that is standard. The other parts are totally original.

Pastry Cream for Five

1¾ tbsp. sugar
8 egg yolks
5 tbsp. flour
2 tsp. grated fresh lemon rind
1½ tsp. vanilla
3 c. whole milk
2½ tbsp. butter
½ tbsp. grated pistachio nuts

1. Place egg yolks, flour, lemon rind, and vanilla in saucepan and mix together.
2. In a separate saucepan, scald the milk.
3. Very slowly, pour milk over egg yolk mixture in a thin stream, beating constantly with rotary beater.
4. Continue cooking on low heat, stirring with a wooden spoon until mixture reaches boiling point.
5. Cook four minutes longer, stirring constantly.
6. Add pistachio and while stirrin, cook one minute longer.
7. Remove pan from heat, add butter and mix well.
8. Pour into bowl and let cool; stir occasionally to prevent skin from forming over the top.
9. Freeze this mixture.

The Cassata

2 tbsp. egg whites
2 c. sugar and some milk
5 c. cream
Candied fruits, orange and citron peel
pieces of unsweetened chocolate
Pound cake (your own recipe, preferably with rum)
Pistachio ice cream
Vanilla ice cream

1. Take the original pastry filling, adding the egg whites.
2. Mix in five cups of cream, some candied fruits and peels, and chocolate.
3. Now line a mold with wax paper, cover with a layer of vanilla ice cream, a layer of pistachio ice cream, and a layer of your pound cake soaked with rum.
4. Fill with the egg white and pastry cream mixture, and finish with ice cream and pistachios.
5. Cover the mould and freeze.
6. Decorate with candied fruits, whipped cream, and orange peel.

CHAPTER FIVE

CANNIBALISM I : THE RELIGIOUS EXPERIENCE
Recipe:
Baklava for Bedu

I became a cannibal after quitting my accordion-playing job in downtown Damascus. But I get ahead of myself, since Turkey preceded Syria, and the desert proceeded from Syria. Let us begin.

Turkey was an endless gourmet experience, but being a poor hitchhiker, I didn't realize it at the time. In fact, riding in the back of endless sheep-hauling trucks, the damned oily ruminants pissing, farting, crapping over endless miles, my vow was never ever to touch these animals again. (That vow was broken several years later, and revealed in Chapter 29, "Where Shepherds Yell By Night.")

Before Syria and cannibalism, I had spent several weeks

in southern Turkey around Adana. Adana had been an Armenian metropolis, but when the two Armenian genocides occurred, in 1897 and the 1920s, the place had become empty and depressing. Wonderful Greek, Roman, Byzantine, and Armenian artifacts had been dug up and were used for doorstops or to hold sheep-droppings. The beach was pleasant enough, but I quickly became bored and repaired instead to nearby Tarsus, the city from whence Paul of Tarsus departed. An invitation from a Turkish farmer allowed me to camp in an orange orchard, imbibing in orange blooms, swims in the stream, served fresh orange juice in the morning with lamb pilaf in the afternoon. Paul of Tarsus made a big mistake leaving.

Traveling southeast, I spent more time in Iskenderum looking at the great mosaics—the finest I ever saw until Sicily years later. Then I hitchhiked into Syria.

Now this was not easy, since at that time, my religion banned me from getting a visa. The solution was simple. I found a terrific group of Irish monks in Ankara, who were happy to make me an "honorary Catholic," with papers to prove it, if I would help them move some ladders and construction equipment.

Finishing the chores, we all laughed and had illegal drinks, and we told some jokes, and the loverly Fathers gave me the papers, assuring me that my new Catholicism was the "Gospel truth."

"Well," said I, "it sure beats my own circumcisial evidence."

We all laughed again, and passed around a drap o' the hard stuff.

So, all decked out as a true believer, I entered Syria, spent several weeks in Homs and Hamma, before that wonderful clifftop view of Damascus. After several weeks, I thought I would never leave, especially with a terrific cushy job.

But again, I get ahead of myself. And please allow a digression.

Relating these experiences at New York dinner tables, I used to assume my audiences would be enchanted with my experiences abroad. Like Desdemona hearing tales from Admiral Othello, women would throw themselves at my feet, the History Channel would devote a series to my perambulations, and Charlie Rose would devote a full hour to my tales of love, tragedy, adventure, and octopus sandwiches.

That, of course, was never true. New York is not, as the platitude goes, the center of the universe. New York is its own universe. Parallel universes may be floating along in other dimensions, but they are unreachable and, frankly, the menu leaves much to be desired.

The exception is cannibalism. According to the prevailing Political Correctness, cannibalism never existed. When I first mentioned that I had once been a cannibal, one acquaintence glared. He hadn't heard my history. Although his own travels had only taken him to Aspen and Atlanta, he informed me that "Cannibalism is a fraud perpetuated by imperialists, missionaries, and racial anthropologists. When I see the DNA evidence, I'll believe this crap."

I pulled out a lock of my hair and asked him to get in analyzed, but he simply sulked into his lettuce. My host, though, seemed to take a minor interest, and, like Sheherezade, I began my tale with a provocative first sentence about becoming a cannibal after losing my job as an accordionist.

"I became a cannibal about three weeks after losing my job as an accordion player at the Casanova Nightclub in downtown Damascus," I told him. (And so the story continues.)

He was astonished.

"How come you lost the job?" my friend asked. "You're not a bad accordion player."

He obviously hadn't heard the "c-word." "Cannibalism" is like flatulence, the skeleton in the closet, the crazy brother-in-law whom we don't bring up. Anyhow, on to the squeezebox.

Briefly, the job entailed playing the accordion at the Casanova Nightclub each night from 9:00 P.M. to 1:00 A.M., with a double bass player from Somalia who was usually stoned on qat. (Since he never learned how to actually tune his instrument, the drug was superfluous.) Sometimes a drummer would turn up. He had learned his trade while studying dishwashing at the American Congregationalist School in Aleppo.

I would lead them in traditional wedding and bar mitzvah stuff, sometimes segueing into Rossini overtures, Lawrence Welk polkas and, if requested, the equivalent of a pop Arab tune from Oum Kalsoum, the Rosemary Clooney of the Arab world.

Whatever made the rich Arabs and their girlfriends or their rouged, kohl-eyed boyfriends jump up and dance was kosher in Damascus.

Anyhow, I wasn't really fired. I was "relieved" for vaguely political and religious reasons. Probably I would be there to this day if I hadn't been informed by Aram, my loveable fat Armenian boss, that I would be murdered if I continued playing.

One afternoon, Aram had come to my rented room in the souk, which was bedecked in roses brought from a poet friend who had won a prize in Beirut. Aram was such a nice man that he was certainly welcome on this festive day.

I guess he had puffed his way from the Casanova, and he was sweating and nervous. But since Aram had come to save my life, I gave him some orange juice and some arak and six glowing pink roses for his wife, and sat him down on one of the wicker chairs, and he gulped the juice and pushed the arak to the side and came to the point.

"Harry, you know I don't give care about a person's religion," said Aram. "But these damned people in the market think you are Israeli."

"The People of the Book," I told him, "along with Moslems and Nazarenes."

"They think Jews are the people of the account book," he said. "Whether you are Jewish or not, it's not my business. To them, a Jewish accordion player is equivalent to an Israeli spy."

He continued quickly.

"So may I suggest that you do not play your accordion any more in the Casanova? I hope you don't think that I'm taking sides with those…those soldiers and street people…"

I knew –and Aram knew– that in Damascus, I had squeezed my last box.

He made it even more clear. "Do you have a visa for Jordan?" he asked. "If not, I could arrange it."

I told him that I always had a Jordanian visa, that I would pack my rucksack (the accordion belonged to the Casanova) and take a bus to the border.

"No," said this ever-generous man. "My driver will take you to the border. In case of any problems."

Aram also gave me about $30.00 in Jordanian money. "Thank you," I said. "Now I don't have to guess who's coming for dinar. It's me."

He looked sad, but it wasn't because of the pun. He felt almost ashamed.

"It isn't that I have any real fear," he said. "But you never can tell."

I never saw Aram after that, and thought it prudent not to write to him. In the 1960s, that could have been very dangerous. I did see his driver, who picked me up in a dusty Toyota, and we made the dusty trip along what had been the Overland Desert Mail

Service route to the border, arriving about 11:00 P.M., when the usual customs people were sleeping.

They were nice enough in a drowsy way, but the chief of customs, who was roused from his cot for my appearance, was curious about my origins. My hair, it seemed, looked…well, Semitic. But my name was hardly Middle Eastern.

"Oh, my father was Polish," I told him (thus, the name), but my mother was Spanish (thus, the kinky hair). I wanted to give him that old chestnut about my sister never sure whether she was Carmen or Cohen, but decided against it. Especially since he embraced me and kissed me on both cheeks.

"You are Spanish. We also once were rulers of the Spanish. We are brothers."

He wanted me to spend the night at the customs post, since the desert area had wolves and "uncivilized Bedu people." But I wanted to get on. Anyway, I enjoyed sleeping in the desert. While the evenings were freezing, the bedroll was warm. Lying on a hill, you could find stars never even imagined in a city.

A three-mile walk in that landscape was a mere jump away. And when I saw out in the fields, about a half-mile from the road, the gray-black tents of the "uncivilized" Bedouin, I had no choice in those early days but to walk over and introduce myself, asking if I could stay for the night.

That night lasted three weeks, since one of the older tribal leaders wanted to speak English again. He also spoke Italian and some Hebrew, all of which he had learned in the Second World War. Since he was out of practice, I was adopted (or abducted) and walked or camped with the Bedu for almost a month.

The whole group consisted of about seventy families, the richer ones with camels, most of the others with mangy dogs and mangy sheep. The Rudolph Valentino picture of Bedouin life was romantic nonsense, of course. The reality was getting up at around

4:30 A.M., putting coffee on the stove, giggling with the children, sitting around, rolling cigarettes from rancid tobacco, and walking around. Once we went to a town to sell some wool, but mainly it was camping for a few days, then marching on to the next campsite, hopefully near a watering hole.

The food was terrible. Essentially, it consisted of Egyptian fava beans bought in the town, along with hard rice and bean sprouts. If lucky, a bit of yogurt from camel milk, and some cumin and cardamom with the rice. Once in the two weeks, a piece of rabbit. The coffee was weak to begin with, and it became more insipid as the week went on, since the original Saturday beans were reboiled each morning until the following Friday.

Nothing changed very much until the third week. Then came the Incident of the Arab Thigh.

The Bedu had several minor chiefs, one of whom was Sheik Abdullah. I hardly saw him, since he was in his tent most of the time, wheezing and coughing, and lighting up his cigarettes and wheezing and coughing again. He had one wife, a crone of about forty-five, I guess, and she would bring him plates of rice. He would take a few bites, presumably, but a few minutes later she would take out the platter and sit down with her kids and they would eat the rest.

One day, Sheik Abdullah died. I knew that he had died that morning since the camels whinnied and moped, the women feebly ululated, and the men sat around and cried in their coffee. I guess they talked about him, but I don't know what they had to say. Maybe in his youth he was a great warrior, a magnificent stealer of sheep. But lately, he had been a bit of a misnomer.

Not having known the Sheik, I went for a quiet walk in the hills. Perhaps I should have ruminated on the frailty of human existence, but I was cussing out the tribe, since they didn't even have any watery coffee.

Nonetheless, I put on a morbid face when returning, hoping they would think I was overcome with grief. Actually, nobody paid attention. The Sheik's body had apparently been dumped in a makeshift wooden crate, and the tribe hoisted him up and walked him out to the hills. While I wondered whether to follow, I was obviously not "family" so I stayed back with the women and camels, trying to find some coffee.

The men were out for about five hours, and I took it for granted they were offering prayers. After burying him, I guessed they would sit around, smoke, have some coffee (they had taken the beanbag with them), and then all would remain the same.

That night, instead of dinner with my adopted clan, I was invited to sit with about fifteen clan leaders outside. A mat was set in front of all of us. Instead of the usual communal pot of beans and rice in the center, from which we would dip our fingers (no utensils were used), we were presented with plate-size sheets of cardboard, from the carton of fava beans they had bought in Amman the month before.

On top of each "plate," used only on special occasions, was a dust-pale disc about the size of a large coin.

Initially, I thought it might have been part of a jackal or a wolf or wild fox, which would have been a treat. But the shape was puzzling. I played the innocent.

"Um...er...rabbit?" I asked my host. His English was learned with the British Army, and he was terse at the best of times.

"No," he said. "It is Abdullah. It is the Sheik."

"Scuse?" I asked, trying to hide my dread.

"It is Sheik Abdullah. We take him inside us."

"Sorry," I said, suspecting nothing. "I thought you had buried the Sheik this morning."

"Yes, yes..." He was a bit impatient, but paused to explain.

"We have buried his body. But his…the piece behin …this we have carefully taken out. We have cut him halal style, so his blood ran out and the skin is pure. Then we cut it. And we give it to those in the tribe whom we admire.

And to you also, Harry. For we admire you."

I was trying to imagine what I could be admired for. Maybe one of the tribe had seen me playing accordion in Damascus. Then I realized they simply liked me. Being liked by them was quite a compliment.

"So we take Sheik Abdullah into our bodies, so that his good qualities will become our good qualities."

I tried to recall what good qualities he had. Outside of rolling cigarettes pretty deftly, he wasn't so great. On the other hand, I was starting to panic inside. I really didn't feel like ingesting the cheek of the Sheik, but tried to put it out of my mind. As well as my mouth.

"You Christians should understand this," said my protector. "It was long ago. But I was told, when I was in your army that even in your service you eat the flesh and blood of the man you consider the Son of God. So when a man is good, you will have his goodness."

The others listened to this, not understanding his English but they looked at me like a child being educated. Which I was. And when my education came to an end, the moment of truth had arrived.

The others proceeded to pick up Sheik Abdullah's ass in their hands and held it aloft.

My first thought was to say: "Just a moment here. The Bible thing is symbolic. I have no intention of…"

The next thought was that they were serious. And that, in a moment more emotional for them than I cared to admit, I would have to be serious as well. They wouldn't have harmed me if I hadn't eaten the Sheik. But they had gone to all this trouble to cut up the fatty part of the man, to boil it for about twenty minutes to make it soft and malleable, the only time that men would do the cooking, and then to offer it to a supposed infidel like myself.

They would have been disappointed, though. So it was time for dinner.

We all held the fractional segment of his ass in our hands, downed it, and had a gulp of water, water that probably was more disease-ridden than the old man. Abdullah's son said a few words in Arabic, probably from the Holy Koran, and the ceremony was over.

The ceremonial cardboard wafer-plates were removed, and the communal pot of fava beans and the fire replaced it. Later, I went into a surprisingly gentle sleep.

Today, friends ask how he tasted.

I try to avoid the platitude that he tasted "like chicken, only gamier." Mostly I tell the truth, that it was the opposite of Bill Clinton's description of pot: I swallowed but didn't taste.

No, Sheik Abdullah's ass was boiled to a pulp, and it was conveniently throat-sized, so one did not have to chew, savor, or swirl in the mouth like a Cabernet Sauvignon. One simply swallowed.

Looking back, it is evident that one swallow does not make a summer. One bit of fat does not make a cannibal. But it certainly was more than a symbolic ritual. I had pleased my hosts and pleased myself.

I left the tribe four days later for more Middle Eastern adventures but, of course, always remembered them. They were good people, taking in a stranger like me. Then again (sometimes I think all too glibly), I took in a stranger myself. In this case, Sheik Abdullah.

Hopefully, his meat made them (if not me) even better.

Recipe:
Baklava for Bedu

It isn't all coffee and rabbit with the Bedouin. Once they get to the decadent city, they might take themselves off for a real banquet, anything from boiled sheep head to baklava. The former is really awful to watch being made (the hair is singed off with flames, the brain is removed; but marinated with bay leaf and onion and cardamom seeds, it can be tasty enough). More practical is that most luscious of all Turkish-style sweets, baklava. A simple recipe can produce ecstatic results.

> ½ kil. gullash
> (This is not the Hungarian stew but a thin pastry, as thin as phyllo pastry. Egyptian grocery stores in New York carry this, and other shops might have it. Otherwise, get phyllo pastry from any good bakery.)
> ½ c. butter
> ¼ kil. fresh cream
> ½ kil. shelled pistachio nuts or almonds
> 1 tsp. nutmeg

1. Spread two-thirds of the gullash on a greased baking tray. Spoon melted butter over the layers.
2. Spread the fresh cream over one layer of the gullash and cover that with the remaining gullash.
3. With the tip of a sharp knife, release this from the sides of the tray.

4. Now add the crushed pistachio nuts with a touch of nutmeg.
5. Cut into 5-7cm squares.
6. Pour the remaining melted butter over the gullash, making sure it seeps through all the sections.
7. Put in the center of a preheated moderate oven until golden brown. Remove from the oven and saturate with cold sugar syrup.

CHAPTER SIX

VATICAN ARCHIVES: "SUDDENLY LAST SUPPER"
Recipe:
Farouk's Bamia

While Egypt was far away on the horizon of my travels, that land had been part of my childhood. In particular, the Howard Hawks classic, "Land of the Pharaohs." William Faulkner had been the screenwriter for this, and later I read about the problems he had had with Hawks. Faulkner had read everything he possibly could about ancient Egypt, but he still had a single problem. As I remember, he wrote to a friend, "Neither Hawks nor I had the slightest idea what Pharaohs did or talked about in their spare time." One could say the same thing about Mao Tse-tung or the Dalai Lamas (before the present one). And I felt the same way when reading the New Testament. Jesus couldn't have spent every spare minute of his time performing miracles or speaking parables. He must have had a sense of humor, or else his Apostles, salts of the earth, would have left him. Even a few practical jokes would have been in the cards, since life in the desert was hardly a bowl of cherries.

Thus, this Napkin Scribble, penned in a Piraeus café.

If Jesus could claim to have two favorite Apostles, they were Jesse and James. Since both disciples were inseparable, they were known simply as the Jesse James brothers. Neither of them had Christian names, but James, the putative brother of Jesus, signed himself into the local bowling alley as "James Christ, the nephew of God."

Now in those ancient days, the people of Palestine were forever gossiping about the friendship of the Jesse James brothers, but nothing was ever proven, even after they had gone together to the Boy Scout jamboree in Sodom.

Quite the opposite.

Mary Magdalene, who claimed to know them in the biblical sense (wink-wink-nudge-nudge), told inquisitive nomads and accusative Pharisees, "If these guys are gay, then I'm the daughter of God.

"Believe me, these guys are Jews: They've never been to Bedouin together in their lives."

Mainly, outside of following Jesus around all day and listening to His sermons, the Jesse James brothers were known around the desert as "the Lazy Apostles."

"We're not lazy," said Jesse once to a chronicler, "we just enjoy hangin' out."

"Hangin' out" to the Romans meant crucifixion, but to the Jesse James brothers it meant goin' down to the Dead Sea, dippin' their poles in the water, and waitin' for a bite. Even though the bite never came.

"You guys," Jesus would smile with mock reprimand. "All

you do is fish and loaf, loaf and fish. It would be a miracle to get you out of your loafs and fishes."

(Once, in a particularly good mood, Jesus actually performed this miracle. But that's another story.)

Anyhow, one fine spring day, the brothers were finally given a responsible task. Jesus had been commanding the bagels to "Slice Thyselves" for the Last Supper when He called the two chums to His side.

"Ummm," sniffed James. "Lox. Bagels."

"Hey," laughed Jesse. "Remember that harelip Samaritan Jesus cured last year? He used to say that Lox Bagels was the big gambling city in Nevada?"

The two chums laughed to beat the band, though Jesus shut His ears. Anyhow, He had more important work for them.

"Look, with Mom bawlin' and the Apostles prayin' and Peter playin' with his cock instead of cookin' it for the main course, I forgot all about the greens. The supermarkets are closed now for Easter. So, though I got everything else for dinner, with all the commotion, would you mind desperately getting off your buns and picking some ingredients for the salad?"

Well, Jesse finished his bun, and James looked at him and laughed. Because they didn't have an idea in hell how to get salad ingredients. Or even what was supposed to go into a salad. The "Lazy Apostles" could wash and dry the dishes after dinner (if necessary), but actually making a salad was for another better world. Not the world of Earth.

"But when Jesus calls," said Jesse, "we better listen."

"Yeah, you better believe it," said James. "Remember that guy he raised from the dead? I mean, this was no Stephen King novel. When I sniffed this guy, I said 'Shalom. I'm goin' home!'"

"You mean 'Arrivederci, aroma,'" said Jesse.

They both laughed again, but knew they had work to do. So

they mused and sauntered and sauntered and mused, and as they started down a path to the Dead Sea, Jesse had a sudden thought.

"Hey, James," Jesse said. "Hey, ya know about that garden around here?"

James giggled. "Oh, the one we can hardly pronounce." They started to do that comic lisp some of the beggars had been afflicted with before Jesus cast His spell.

"Geth…Geth, themany." They laughed so hard they could hardly stand.

"No, actually," said Jesse, "down in that Geth…er, garden, they grow some good stuff there. We could sneak in after sunset…"

"You mean like a thief in the night?" asked James.

"Sure. That's the way Jesus does it. You know Mr. Honesty and Integrity. He says He comes in like a thief in the night and gets all His ingredients."

"Okay," said James. "Let's go for it."

Which is just what they did. They went into the Garden of Gethsemane, and before the Roman watchman could see them, they were rassling up a terrific salad for all their pals on this special occasion.

First, James scurried up a palm tree and shouted down to Jesse: "Hey, which part do you want? Palm tongue? Palm foot? Palm eye?"

Jesse did some calculations. "Hey, James, how much is it in the market?"

"Umm," thought James. "I think it's the same as bread. One palm-per-nickel. So we'd better get the best part. I'll bring down the palm heart. Jesus always likes heart anyway."

Next thing, the two Apostles scurried over to the arugula patch.

"Wow," said Jesse. "Will you look at all that arugula? There must be a thousand miles of arugula here."

Well, neither of them had ever seen arugula before, nor did they know what it looked like or anything about it, or whether it was poisonous or tasty, but still they filled up their baskets and went on to the next challenge.

What a day it was! When they came back to the house, their arms were filled with avocados, carrots, eggs, salt, pepper … They'd even stolen a clove of garlic from the Witch of Endor.

"And now," said James, "how about this? In honor of our beloved Emperor, we have a Caesar salad."

"Hail, Caesar salad," said the Apostles in unison.

Not only Jesus, but all the other Apostles – even the usually dour Judas Iscariot – looked on in appreciation.

"You guys," said Jesus, who was rarely awestruck. "I'm not going to call you the Lazy Apostles any more. From now on, you will be called, in honor of the garden, the Eden brothers."

"That's all we ever wanted to be," said James. "Eden and sleepin' and lookin' cool."

Well, children, that called for some music. So Judas took off to get the local hour band from the local hora-house, and soon the whole place was rockin' and rollin'.

"It's been," said an exhausted James to Jesse, "a really nice Friday. A terrifically Good Friday."

"The problem is," said Jesse to James, "that somebody has to pay for this stuff. And it won't be me. And it won't be you…"

"You mean Jesus has to pick up the bill? Oh, God! That's not good news. Still, Jesus is a philosopher. So He'll probably just say that we all have our cross to bear."

And the two chums roared with eternal happiness.

Recipe: Farouk's Bamia

As the staple meat of the entire Middle East, virtually every metaphor in the New Testament uses sheep or lamb. Bamia is a basic lamb dish eaten everywhere in the region, and while the recipe is simple, the taste is exquisite. This recipe comes from the diplomat-Arabist Farouk el Hussein, whose roots go back to Yemen, and whose recipes go forward to heaven itself.

> 2 chopped onions
> 4-5 cloves garlic
> 1 lb. okra, cleaned and chopped
> 2 lb. lamb, cubed
> Juice of 2 lemons
> Salt and pepper to taste
> Pinch of cumin
> Olive oil

1. Sauté the onions and garlic with olive oil in a pan with salt and pepper until brown.
2. Now add the lamb, browning the mixture together with lemon juice. Marinate this until the lamb is tender.
3. Add the okra and cook over a low light until it becomes "stewy." You may add some cumin now, more salt and pepper to taste.
4. Cover and simmer for a few minutes.
5. Serve as a main dish or with pita bread as a dip.

CHAPTER SEVEN

MYSTERIES OF THE BOTTOMLESS PIT

Recipe:
Coffee Glazed Peaches

Before Damascus, I had spent a strange night in Aleppo, across the border from Turkey. There, I had a discouraging start of a three-decade search for the Meaning of Coffee. Needing a place to stay, I found a missionary college in the town where I was permitted to sleep on the grass. The next morning, I was offered my first—ever—cup of coffee.

The American women had told me that I was in for a treat: Real American Coffee.

"Not," they said with less than Christian charity, "this Arabic mud."

It is no secret that at this time, before the espresso and latté revolutions of Greenwich Village and Seattle, American coffee tasted like water, stained brown. What I was given in Aleppo was my very first American-style coffee. It was an abhorrent brew, and I came close to never drinking another.

Fortunately, not only did I soon become used to Turkish "mud," but I soon became something of a connoisseur on the worst coffees of the world – which I loved and widely publicized in my restaurant columns. But throughout extended stays in Syria, Egypt, Libya, and Yemen, I realized that coffee and the Middle East go together like ham and eggs. (Um, that "ham" part isn't exactly kosher. Let's say coffee and the Middle East go together like hummus and felafel or Laurel and Hardy.)

So when I reached Hong Kong and was commissioned by a German coffee company to write a pamplet about coffee, I decided—after several mugs-full—to write a complete book for them: a 280-page coffee table book on the idiosyncrasies of coffee—its history, anecdotes, and celebrities.

The Melitta Company was a bit upset that I had written very little about coffee itself, and virtually nothing about their esteemed company. So, against my better judgment, I added those pages. But the peculiarities are still my favorite parts. The Complete Book of Coffee is available on the Internet from some shops. But for those who don't need it, allow me to offer fifty-one discoveries, each as short and disordered as a pile of coffee pits themselves.

1. Pits? That's correct. Coffee is not a bean. It is the pit of a fruit that looks like a cherry but has no relation to the cherry.

2. Coffee arabica isn't Arabic at all. The botanist Linnaeus thought it grew in southern Arabia. Of course, its homeland is Ethiopia.

3. Moslems banned coffee because fourteenth-century parishioners used it to stay awake during services. Religious leaders said the Word of God was sufficient; none of these artificial pills.

4. Christians banned coffee because they said only Moslems

used it. Fortunately, Pope Clement VIII in the sixteenth century decided to try it on his own, and announced that coffee was so delicious, it overrode the fact that unbelievers and heretics also enjoyed it. How nice that the brew was given clemency so early in its career.

5. How about Jews? Look in II Samuel, where King David is given a present of "dried beans." Couldn't he have been drinking a cuppa Java?

6. And Buddhists, too, have a share, although this is a tea-drinking religion. Still, Norman Mailer, in Of a Fire on the Moon, speaks of the Apollo News Center, consisting of endless aisles of desks, telephones, and typewriters, plus "one giant Buddha of a coffee urn." "Coffee," writes Mailer, "is the closest the press ever comes to satori."

7. Finally, on religion, the Puritans brought coffee-making equipment with them, but in 1674, The Woman's Petition Against Coffee said that coffee not only kept men from work and prayer but "they trifle away their time, scald their chops, and spend their money, all for a little base, black, thick, nasty, bitter, stinking, nauseous puddle of water."

8. The first Viennese coffeehouse was founded by a Hungarian merchant who drove away Turkish invaders. As a gift, all he wanted was "a house of my own and possession of the heavy sacks of beans left behind by the Turks." Together, they made a coffeehouse.

9. The Viennese coffee house was for more than coffee. It was a center for musicians and artists to gather. And who could forget Orson Welles in Café Mozart with zither, spies, and coffee?

10. Frederick the Great was a good flute-player and musician, but he drank his coffee with champagne. So did I once, for an experiment. Ugghh!

11. On the other hand, in Zanzibar they have the right idea. Coffee is taken with a handful of cloves. Not bad at all.

12. More clove-making coffee. In Sudanese villages, coffee beans are roasted dark over charcoal, then ground and mixed with minced cloves, then brewed and steeped and poured through a woven grass sieve into tiny glasses.

13. The Libyans in the desert are the most romantic coffee makers. The coffee pot sits on a glowing fire and the brew is poured into handle-less porcelain cups like oversized thimbles. With this comes a copper pot of goat curd followed by a black wad of dates. The dates are dipped into the curd, and followed by sips of the coffee.

14. The Moroccans sometimes add peppercorn to their coffee, as well as salt.

15. The world's toughest coffee beans? Go to Liberia, where Coffca liberica grows wild. Almost immune to disease, the pits can even grow at sea level and nothing kills them. The coffee itself tastes like weed-water.

16. Ludwig van Beethoven was never interested in food (his favorite dish was mashed eggs), but coffee was the exception. Each morning he would carefully measure out exactly sixty beans per cup.

17. The second "B," Johannes Brahms, also had a special obsession with coffee. At 5:00 A.M., he would wake up and take out his most treasured materials: music composition paper, a box of cheap cigars, and a coffee-making machine. He was never modest, either about his music or his coffee. "Nobody," he told friends, "can make coffee as strongly as I can."

18. But J.S. Bach, the third "B," was the most important to coffee, with his Coffee Cantata, a satire (when not playing the organ, making children, or composing the B Minor Mass, Bach was a stand-up comic) about the banning of coffee. A girl tells

her prospective husband that "no wooer need come to the house unless he will promise, and have put into the marriage settlement, that I may have the freedom to make coffee whenever I want." Some say that after this "Bach's breakfast," he was preparing a "sandwich cantata" as a sort of "Bach's lunch."

19. Actually, in 1703 a whole series of cantatas about coffee was published in Paris. None survives to this day.

20. The most useless question – when was cream first put into coffee? – has the wrong answer. The conventional wisdom is that the eighteenth-century British Ambassador to China added cream, since he saw the Chinese adding cream to tea. However, the Chinese do not put cream in their tea. This is yet another insidious British invention.

21. Nor are the British congenitally capable of preparing coffee. The great comic Fred Allen said: "English coffee tastes like water that has been squeezed out of a wet sieve."

22. The eighteenth-century statesman Charles-Maurice de Talleyrand-Périgord was a plagiarist. It was he who wrote: "Coffee should be sweet as love, black as hell and strong as death." Except that a Turkish mystic said the same thing three hundred years before. Nor did the wily politician inspire the song lyric "Hey, Mr, Talleyrand, tally me banana."

23. In 1623, the Sultan of Turkey found his subjects were discussing politics in the coffeehouses. So, he decided to punish coffee drinkers. For the first drink, one was beaten with a stick. For the second, one was sewn into a leather bag and dumped into the sea.

24. No greater lover of coffee ever existed than the philosopher Immanuel Kant. He would scream in apoplectic fury if his coffee was delayed. If his servant said the coffee would be ready in a moment, he would rage: "Will be! There's the rub, that it only will be." And if it finally arrived, he would turn around and

shout to his friends: "Land! Land! My dear friends, I see land." Then he once said that heaven would never have coffee "since in waiting for coffee one sees only hell." These sentiments, fascinating as they may be, were related by Thomas DeQuincy, who did not know Kant personally and may have been influenced himself by his penchant for good opium.

25. Napoleon Bonaparte was no coffee slouch himself. "Coffee gives warmth, force, and a pain that is not without any very great pleasure. I would rather suffer with coffee than be senseless."

26. Talking about pain, let's get to the Marquis de Sade. In 120 Days of Sodom, he discovers a unique use for coffee. On the twenty-sixth day, the coffee is served, but not in a cup. "It is in the children's mouths, and one had to sip it therefrom. They took a mouthful, swished it around in their mouth and returned it into the mouth of him who served them…" (The rest is unprintable. And probably impossible to do.)

27. Two origins of coffee. One is the conventional wisdom, that coffee was "discovered" in AD 850 by Khaldi, a goatherd in what is now Ethiopia. He woke up one morning to see his goats wildly dancing around, bleating and happy as clams (or goats). When he discovered that they had been eating a plant, he tried it himself, and was suddenly excited, clear thinking, and abnormally cheerful. Well, his wife suspected something weird was going on, so she took these pits to the local monastery, where the chief monk, in anger, threw the seeds into the fire. "If these seeds are the Devil's work, then back to the Devil they shall go," he said. Then everybody was intoxicated by the smoke and they dunked the residue into a ewer of water, and everybody lived happily ever after. Thus, coffee. Thus, the usual legend.

28. But the English classicist Sir Henry Blount has a different story. A careful reading of the eating habits of the Spartans of

ancient Sparta (where else?) has them drinking "a black broth" when preparing to fight. So, he divined that this was coffee. But with no other grounds of proof.

29. Why is Sri Lanka the home of tea growing instead of coffee? Blame it on pure greed – because Ceylon was once covered with coffee plantations. In 1877, a small fungus began to destroy the coffee bushes. Rather than trying to eliminate it, the British merchants enjoyed the fact that the price of coffee was actually increasing, so they encouraged the blight. The following year, the happy fungus went all the way and destroyed the whole crop. Ceylon was left barren until tea was planted, and all were happy again.

30. Charles II of England was not very wise. Like so many other rulers, in 1675 he banned the coffeehouse. When his subjects revolted, he immediately rescinded the order, but it was too late. Everybody began to hate him, and he soon lost his head.

31. What do you call coffee in other languages? Mostly, the word is a variation of the original Arabic Qahwa. But there are a few exceptions. The Egyptians call it Masbout, the Japanese call it Koohii, the Iranians call it Gehve, and in Swahili it's Kahawa. But it's always coffee.

32. Try to bring up this word at your next dinner table: Garboon. It seems unlikely that anyone will know what it is, but if the subject happens to be the history of spittoons, you can mention that nineteenth-century coffee tasters in New York called their professional spitting bowls garboons.

33. When do you know if you have the perfect coffee? Try the point system. Actually, there is only one point. Tasters say that when coffee has reached its ideal sharpness, without the bitterness, then it has reached its point.

34. The possible health question of coffee was brought to the attention of Voltaire. The great French philosopher was

addicted, and he was warned by a French doctor to give it up, since "coffee is a slow killer." "It must be slow," said Voltaire, "since I've been drinking sixty cups a day for fifty years, and it hasn't killed me yet." Voltaire, for the record, died at the age of eighty-four, still downing his poisonous cup.

35. The other side of the coin comes from a Persian poet, who tells about the effects of coffee on the prophet Mohammed. "When the angel Gabriel presented the prophet with coffee, he felt able to unseat forty horsemen and possess fifty women."

36. Those allergic to coffee or fearful of its medicinal (or libidinous) qualities might try other uses. In the nineteenth century, coffee was used as money in Hawaii between 1810 and 1825. When asked for taxes, the people of Kona would pay in coffee.

37. Readers probably know that in marriage ceremonies in Lapland, asking for the hand of one's beloved involves coffee. The girl's suitor will have a "spokesman" who will enter the house and speak with the prospective father-in-law, usually in riddles, while the real swain drives around the house with his reindeer. If the father-in-law is impressed with the spokesman, then the spokesman is asked to make some coffee. If no coffee ritual is performed, he will leave without the girl.

38. More Lapland. The game of talo, which vaguely resembles backgammon, is played with coffee beans as markers.

39. Gypsies around the world are known for telling fortunes through tealeaves. In Romania, though, they make their divinations through coffee grounds, usually with the same results.

40. Then you have coffee as a reason for divorce. If a Turkish wife does not keep an adequate supply, the husband has grounds (so to speak) for divorce. I would imagine in California the same rules for divorce would be acceptable. (See 43. below.)

41. Brazil should really value coffee too much for use outside of the cup. However, during a particularly bountiful season, they

tried to keep up the prices by using the coffee in different ways. One was on the railways, where they would shovel coffee into the boilers to make the trains go faster. The results are not known to this writer, but they must have had a loco motive for doing it.

42. Only the Japanese could come up with a more loco motive in the use of coffee. This is the Japanese coffee sauna. Customers wear paper bikinis and are buried in thirteen tonnes of ground coffee and pineapple pulp in a huge brown pool. The pineapple pulp induces fermentation, so the grounds heat up to 140 degrees Fahrenheit. One sits in this mixture for an hour, and the therapeutic values are said to be good for almost anything. Or possibly it's for those who like lots of body in their coffee!

43. Why only one previous mention of Turkish coffee here? The method of preparation is intriguing. But Mark Twain, who wrote so much about coffee, has put this writer off Turkish coffee forever. "The servant brought the world-renowned Turkish coffee about which poets have sung so rapturously for many generations. It was a fraud. Of all the unchristian beverages that ever passed my lips, Turkish coffee is the worst. The cup is small, it is smeared with grounds; the coffee is black, thick, and unsavory of smell and execrable taste. The bottom of the cup has a muddy sediment in it half an inch deep. This goes down your throat, and portions of it lodge by the way and produce a tickling aggravation that keeps you barking and coughing for an hour."

44. Everybody knows Kahlua and Tia Maria (the latter given the feminine name in English bars, where the drink was ordered for women in lieu of wine). But in Ethiopia, there is a more potent coffee liqueur. Here, the coffee pulp is fermented and somehow made drinkable. Ethiopian soldiers in the eighteenth century used to eat the bean whole, saying it gave them courage.

45. Who is Madame Blue? Ah, for this you go to Denmark, where they drink coffee with and for everything. When they drink

coffee and aquavit, Madame Blue – named after the lovely blue coffee cups of Denmark – become part of the ritual. Here are the instructions: (a) Take a Danish copper coin and put it in the bottom of the cup, with the picture of the monarch looking up; (b) fill the cup with strong coffee until one cannot see the eyes of the monarch; (c) count to three; (d) fill up the rest of the cup with the aquavit until you can once again see the eyes of the monarch; (e) drink.

46. The Belgians don't have those charming customs. They drink their coffee in big plain bowls that can hold up to two cups. This café au lait dans un grand bol with big lumps of sugar is accompanied by thick slabs of heavily-buttered white bread, which are dunked into the bowl. The result is coffee-bread and breaded-coffee, and the Belgians love it. This says much about Belgium.

47. English coffeehouses? They were started by Middle Easterners. The first was by a Jewish emigrant in the sixteenth century. The next was a Greek-Egyptian manager who opened his shop in what is today Threadneedle Street. His coffee then was offered as medicine (i.e., "It is a remedy for dropsy, gout, scurvy, the king's evil and hypochondriac winds. It so incloseth the orifice of the stomach and fortifies the heat within, that it is very good to help digestion. It much quiets the spirits and makes the heart lightsome.").

48. A century later, Jonathan Swift spent most of his time in the coffeehouse, composing this quatrain (though some say he would have done better with a rhymed "cup-let"):

> "A fig for partridges and quails,
> Ye dainties I know nothing of ye;
> But on the highest mount in Wales
> Would choose in peace to drink my coffee."

49. Far more eloquent was Balzac who wrote that "coffee falls into the stomach and there is general commotion. Ideas begin to move like the battalions of the Grand Army... Similes arise, the paper is covered with ink; for the struggle begins and is concluded with torrents of black water – just like a battle with powder."

50. But the finest tribute is, obviously, from the world of Islam. Of all the great poetry about coffee, the sixteenth-century Sheikh Ansari Djerzeri Hanball Abd-al-Kadir was the most effusive. He must be quoted, but not in full, since he wrote thousands of pages. Here is an example: "Coffee, you dispel the worries of the great...you are the gift of the friends of God...you are the common man's gold, and, like gold, you bring to every man the feeling of luxury and nobility. Where coffee is served, there is grace, splendor, friendship and happiness. You flow through the body as freely as life's blood, refreshing all that you touch. Oh drink of God's glory, your purity brings to man only wellbeing and nobility."

51. Not to be outdone, Elizabeth Barrett Roasting (née Browning) penned the following poem for coffee (along with a variation which appears at the end of this book.

> How do I drink thee? Let me count the ways.
> I drink thee for the taste and scent and roast
> My senses feel. And even more engrossed,
> For time alone improves thy fine bouquets.
> The memories of coffee nights and days
> Are pure solace. If by myself, my cup
> Becomes my confidante, my lover and my host;
> With friends, small rooms are Mozart-filled cafés.
> With thee are confined history and the world.
> To Mocha first I soar, then Java and Versailles,
> To King and Pope and Sultan, all have swirled
> And supped of thee, thy praise to amplify.
> So rich, so gentle and so designed,
> That thee and thy world should mutually glorify.

Recipe: Coffee Glazed Peaches

Recipes from The Complete Book of Coffee, provided by the sponsoring company, are excellent. Here is one of my favorites.

> 8 tbsp. canned peach halves
> 1 tbsp. Kirsch
> ½ pt. fresh cream
> 2 tbsp. strong, fresh-brewed coffee
> 2 tbsp. sugar
> Pinch of powdered cinnamon
> 9 oz. fresh raspberries

1. Sprinkle the peaches with Kirsch.
2. Whip the cream and mix in the coffee, sugar, and cinnamon.
3. Layer the bottom of an ovenproof dish with the cream, add the peaches (inside uppermost), cover with remaining cream, and glaze in a very hot oven.

CHAPTER EIGHT

ODES TO A LARGE FISH: "CAVIARS LONGA, PITA BREVIS"

(Translation: "Beluga doesn't go so good with Arab bread.")

Recipe:

Caviar

To reach Iran, I had taken more remote highways and biways than Alexander the Great. After teachng, traveling, living in caves, then taking weird miscellaneous jobs in Syria, Jordan, Israel, and Cyprus, I returned to Turkey again. There, at a tiny port where the Cyprus boat docked, I had one of the great meals of my life: a simple freshly-caught fish with a few drops of lemon juice, a side dish of eggplant, some yogurt, and a pretzel-shaped honey sweet for dessert. And no, I don't know the name of the fish. But I do know that simplicity is the key. To everything.

Eastern Turkey included more non-food adventures than can be counted here. But finally, Turkish militarism became too grinding, too grating. I kept asking, "How can such confined, intellectually dead country have the most luxuriously sensuous food in the world?" So I stayed at the border with Iran and finally got over there for six months of more adventures.

No matter what happened, though, my saving grace was caviar. Yes, it was a luxury in Teheran, since it was mainly for export. But each Monday I would take the shuttle bus to Mehrabad airport. Bearded, wild-eyed, with grimy shirt and filthy trousers, I resembled a typical Iranian zealot, so I could easily go up the back steps to the second floor, where cartons of caviar were stored. There, the guard could be bribed (about $6.00 a can) for as much as I needed. That night was gorging night.

Fellow travelers got their thrills with cheap grass. I preferred the blending of silken/salty/smooth Beluga with rough/fiery/bitter Persian vodka and the adventure of being a religious fanatic. One gets one's thrills where one can.

A year later, I was in caviar-poor Bangkok. But the Thais have their own "poor man's caviar," which was almost as relishing. This is called "kai pla duk," or catfish eggs. The eggs are the size and color of Beluga, and perfectly acceptable in a salad with fresh onion slices and ground-up green papaya. (Are you jealous, Mr. Petrossian?)

Fortune smiled upon us when the Thai government recognized the Soviet Union in 1972. In honor of the first Soviet ship landing, a grand party was thrown, which I attended with a colleague from the Bangkok Post. At my suggestion, she beguiled the already sloshed Russian captain into revealing the caviar larder to us. Then we all went down, he pulled out his caviar-larder-opening key, we took about two hundred cans of caviar, loaded it into her car, and invited the captain back to my apartment with promises that he could seduce her for his efforts.

He was not disappointed, although his feeble attempts at love ("Better in the desire than the performance," said Shakespeare) were useless. He left in an hour while we surfeited ourselves for weeks. For Sunday brunches, in fact, we entertained goggle-eyed friends by serving bagels, cream cheese, and caviar.

Hong Kong was a different story. Those of us in the know knew that up in Manchuria, fishermen preferred the five-hundred-pound pearly saline meat of the sturgeon to the eggs. They did collect the eggs and preserved them in brine, but neither they nor the Communist bureaucrats had any idea of their worth in the world. Each week, one of us Hong Kong people would make the milk run to a town on the Kaluga River and bring back eight or nine pounds of Kaluga caviar. The eggs had the same quality as Iranian, but we had to salt our own. Still, paying a few dollars for so much caviar was a treat. We had many a Kaluga party accompanied by pink Portuguese champagne.

Alas, this caviar became extinct after a while when a nasty Swedish company used the Kaluga fishermen as Manchurian candidates for exploitation. They corrected salting, packing, and pricing, putting an end to our joys.

However, when it comes to Have-I-Got-A-Caviar-Deal-For-You stories, nothing beats the caviar-for-Levi's-Jeans transactions of the 1980s. While I had long since left Thailand, I regularly paid court to the new offices of the Bangkok Post in the port area of Klong Toey. Here, friends would chaperone me to a clothing shop that had a big freezer by the cash register. And there we would buy caviar.

This was part of the barter system. Russian sailors, who would never be paid anyhow, would steal caviar from the ship's refrigerator and barter the cans for rare, real Levi's jeans. About fifty cans (which were free for them) for one pair of Levi's. The purloined caviar would then go into the freezer of the shop, and we would purchase them for fifty baht each, then $2.50. With an egocentric mania equal to bathing in mare's milk or coating oneself with gold, we would order some kwaiteo ladna kung – noodles with shrimp – and pour a can of caviar into the mixture. An act that was obviously heretical, indefensible, and utterly delicious.

Below are some musings on caviar done over the years.

ODE OF THE HAPPY CAVIAR PHILISTINE

They say the Caspian has the best,
Russia, Iran, or even Romania:
But caviar east or caviar west
May make major mouthfuls of mania.

So when dining with friends or dining at home,
The taste is always the crème de la crème.
Ask not from whence your fishy joys come:
They are the roes by any other name.

MAE WEST'S PERSONAL CAVIAR'S CRY OF HELP TO AN IGNORANT PURCHASER, FEARING UNSEEMLY TEMPERATURE FLUCTUATIONS

"Is that a Beluga in your pocket, or are you simply glad to freeze me?"

A WARNING TO FRAUDULENT EVANGELISTS

You'd best seduce less
And not tempt more:
With bad eggs, do not mess:
Caviar emptor!

A CAVIAR LIMERICK

A Caesarean birth specialist surgeon
Gives up his trade without urgin':
If no money he begs
Then he takes eggs
From the patient, if primitive, sturgeon.

SONNET FOR A CASPIAN TREASURE

Shall I compare thee to a cheese soufflé?
Thou art crunchier, popping, salty, light.
In noontime sun or darling bowls in May
As ebon as the prehistoric night.
Sometimes too hot a soufflé burns,
And often is its gold complexion browned.
Its crust is warped or its freshness turns.
But thou need no top, not even lemon crown'd.
From thy mighty mother art thou plucked,
Each ovum carefully, delicately stroked
With saline spray, each skin is safely tucked
Finally in thy barrel art thou cloaked.
Then consumed upon a gentle blinis:
As mortal life: eat and love from start to finis!

(Alternative last lines)
Now I know what enthralling sin is:
Sour cream, onions, caviar and blinis.

Recipe: Caviar

No secret recipe here. Put a tiny spoonful on rye bread, which has a little unsalted butter. Toast or blinis pancakes Russian style are fine. (Blinis comes from fermented buckwheat batter.) The Russians may serve it with sour cream, but that's why Communism failed. You could also roll caviar with Scottish salmon, but why mix apples with oranges? Or caviar with salmon?

CHAPTER NINE

THE VEAL OF TURIN: A MIRACULOUS TAIL
Recipe:
Peppers Stuffed with Pasta

The most fascinating trial I ever saw was in the outdoor square of a Central Turkey village some years ago, where a donkey had been accused of kicking its master to death. In front of three judges, the donkey had a defense attorney, prosecutor, and enthusiastic partisan crowd of spectators. Found guilty, the donkey was hanged that very afternoon. If donkeys can be tried for murder, if Emperor Caligula can make his horse a senator, why can't the world's oldest veal be turned into a saint?

Thus, the following musing on a napkin in Istanbul.

VATICAN CITY, May 18 (Wire Services). For the first time in the history of the Roman Catholic Church, a quadruped was declared an applicant for sainthood. Pope Gouda IX yesterday declared that the "most venerable and delicate of vertebrates, the Holy Veal," was to be presented before the Sacred College of Cardinals, to go through the arduous process of both beatification and canonization, at the end of which the dish could be worshipped.

Sweeping through the poorer districts of Turin is itself a miracle, since, as one parishioner has said, "Nobody ever swept up the place before. The garbage collectors are always on strike." Nonetheless, this particular animal has been worshipped for more than five years, and devotees line up for miles each day to pray to the sacred animal.

What distinguishes this veal from all other veal?

"For one thing," said Sister Ricotta, who has resided in Turin for more than sixty years, "Holy Cow is the oldest veal in the district. Usually, veals die before they are one year old. This veal, Holy Cow, is now about six, maybe seven years old, and is as sweet as the day he was born. Holy Cow is really ancient. For a veal, that is.

"Second thing is that Holy Cow got such a pretty face. The long eyelashes, the mournful mouth, those sad trusting eyes. We really get inspired by that sort of thing.

"But what makes Holy Cow special is that many people hear him talking. Not just veal language, which nobody around here understands. But Holy Cow sometimes says stuff. I haven't heard it myself, but lots of people hear Holy Cow say things in Italian like 'Be good.' Or 'Give all your money to the poor.'"

"In both testaments," explained Father Franco Roquefort, Dean of the College of Cardinals and advisor to the College Homecoming Prom, "the veal has been a spiritual animal. In one of Noah's forgiven transgressions, he allowed three veals to board his ark, in case one of the veals didn't want to 'do' it.

"The Jewish Talmud has an aphorism that says the presence

of this animal is a sign of Jewish presence. I believe it is written, 'Where there's a veal, there's oy veh.'"

"Another story, which has never been verified, has stated that during the Sermon on the Mount, the actual 'mount' was in fact one of the many veals in the area, taken by our Savior from the herd of veals. While the animal was relatively unknown, today everybody has heard of veals. And during the first days of the Holy Mother Church, according to the Acts of the Apostles, women who proclaimed vows of chastity would be known in the vernacular as 'taking the veal.'"

With a laugh, Father Roquefort admitted that not all of veal theology is necessarily 'gospel truth.' "Archives from the cellars of the Vatican have alluded to a third-century Encyclical proclaiming martyrdom when veal is roasted," he noted. "But most of us call this the 'Silly Encyclical.'"

In the sixth-century Council of Vinaigrette, several holy fathers decreed one of the original animals in the stable of the birthplace of Our Savior was actually a veal, not an ox, since oxen were traditionally grazing in mountainous pastureland during the winter season.

(Several delegates to the Council left the mother church that morning, led by the charismatic Father Cambinzola, to form what later became the Church of the Alternative Nativity. In what became known as the Schism á Fromage, they declared that in a Hebrew mistranslation, the "ox" was actually "a hunting dog." This led to a nine-hundred-year heterodoxy later celebrated as the "Breakfast of Beagles and Ox".)*

Since taking note of the Turin phenomenon, the process of making the veal into a saint goes through several stages. The first is, of course, beautification. "That," said Monsignor Thomas Pecorino, "is actually a formality. To 'beautify' the meal is simply to make a decent marinade, like the one you will see below.

"And maybe add some parsley."

After this comes the real test: the canonization of the animal. (The church frowns on jokes about the "cow-nonization" of the veal.) The parties involved in this include the Protector of the Faith, the Advocatus Diaboli (or Devil's Advocate), and the Sacred Curdler of Rites.

"What happens," explained Msgr. Patrick Pecorino, "is that we have this big cocktail party right in the Sistine Chapel. We got everything there. A band with piano and drums and guitar, a singer, some very good hors d'oeuvres with those little sausages (some of the fathers call them 'hot dog-mas'), a few bottles of Italian wine, beer, and a sainthood cake, where the Pope makes a nice speech before he cuts it.

"Very classy altogether."

But the cocktail party is more than just sausages and dancing. Serious work goes on here. Usually, the Protector of the Faith and the Devil's Advocate have contests, like Twenty Questions or arm-wrestling or Latin Scrabble. Nor does the Sacred Congregation of Rites just sit around and nibble on crackers and cheese.

"Usually, they have to make up holy riddles based upon the Liturgy," said Msgr. Pecorino. "Or they divide themselves up into Franciscan, Augustinian, Jesuit, and Dominican, and they have a baseball tournament. Inevitably, the Dominicans win. They win the car rallies, too, with their autos-da-fé."

But at the end of the cocktail party, all the participants have to talk about canonization of Holy Cow. And for this, they need to mention two miracles ascribed to the animal.

"Still we don't know what these miracles will be," said Sister Ricotta. "Maybe eating the sauce without dribbling, or cooking the veal so it comes out juicy and not dry but not too rare, either. At any rate, my job is to train the choir. So should the miracles be performed, we will have a special song for the occasion."

The song is still secret writ, of course. But already those in the know know that in the beginning are the words…

"It was only a Papal Bull

   Looking over a Papal See…"

*Another theory in discussing the animals was that they were meant to be sacrificed. Apparently, on the walls of the crèche in the holy stable was pinned a sign from God proclaiming "On peut manger ici."

Recipe:
Peppers Stuffed with Pasta

After such a saintly tale, it would be iniquitous to simply write down one's favorite recipe for escalope of veal or saltimbocca. Instead, here is a more pristine dish, coming from a far from pristine city, Naples. The great composer Giacomo Rossini loved Naples. And even after being robbed once, I returned for a few days, visiting the Cabinetto Secreto in the museum, whose sexual paintings and mosaics are quite the most phenomenal in the world. At an outdoor restaurant, I enjoyed some Neapolitan peppers stuffed with a kind of spaghetti. It was highly original, and with the help of a translator I took down the recipe while watching them prepare it. The measurements are only approximate for about four people.

4 large yellow peppers
½ c. black olives, pitted and chopped
2 tbsp. parsley, chopped
2 anchovy fillets, chopped
1 garlic clove, peeled and chopped
½ small dried chili pepper, seeded and chopped
1 tbsp. capers, rinsed
Salt and pepper
5 tbsp. extra virgin olive oil
10 oz. spaghetti
2 tbsp. dried breadcrumbs

1. Grill the peppers until the skin is charred and, with dexterity, remove the skin with a sharp knife. (This was done quickly and viciously: Perhaps the best thing is to place the peppers in a bag or the fridge until they are cool enough to handle.)

2. Cut them in half, remove the core and ribs, and wipe clean.

3. Combine the chopped ingredients with the capers, salt and pepper, and half the oil.

4. Cook the spaghetti and drain when slightly undercooked. Transfer that to the bowl of chopped ingredients and mix thoroughly. Add the seasonings.

5. Heat the oven to 425 degrees. Brush a roasting pan with some of the oil, place the pepper halves in the roasting pan, and fill with the spaghetti mixture. Sprinkle with crumbs and oil.

6. Bake for about 10 minutes until a light crust has formed.

Chapter Ten

ONE OCTOPUS SANDWICH, AND HOLD THE DODO!
Recipes:
Octopus Vindaye/Fried Wasp Grub and Onions

Another public relations disaster was overcome when I was invited by a friend from the Air Mauritius Bangkok office, one Rupert Russell-Cobb Esquire, to describe the resorts. The mixture of peoples—African, European, Malay, Chinese—were ethnically interesting enough, but the resorts rather tawdry. On the surface, the resorts advertised extraordinary deep-sea fishing. But the real reason was that South Africans, some twenty years ago, could have sexual experiences denied them in their own country.

Outside of [what Shakespeare called] the "naughty house," or the "leaping house," Mauritius had sugar plantations, a light industry then stocked with Mainland Chinese laborers who lived in appalling conditions. It also had an airport, and I took my little legs as quickly as possible to the French island of Réunion, a mere fifteen minutes away. As the French believe their civilization should extend to the ends of the earth, daily planeloads of French produce are dispensed to the otherwise unemployed residents of this territory. Thus, in the middle of the Indian Ocean, far away from anything remotely approaching the Champs Elysées, auberge restaurants serve up escargots, gigot d'agneau, fondant au chocolat, and a host of great Burgundy wines, under the torrid Indian Ocean sun.

But my favorite Réunion description comes from an old computer geography program called PC-Globe. Under Réunion's "Major Exports" were given products about which any decadent French poet, lolling about in his drug-induced cloud, would have been proud. Réunion's major exports were listed as "Sugar. Rum. Molasses. Lobster. Perfume essences. Tea. Vanilla."

The only necessity lacking for a fin de siécle poet is absinthe, to make the heart grow fonder.

Back to Mauritius, though. And food. Ordering breakfast in Mauritius can be dangerous. Reckless tourists who order "black coffee" in a republic that relies on the sugar industry may be crucified on coconut trees. Asking for "a breakfast sandwich" in the town of Flic-en-Flac is asking for trouble. Sandwiches in Flic-en-Flac are touch-and-go situations. In fact, most travelers touching a Flic-en-Flac sandwich immediately go. And always elsewhere.

On my first morning in Flic-en-Flac, I pulled up a three-legged wooden stool on the pavement at Rajeesh's Breakfast Stand, a wood shack on the main street, and asked for black coffee and their local sandwich offering.

Mistake number one. Café noir does not exist in Mauritius. One may as well ask for a singing rhinoceros. So, while Rajeesh's son, a six-year-old boy with eyes the size of basketballs, was brewing up the French roast coffee, Rajeesh was assiduously pulling down sugarcane trunks from a nearby truck and pressing them through a sugarcane pressing machine that was antediluvian when Napoleon's troops came invading here some two centuries ago. As they say in the coffee business, I took my lumps without complaining.

The sandwich was the specialité de la shack. An octopus sandwich, fresh from the waters around Flic-en-Flac which, as Rajeesh explained, swarm with primitive beasts.

"Like South African tourists?" I laughed.

"No," said Rajeesh, seriously. "We have giant squid and octopus, and sharks and sponges."

"I would imagine that the waters would be much deeper without all the sponges," I said. Rajeesh wisely paid no attention.

"Do you want some ghee with your octopus sandwich?" he asked, as if asking if I wanted a pickle with my corned-beef sandwich. I told him that Flic-en-Flac mayo-and-octo was very Noo Yawk Noo Yawk.

"But you fix it up the way you want," I smiled. "And tell me how you make it. Don't spare the details."

"The tails?" he asked. "I am afraid we cannot give you the tails, as we use only the meat from the arms. And the flesh from the belly, and…"

"Never mind," I said. "Describe for me the preparation."

Rajeesh became serious. The Confederation of Deep-Six Gourmets had come to session.

"First," he said, "we make a rougaille. A traditional Mauritian method of browning the oil. We use rougaille everywhere here, browning tomato paste, garlic, and onions."

He offered me the pan, which had a light brownish sauce at the bottom, already percolating little bubbles. Then Rajeesh reached into a box and pulled out some white-pinkish cubes, which he threw into the pan. Then little pods, like the bottom of snowshoe tires, the tips of the octo-arms. He threw them into the pan, too, raised the flames, and the sizzling began as he served another customer.

He returned to finish talk of the preparation.

"And now," he said, reaching for a yeasty white roll on the counter, "we take a roll and cut it in half."

Rajeesh took a wooden spatula, turned over the meat in the pan, and turned up the flames to the max for a minute. Then he spooned out the meat.

"Now the mystery is revealed. We place the octopus on the bottom half of the roll, we put ghee on the top half, and then ... voila! Octopus sandwich!"

The "voila" part is less exclamation than affirmation that Mauritians speak so many languages that Sir Richard Burton, reputed to speak close to a hundred tongues, would be considered illiterate. Added to that, Mauritius has more types of food than any other obscure remote ocean republic that is usually confused with Mauritania, Madagascar, Malaysia, and Mali.

Octo and ghee. I took the sandwich and coffee out to the seaside, pulled and tugged at the octo, let the syrupy coffee mixture drip down my gullet, threw the ghee-covered bread to the gulls, and had a downright delicious Flic-en-Flac feast.

Food choices start with Indian, French, Creole, and Chinese (the latter of the sweet-and-sour variety). Then you have a Malay intermixture of tiny peppers, tomato paste (the word "ketchup" is itself of Chinese extraction), and garlic. This comes from the original Malay inhabitants of nearby Madagascar, which adds peppercorns to the brew.

The fish is blue marlin, and is on every menu, and when the octopus is "off," blue marlin sandwiches are equally appetizing.

Mauritians are fishermen, but also hunters. One area is called Domaine du Chasseur. Here, you catch your own stag in the Mauritian equivalent of the Versailles deer park, and stag chefs cook them for you. They also insist in Mauritius that the wild boar is the sweetest in the world, since it relies on guava.

"Guava," said Patrick Maurel, a noted chef, "is of course fruity. And because it does not digest as well as other fruits, the taste stays with the animal even after cooking. I have had suckling pig in Hong Kong and barbecued spareribs in Memphis. But no pork dish matches that of Mauritian wild pig. Of that you can be assured.

"We also have palmier, hearts of palm, which are boiled with a smooth vinaigrette sauce. But I prefer to quickly fry them, giving them a crispy taste."

But the ultimate Mauritian taste experience is neither octopus nor stag, nor hearts of palm. It is a restaurant that can be duplicated nowhere else in the world, and called, with severe understatement, Carnivore Restaurant.

Carnivore Restaurant does not prohibit vegetarians. But truth to tell, vegetarians here are as welcome as Colonel Gaddafi at a bar mitzvah.

This is animal flesh country. Before eating, customers gulp down one of the ten-odd Mauritian rums that stand in miniature bottles on each table. The mildest rum – which Mauritians presumably feed rambunctious babies to make them sleep – could be labeled "Nuclear trigger." Rum for teetotal tourists could be titled "War of the Worlds."

The strongest Mauritian rum cannot be drunk by earthlings. Consequently, it could be compared to the big bang theory for the genesis of the universe.

Creationists are not welcome.

Some customers do mix their rums, with fruit juice or plain old whiskey. But this is a waste of rum, something like pouring uranium into a water pistol.

Nobody uses a menu at Carnivore Restaurant. You sit

at tables under the sun in a yard dominated by a barbecue grill that seems about a hundred feet around, the flames bursting out, sizzling with beef, chicken, suckling pig, sausages, lamb, mutton, and fish.

Where did this barbecue come from? The word itself is derived from another French island colony, Haiti. It referred to a torture device, where one hung people over a fire until well cooked. In this setting, that seems most appropriate. You can add the sauce of soy, honey, garlic and pepper, but nobody bothers to, as the meat is so tender.

Pounds and pounds of dead fowl, fish, and mammals are blackened, skin popping off, and ravenous guests gorge themselves into a carnivorous Nirvana, far into the night.

My host, Marcel Noe, is the editor of a Mauritian newspaper and a noted gourmet, and he told me why Mauritians love their meat. The reason is exactly why Fijians originally loved human flesh. Because there was virtually no mammal to eat here when the Europeans arrived, and man cannot live on coconut and hearts of palm alone.

"Flesh to flesh I call it," said Marcel. "We didn't have mammals here until the Dutch landed some four hundred years ago. They brought with them macaque monkeys, deer, and presumably they brought the rats, too. We have them all."

Monkey kharri is typical of the wild animal fare, he told me, the curry strung together with a marinade of garlic, cloves, cinnamon and, of course, tomato paste.

This did not sound appetizing at all, and I told him so.

First, the monkey. I have not eaten, and will not eat, monkey. Monkey is the creator of a grand lie (i.e., monkey brain). The legend is that Chinese sit around a table with a hole cut in the center. The inebriated monkey sits under the table, its brainpan removed. The brains are spooned out and put on to a sizzling plate and then consumed like sweetbreads.

Countless times I have been asked if I had eaten this, and countless times I tell them that it is not true. William Mark, the most esteemed Hong Kong expert on Chinese food legends, with whom I had the honor of co-authoring a book, told me that it is "a Chinese urban legend, based upon the Mongolian barbecue table. But no monkey brain has ever been eaten." I believe Willie.

But it was the curry part that was off-putting. I can take strong Thai or Ceylonese curries without fear, thinking of them as the musical dissonance of Charles Ives or Edgar Varèse. Milder Malayan curries or Indian kormas, made with sour curds and coconut milk, have an equal attraction to the taste buds, like eighteenth-century French harpsichord music is to the ear.

Hélas, these Creole-Mauritian curries are usually botched up a tomato dressing which is gloppy, gunky, and sloppy. Which was exactly what I told Marcel Noe.

He shrugged his shoulders and said: "Well, then, I suppose you are not interested in how we curry our roast tenrec."

"Roast…er, what?"

"The tenrec," he said. He looked at me as if he were facing an inner city child who had never heard of Shakespeare. And years later I have exercised unfair one-upmanship at Manhattan gourmet dinner parties by inquiring about one's favorite tenrec recipe. When ignorance is expressed, I close my eyes in exasperation and explain that tenrec is – as anybody should know – the Madagascar hedgehog.

"Oh," these putative gourmands say, hanging their heads in shame, their ignorance on display. "We had no idea…" (I actually have never done this, but dream of doing it some day.)

Mauritians, though, do have the idea. The cooking isn't as meaningful as the hunting.

"Our tenrec," said Noe, "lives six months on land, then six months in a cave, hibernating. The time to catch it is in mid-April, just before it goes burrowing into the ground. That is when the tenrec is at its fattest and juiciest.

"We trap the hedgehog in the forest and skin it. Then we marinate it with onions, garlic, ginger, and cinnamon and put it in tinfoil. Then we put it into the oven for two hours."

Noe also remembered a childhood treat in Mauritius – wasp grub. He tried to impress me, but I told him how the Northeast Thais take combs of wasp honey, eat all around, then swallow the grub live. A deliciously sweet treat.

This, though, was primitive at best. "We spoon out the grub in Mauritius," Noe explained, "and mix it with honey and Ajinomoto. Then we fry it with onions in a large Chinese wok."

While this was all interesting, nobody was talking about the single creature that gives Mauritius its questionable influence in the world of food. For this I had to repair to the museum, where on display are the only known supposed bones of the Mauritian dodo.

The dodo, both in looks and attitude, had to be compared to the legendary Shmoo, a mythical animal created by Al Capp, creator of Li'l Abner. The Shmoo loved humanity so much that it would waddle up to men and women and fall down dead in order to be eaten, its meat tastier than anything in existence.

According to Dutch sailors, the dodo, the only known creature on the island, was big, fat, friendly, and goofy. With no fear of humankind (or human-unkind, as it transpired), the dodo would wander up curiously, only to be battered down with clubs or blasted with buckshot.

An anonymous seventeenth-century "frying Dutchman," who described the meat in his diary as being "oily and fatty," gave the only known description.

Nonetheless, within a hundred years Mauritians had to revert to octopus sandwiches, since every known dodo had gone to dodo heaven.

As for the dodo-dining Dutchmen, their diets were soon supplanted with their favorite cheese. So, with the dodo, demised and gone with the Indian Ocean wind, their chefs would have exclaimed, "Frankly, my dears, we don't give Edam."

Recipe:
Octopus Vindaye

Since the creator of this dish, Guy Felix, was chief physiotherapist for the Mauritius Ministry of Health, you certainly won't get sick with this. Vindaye is the Mauritian name for the French vin d'aile, a garlic/wine covering used a hundred years ago. The Mauritians all make their own covering with green mustard powder, green chilies, garlic, sometimes peppercorn and saffron. This is the recipe:

    2.2 lb. tender octopus
    4.4 oz. ginger
    4.4 oz. garlic
    4.4 oz. grams green saffron diluted into ½ c. of vinegar
    6 large red peppers halves
    40 cl. mustard oil
    9 oz. of small onions

Preliminaries:
1. Wash the octopus and rub with coarse salt until the mucous has disappeared.
2. Pound them on the grinding slab. Cut into pieces.
3. Wash, drain, then mix with table salt and a pinch of ground pepper.

Cooking:

1. Pour all the oil into a Chinese wok, turn up the heat, and fry the octopus.
2. As soon as it becomes red, reduce the heat and cook over a moderate heat for half an hour. Stir frequently.
3. Remove from the pan and drain. Brown the garlic and the ginger, and add the pepper with optional very hot pepper.
4. Add the crushed green saffron diluted into vinegar and cook for 2-3 minutes.
5. Add the small onions, cook for 5 minutes, then add the octopus and cook for a few minutes.
6. Sterilize glassware by boiling for 15 minutes. Dry and pour the vinegar with hot oil. You can substitute tuna for octopus.

Recipe:
Fried Wasp Grub and Onions

This is a Mauritian dish favored in the countryside. Guy Felix gives his own special impact to the recipe:

2 twists oil
1 tbsp. vinegar
1 tsp. soy sauce
1 large wasp comb
2 large Bombay onions (or Georgia onions)
1 teaspoon Ajinomoto

Preliminaries:

1. Pass the comb over a flame, knock lightly with the palm of the hand, and the grub will fall onto the plate. The grub must be sorted out and only the larva kept, because some may have started changing into adult wasps.
2. Place this larva into a bowl, adding Ajinomoto and soy sauce. Mix well. Mince the large onions.

Preparation:
1. Put oil into a wok. Put the grub into hot oil, stirring continuously for 2 minutes.
2. Make a hole in the midst of the grub and place the onions.
3. Fry for 30 seconds and stir for another 2 minutes. Before retrieving from the fire, add a spoonful of white vinegar and restir.
4. Serve hot with rice and a hot chili sauce. You can have a vegetable fricassee with the same dish.

P.S. Guy Felix gives instructions on how to get wasp grub on the top of trees. "One must use a long stick, at the end of which are attached old pieces of cloth set to flame. The smoke frightens the adult insects. When the adults are really gone – and this is very important, since a wasp bite is everything but interesting – a blow with the stick on the comb makes the latter fall. I can only hope for you that the comb will be full of grub."

Chapter Eleven

Federico Garcia Lorca: The Gravy of Redemption
Recipe:
Tortilla à la Española

In my New York junior high school, the Literary Society once invited a famous, young, intense, very beautiful Filipino poet to address us. He asked us what we wanted to be when we grew up, and with the joy of being in the company of an angel we informed him of our goals to mature into eminent essayists, philosophers, painters, composers of great operas, historians, theologians, and (did we dare utter this?) even poets. I asked whether he had always wanted to be a poet. "No," he said, with mock-seriousness. "I wanted to be a window washer." We laughed, hesitantly, then he changed his mind.

"Poetry," he said, "is only my avocation. But I have always dreamed of being a pastry chef."

In his honor is this faux-biography and faux-poem of a real poet.

Before Federico Garcia Lorca discovered what he called "big bucks through small books," he was employed as a short-order cook in a Barcelona cantina. In short order, he realized that this work was ideal for his way of life. Years later, he reminisced about his life there.

"If it wasn't for the mega-dollars I make as a bard," he confessed to President Herbert Hoover during one of the celebrity galas in his Jackson, Wyoming, chalet, "I'd give up ode-making altogether. Sandwiches, you see, are useful. Unlike poetry, sandwiches belong to the world, regardless of race, class, or sexual orientation." (The President, who had once likened his Herbert Hoover Dam to a Rilke Elegie, stomped out of the chalet and spent the rest of the night vehemently skiing.) This, one of Garcia Lorca's early poems, penned on the back of a donkey saddle, exhibits the same abject remorse he felt in his later mucho dinero years. (Actually, it was scribbled while waiting for a ride from Meshed, Iran, to Afghanistan in another happier time.)

> Culpa mea! I'm a tortilla!
> The slivers of jalapeno
> Chilies burst my skin
> As arrows burst
> The nakedness
> Of Sebastian, our Saint.
> "Mother, mother," I call, but she stares blindly, eyeless,
> Gazes hopeless at that gravy-greyed orb on the sidewalk.
> "It is me, me, Madre," I wail, like the wounded soldier.
> From the reeking dough that has become my Iberian skin.
> "Touch me, feel my crust," I whisper and genuflect to her.
> With rainbow tears, she cries

For her long-lost son.
Gazing at the sepulcher.
On the tortilla floating
In the iridescent gutter.
"Yes, my body is pastry,
Trembling as you touch."
Here in the pepper sleet
She listens to the wind
And in the tapas of her mind
She stops and cries and howls.
"Oh howl, my stillborn son."
Now she raises me, her child.
But this tortilla is as a wafer.
She continues to devour me.
Ah, communion! In her mouth
How warm is mother's tongue.
How flush the potato freshness
Of her breath.

Recipe:
Tortilla à la Española

The Spanish tortilla is the simple omelet, which Garcia Lorca would have enjoyed as a youngster in the slums of Madrid. The "potato freshness" is echoed in the filling, which is really terrific. Although he was very much a loner, this recipe serves four, so the poet would have had to go out and find three amigos.

    4 small potatoes
    ½ c. oil
    ½ tsp. salt
    8 eggs

1. Peel the potatoes and cut into very thin slices. Dry them on paper towels.
2. Fry in hot oil until tender and lightly browned.
3. Drain off the excess oil and season the potatoes with ¼ tsp. salt.
4. Beat the eggs (a chore in which Garcia Lorca took special pleasure). Put them in a bowl, and add the remaining salt.
5. Pour over the potatoes to form a round flat omelet.
6. Brown the omelet on both sides and serve with salad.
7. (Suggestions for the salad would include tuna, onion, olives and lettuce.)

CHAPTER TWELVE

THE GREAT DURIAN AIRLINE DISASTER
Recipe:
Terengganu Laksa

"And we'll live and laugh and tell old tales of durian."
—King Lear (revised)

A year was spent in India and Nepal, a year best written in another volume. One night you relish a sweet of incomparable sweetness, with rosewater, milk, sugar, honey, and pistachios. You learn the name, you put it in a notebook, and three miles along is another village. Here, you ask for that sweet. They do not comprehend. They look at you and smile as they would smile at a madman. The teacher of the village will come to see you and cluck sympathetically.

"No, no," he clucks. "That was another village. They speak a different language. They have different foods. They are different people. Here we do not do such things."

Thus, the philosophy of Indian desserts. They are created

by women as the sun comes up over the river, they are consumed at night as the sun goes down over the mountain. You move on. The sweets are ephemeral wisps, the memories are glued to the mind with cloying persistence.

That wasn't true in Goa, the ex-Portuguese colony with its little old hippy territories, endless beach, churches, mosques, temples, and—best of all—the roadside stalls selling brandies of the most dubious labels. Goa also has a cashew wine! Yes!!! It is evil and terrible, but if you happen to have a longing for cashew wine, well, get thee a ticket to Bombay and a train trip to the south. Goa will satisfy your desires.

Goa was also the Asian fount of the original Inquisition, and many a burning took place here. Visiting the home of the Archbishop of Goa, I asked to see the section of Old Goa where the autos-da-fé took place and was taken with some reluctance, to a middle-class apartment complex. And truly, I did feel noticeable vibes coming from this haunted ground. My guide, a young priest, told me that the vibrations were from a broken-down electrical generator, but I never lost my faith.

The boat taking me to Penang from outside Madras had docked in the early morning. I took a room in a Sikh temple and was accosted by two young Chinese gentlemen who told me that they had a wonderful position in their entrepenurial enterprise. Specifically, selling cod-liver oil to the starving headhunters of Borneo.

My only requirements were that I wear a necktie (which they provided), and that I approximate the mien and character of a medical doctor. A quick learner, it took me only a few hours to practice scowling in the little mirror of my temple communal room, lifting my finger in admonition, raising my eyebrows, then lowering my lips in sympathy.

That, with the necktie, seemed doctor-ish enough, so my ticket was purchased, and we flew to Kuching and began to traipse through the villages.

Thus, Sarawak was my first extended sojourn in Southeast Asia, though today I am hardly proud of my achievements there.

Our marks...er, customers were the Sea Dyaks (or Ibans) of Sarawak, who had been notable head-hunters until recently, and usually, we would see a few skulls peeking out from an old wardrobe or hanging unobtrusively under the rafters.

But if their heads were concealed, their medicine bottles were put on public display. Almost exclusively, these medicine bottles contained cod-liver oil. They were identical capsules, identical bottles—but the labels changed almost weekly, depending on which Chinese salesman was in the village. As I learned later, the salespeople would sit over a few beers in Singapore and make up exciting label-names, much as I did for products I was selling as an advertising creative writer in Hong Kong many years later.

On the label might be printed "Thousand Roses Cod-Liver Oil or "Eternally Life Cod-Liver Oil" or "Guarantee Happy Joy Cod-Liver Oil" or "Winston Churchill Healthy Cod-Liver Oil."

My group had a bottle called "Palmtree Lively Cod-Liver Oil." We would enter a house and my salespeople would look carefully at the other bottles, with disapproving sneers. They would confer with me in English and I would shake my head sadly, no matter what they said. Then they would speak in the Malay language, that selfsame patent-medicine-salesman-patter that predates Hippocrates. The patter would slowly be translated into Iban.

The litany recited, they would give a capsule of Palmtree Lively Cod-Liver Oil to me, the doctor. I would take a pill, hold it to the candlelight, bounce it once on a table (after all, cod-liver was supposed to give life and vibrancy), and finally pop it in my serious mouth, upon which a smile of contentment would appear.

Smiles would appear on all faces: The Doctor Approved! The Ibans would hunt for some old currency hidden away behind the heads, they would buy, we would give them ten or twelve bottles, and would take a boat or walk to the next village. At night we would divvy up the profits, they would go to the brothel, and I would go to bed with a mild case of acid indigestion.

I do feel guilty today that they paid for medicine they didn't need, but, like the world, I too have changed. The cod-liver oil, by the way, was real.

I learned much about Sarawak, through which I traveled for a few months after the salesguys got more sincere companions. But for the sake of this volume, my main knowledge came with my first taste of the durian. And the durian, to these lips, made my many trips to Borneo, Thailand and, of course, Malaysia, well worthwhile.

Sarawak is the home of this, the most fetid of all fruits, although its cultivation is best in other countries. Most foreigners hate it. I love it. In musical terms, the mango has the sweetness of Schubert, the papaya has the joy of Mozart, but the durian exemplifies the most recondite atonal music: difficult, alien, almost repulsive at first taste, but with a depth of flavor and penetration of emotions far more profound than its spiky surface. On those rare moments when one meets fellow durian devotees, talk and adventures are inevitable.

We switch now to a variety of countries, which include Malaysia, Thailand, and Laos. And we happily switch to one of my favorite Asian people, John Everingham.

Everingham is an Australian photographer who lived in Laos for many years, was thrown out by the left-wing Pathet Lao, crept back one midnight by swimming the Mekong River, then rescued his girlfriend and swam back with her to Thailand. Later, a movie was made of his exploits, and while John liked the actor who played him, the late Michael Landon, he found the whole film ridiculous.

"What happened was that the producer flew to the Mekong River and found that it wasn't 'Lao enough.' So he took the whole crew to Jamaica or Bermuda, where it was much prettier."

John and I share the same love of durian, but where I could indulge endlessly in Thailand, he was in durian-devoid Laos, so he took every opportunity to procure them. He joined me in northeast Malaysia to shoot a story on the breeding habits of the leatherback turtle mainly so he could buy durians on the way back, in southern Thailand.

If one must stay up all night on a beach waiting for half-ton female turtles to trundle up the sand to lay eggs, it's easiest with somebody else who relishes Southeast Asian food. And that was the enthusiastic John. Under the moon, while waiting for Ms. Turtle to take her own damned time, we argued about which country had the hottest curries, the spiciest peppers, Lao barbecued chicken versus Thai grilled chicken.

Each time the turtles made their perambulatory strolls, we stopped talking. He shot, I wrote. At about 4:00 A.M., the show was over, and we prepared for a three-hour wait for the bus, without coffee or beds or food. So the talk naturally turned to durians.

At first we were sensible. We spoke of the different kinds of durian, from the "Gibbon" to the ethereal "Golden Pillow."

"It's like butter," described John. "Butter and sweet almonds." He looked like TV's Homer Simpson, eyes rolling over the thought of a great meal.

"Nah," I said. "You can't even taste Golden Pillow. It's like a perfume, like a creamy perfume where you catch the essence, not the flavor."

Then we discussed the aroma, cursing out those visiting writers who themselves cursed the smell as a combination of rotten onions, sewage, New York subways, or dogs in heat.

"Those poor writers," said John. "They look at the silkworm, not the silk. Shit, anybody can eat a mango or an orange. Durians are for the elite."

Sunrise over the South China Sea is so glorious that even we were silent watching it ascend. Then we began to tell durian stories.

We spoke fondly about Robert Halliday, a renowned American music/food critic in Bangkok who, during the season, would visit a durian warehouse with a special "durian stick." He would pat each durian until he found the perfect resonance.

Then I recalled the famous durian court case, which John hadn't heard of.

"You don't know the story of the bar girl, the GI and the durian?" I asked in mock astonishment. Since the bus was coming in fifteen minutes, I truncated the tale along with the O. Henry conclusion.

"Well, last year, a GI in a Patpong Road bar was complaining about the 'crappy' smell coming from behind the bar. So up from the floor came this hooker who was eating a durian. I guess she was a bit drunk, too, and she took the husk with all those pointed spikes and attacked the GI in the face. The poor guy looked like he'd been with Mike Tyson for ten rounds, with blood pouring from his nose and his mouth. He needed emergency treatment. So he went after the girl and sued her for damages."

Astonished that somebody would besmirch the feelings of the durian by holding judicial hearings, John exclaimed: "Nobody could ever find her guilty, right? They found extenuating evidence, okay? She must have been found innocent."

"Not exactly," I told him. "By Thai law, she had attacked, and she was found guilty."

John looked crestfallen.

"But," I continued, "the judge, a patriotic Thai durian eater himself, while finding the attack not quite justified, fined her a mere two hundred baht – about ten dollars. And then he paid the fine himself."

"Wow!" said John, impressed. "I've always said that the Thais were real nobles."

We talked about great durian recipes. The ice cream, of course, and durian stuffed into bamboo. But John remembered a Sri Lankan specialty.

"They take fresh buffalo curd. Then they roll durian meat around until it's pliable, and they combine the two. It's heaven on earth."

For the next hour, we laughed about durian tales, scatological and juicy. When the bus for the Thai border arrived, we found our seat, stowed our bags, and continued spinning tales about our favorite fruit.

Once we arrived in Songkhla, Thailand, John was determined to buy at least two dozen durians and smuggle them into Laos. The job was cloak and dagger, since no airline will allow durian on board. The aroma is supposed to annoy the passengers, turn them woozy. We had to fly to Bangkok (challenge one), and John had to fly to Vientiane (challenge two, which he would confront in Bangkok).

So that night, after we had procured two dozen big fruit, each about the size of a football, we searched around for a way to hide them from nosy airline personnel.

First, we scraped together tinfoil and plastic bags from a dumpster near the hotel and a tiny hardware shop. Then, under the sky on the beach, we took reams and reams of plastic, covered each durian carefully, and canopied it with tinfoil. To finish the operation, we put each fruit into the bags John usually uses for sealing rolls of film in tropical climates.

To be on the safe side, though, we took this bundle of plastic-wrapped, foiled, bagged fruit and locked it in a big suitcase, which we could store in the baggage compartment. To celebrate these labors of Hercules, we shared a durian, and prayed that the gods would bless our efforts.

The next morning we innocently, insouciantly checked this contraband suitcase into the baggage compartment of Thai Airways and boarded. The plane was due to leave at 10:00 A.M., but as usual it was running late, and at 11:00 A.M. we were still on the ground. Hardly serious, we thought.

That, though, was when the stewardess stood in front of the plane and asked for our full attention. Being Thai, she tried to speak loudly, but her voice came out in a whisper announcing a serious problem on board.

In the translation from Thai, she said: "Somebody on this plane is not polite. Even though we have rules, a passenger has brought many durians on board. And the aroma has reached the cockpit. And the pilots are very unhappy. They will not leave the ground."

She was silent, thinking what next to say. Then she must have remembered her school days.

"Would the impolite people," she asked, "please raise their hands?"

We looked around to see if somebody else would take the blame. But John finally owned up to his crime and reluctantly obeyed, raising his hand like a schoolboy caught smoking. Then I raised my own hand, almost prepared to ask the teacher if I could make a wee-wee. Our stewardess looked embarrassed to see such nice foreigners feeling so guilty. She darted back to the cockpit, and then returned.

"Please," she said in halting English. "Please do something with the durian. Please go outside. We will find the durian for you. We will help you." Both John and I prayed silently that she wouldn't cry.

After a moment of silence, a magisterial "harrumph" came from two seats behind us. First, a short elderly man, dressed in wrinkled khakis laden with ribbons and medals, stood up. He was a colonel in the Royal Thai Army, now retired, but still ready to do his duty. He asked us with avuncular kindness how many durians we had. We told him we were carrying them for friends in a country that was bereft of durian. Like military orderlies from A Farewell to Arms, we were carrying blood to the wounded in an Asian Catalonia.

The colonel hesitated for a moment and then declared his plan to the other passengers. In military language, he announced that if it was all right with the farangs (us), everybody would disembark and share the durians together.

"It is," he said in Thai, "fair. It is the Thai way."

The episode, faintly reminiscent of those James Cagney prison movies, where all the inmates take blame for a crime, continued in good Thai fashion.

The stewardess darted back to the cockpit and the pilots agreed to the plan. The controls were dis-controlled, the doors opened, and every passenger disembarked. Our suitcase came out of the hold, bags were opened, storage container unglued, tinfoil removed, plastic unwrapped, and one of the passengers (presumably a terrorist) took out a carving knife to cut open the fruit.

Thus, for the next hour, while the plane lolled on the runway, we sat on the tarmac and ate durian and told stories and laughed and became soppy with the fruits and our new friends: passengers, pilots and, of course, our newest friend, the stewardess.

The sun was scorching us, but the durian cooled us, and the thought that we could recite yet another Homeric tale of durians cheered us and made us giddy with pleasure.

When we finally boarded, a mere ninety minutes late at high noon, every breath we took over the next two hours back to Bangkok breathed out the delicate aroma of Limburger cheese, old socks, and that oh-so-sweet taste of Thailand.

We, the fellowship of durian lovers, soaring as near to heaven as our sulfuric odors would allow. As durable, acrid, and luscious as life itself.

Recipe: Terengganu Laksa

The leatherback turtle is limited to the beach village of Rantau Abang, just twenty miles south of Terengganu on Malaysia's east coast. Until recently, this was an idyllic province, not corrupted either by religious fundamentalism or secular materialism. The food was wonderful, too. This recipe was given by a man whose name was Mohammed. He said that no last name was necessary, but I do thank him, wherever he is, for this spicy masterpiece takes advantage both of the seafood and spices of the region.

This recipe is for about five hungry people.

600 grams mackerel or herring

300 grams prawns

150 grams salted fish (Chinese groceries carry it)

150 grams coriander

80 grams cumin

A ground-up powder of about 100 grams dried chilies, 150 grams shallots, 50 grams garlic, 80 grams galangal, 80 grams ginger

50 grams turmeric powder

150 grams lemon grass

30 grams pepper powder

1 liter coconut milk
150 grams dried tamarind
100 grams sugar
30 grams salt
100 grams dried shredded coconut
600 grams soft noodles

1. Marinate the fish with salt for 15 minutes.
2. Steam the fish for 15 minutes and remove the bones.
3. Mix with coconut milk, pepper powder, tamarind, dried coconut, the ground-up mixture, salt and sugar, then bring to a boil.
4. Stir constantly and simmer for 20 minutes.
5. Place noodles in a bowl and garnish with prawns and salted fish.
6. Pour the sauce over the noodles and serve hot.

CHAPTER THIRTEEN

IN DARKEST BORNEO, WITH ANDY AND MAYONNAISE JAR
Recipe:
Spicy Stuffed Eggplant

Dark hours have been spent in sunlit Borneo. The Sarawak sojourn was described in Chapter 12. Brunei is in Chapter 15. Sabah was visited because, after some years in Asia, myths of an infernally hot sauce came to my nasal attention.

Now when it comes to the hautest of cuisines, Borneo is not on the top of the pedestal (except if you're standing on your head after a night trying to get rid of a hangover from tuak, a liquor made with rubber sap, viper skin, and rusty razor blades). Not a single epic poem has been composed for the lowly cassava or yam.

Still, Sabah does have one extraordinary dish, and this story tells of its mysterious discovery.

It begins with groups of Old Asian Hands, found on any beach in the Far East. One recognizes Old Asian Hands, since they are usually freckled, lined, brown with tobacco stains, fingernails dungy and cracking, and frequently shaking with palsy, rage, drink, and sudden spasms as cigarette butts burn down to the skin.

Old Asian Hands are also identified by their memories of hot food. When not comparing the women of Asia or the politics of Asia or the beers of Asia, they compare peppers. They vie with each other, contrasting curries from Ceylon (never Sri Lanka) with rendang beef in Sumatra and with Siracha fish sauce in Thailand. And they go on and on and on.

Although a non-smoker and a non-beer drinker, I participated sporadically in their chili discussions. We compared green Thai chilies with the yellow Mexican jalapeno. Szechuan fagara beans with Xinjiang Moslem hot pots. But always in these hot-tempered discussions, somebody would come up with the hottest food, silencing others ... until the next kaffeeklatsch.

Yes, in the old days I would partake of these burning talks. But having found the hottest condiment in the history of the universe, I have no intention of participating any longer. They can have their Ceylon, Thailand, Malaysia, Mexico…I (to paraphrase from Bergman in Casablanca) will always have Borneo.

More specifically, I will always have two different Borneos. I speak of a sauce that came secretly across the border from Indonesian Borneo to Malaysian Borneo, specifically the northeastern Malaysian state of Sabah. Perhaps transported by native carrier, perhaps on the backs of water buffalo tramping through remote rice fields, perhaps by the Punan people, who hide in the forest and appear like spirits…

But I get ahead of myself. For my own pilgrimage to find that hottest of hots, started with a simple trip to Sabah, on the northwest coast of Borneo island. The trip was taken in the company of a one-time actor, Andy Chworowsky, who today is distinguished by having the best restaurants (and least pronounceable name) in Hong Kong.

Like the Komodo dragon, Andy has no natural enemies, and while I usually travel alone, Andy, when he volunteered to come with me on a trip to Sabah, was a welcome companion.

Sabah, with a few exceptions, is more exotic in name than in sights. The capital, Kota Kinabalu, is flat and boring. Sandakan, on the eastern coast, has one of the great orangutan sanctuaries. Mount Kinabalu is the highest mountain in Southeast Asia, at more than twelve thousand sheer feet, and we actually almost climbed it. Fortunately, as we were driving to the base of the mountain seeing the primordial trail disappear through the trees and crevices preparing to ascend its mighty peak ... well, either Andy or I may have felt a drop of rain.

"Guess it's gonna rain," said Andy.

"Yep. Too bad. It woulda been nice to climb to the top," said I.

"Sure would have. Better turn back," said Andy. "We can look at the Venus flytraps." (That carnivorous blossom being the second local attraction.)

Okay, so that was the only drop of rain to fall in Borneo that summer. But it could have been a torrent; we could have been washed away, a loss to our near and dear ones. Right?

Anyhow, back to the chilies. In Kota Kinabalu, Andy and I had been standing on the port street during our first night, watching the fast-talking patent medicine salesmen telling how their potions would cure blood poisoning, toothaches, and curses from spurned girlfriends. Seeing our interest, an urbanized gentleman from the dominant tribe, the Kadazan, approached us and inquired why we had come to Sabah. We mentioned various exotic sights to see. He looked at us curiously, then shook his head. And scoffed.

"I see no particular reason why you should have come here," he told us. "Outside of this city, Sabah is only wild jungle. No roads are built. It would have been better if you hadn't come at all. Or, since you are already here, then stay in the city. Out there is too much jungle. Too many trees."

Having made his point, he turned away, while we pondered on the possible nastiness of trees.

Then he turned to us again and revealed what he could not reveal before. That, yes, Sabah did have one reason for being. And that single reason was enough to justify our journey.

"We have," he said with dark and heavy foreboding, "the hottest chili sauce in existence."

Well, of course we grinned. Foolishly, as it turned out. We, as American sophisticates living in Asia, laughed with a hearty guffaw. Yes, we'd heard that one before. We knew all the tales, we'd tasted all the peppers. And what did Borneo have anyway? Sago, cassava, rice, papaya … Never heard of no peppers here. Somerset Maugham's tongue was never burned enough for him to write Of Human Bandage. Joseph Conrad never tasted peppers spicy enough to jump back and shout "Lord! Grim!"

But the man who took us aside on that main street in Kota Kinabalu was not so easily put off. Like a narrator from Edgar Allan Poe, he spoke not in words but in italics and underlines and whispers.

"I tell you, having heard from B---, the great taster of chilies, that they do exist! That the torridity is deserving of a Latin curse! That across the wide expanse of the jungle, lying outstretched and lit by a white crest, is the blood-red oh so curséd pepper plant which, though remote, has the fervid savagery of the ancient Babylonians within its blasted stem."

He sighed, wrapped a black cloak around his shoulders, buttoned his Burberry raincoat, and hastened off into the night.

(No, no, you're right. It didn't happen that way. Actually, he said: "Hey, you gotta eat Borneo chilies. Hotter'n anything you ever tried before.")

Well, neither Andy nor I believed him, but we remained on the lookout. We were told that this sauce came not from Sabah itself (the British one-time colonialists having banned the pepper) but from Indonesian Borneo, a hundred miles to the south.

Since we were never to climb Mount Kinabalu, we decided to make another pilgrimage, this for the sacred pepper. Easier than climbing a mountain, we resolved to find the pepper on the Tenom express.

Tenom was the obvious destination, for (a) it was located right in the middle of the jungle, with no roads going in either direction, and (b) railroad tracks were actually laid down for Tenom in about 1890. They were supposed to continue to the coast, but through bad engineering and the usual corruption, the money ran out. So today the train runs along the coast from Kota Kinabalu, then down through the jungle, ending at Tenom, a town that goes into the mysterious interior.

"If the chilies are anywhere," I told Andy in italics, "they will be in Tenom."

We boarded the seven-car diesel engine train early one morning, and started peacefully chugging along at eight miles an hour. Not only is this train spotlessly clean, but it is the quietest in Asia. No restaurant car here: One loads up on papaya and pineapple and bread at the first station, Tanjung Aru. Within a minute, one is lounging in the countryside. To one side is the South China Sea, with a few islands jutting out, a few cargo boats taking timber, tankers on the horizon heading to nearby Brunei.

The other side of the train has more variety. Open lawns running into glistening rice fields. Children running outside the schools. Twenty miles on, the scenery became dense with the roots of a sadly depleted jungle. Potholed roads with sixteen-wheel trucks dragging big trees from the interior. Mangroves and casuarina trees guarded the train from the sky, with the vast empty beaches leading to the pine-brown sea.

At each tiny town – towns with a few palms, a main street of Chinese concrete shophouses, a mosque, a Buddhist temple and a church – the train would creak to a halt. Mail would be thrown over the side, fruit-sellers walk up to the windows, a few passengers saunter aboard, their clothing more varied than the scenery. Teenage girls in T-shirts and sarongs; old ladies in cheap cheongsams and Malay scarves; men in shorts and fedoras; children wearing starched white shirts, green shorts, and Malay flat hats. They sat quietly and munched fruit and stared at us, then back at the scenery.

Four hours later we arrived in the final coastal town, Beaufort, waited two hours, and then plunged into the jungle. The accursed jungle, which Borneo people call, with onomatopoeic justification, the ulu.

Only the trains can crawl through the ulu, since any roads would be quickly overgrown by the vegetation. The exuberant Kadazan passengers were replaced by the more morose jungle-dwelling Murut people. The train was now cruising in the huge Crocker Gorge, rising two hundred feet from the Padas River. We could see a few flat rafts and boats paddled desperately in the brown flowing street.

On the banks far below, an old man stood with a three-foot lizard he had just caught, waving the poor reptile to us on the train.

"A strange pet," said Andy.

"A momentary pet, destined for the cooking pot."

We both considered the ephemerally of reptilian life, but then moved on.

This was the scenery we expected in Borneo. The forest primeval, beautiful, impenetrable. And somehow comfortable. We imagined ourselves in a nineteenth-century barouche jiggling through the English Lake District.

At the end of the journey we, like Gertrude Stein speaking of Los Angeles, found there was no there there. Tenom was a square block of concrete shops around a dismal park. Three tiny shops, a dozen poolrooms, a few Chinese and Malay restaurants, and one hotel perched irrationally seven hundred feet up a hill. With a picture-postcard view of the tiny town and the surrounding jungle.

Nobody stays here, but since the hotel is owned by the government, a half-dozen girls from the capital staff it. Their main diversion is watching the train arrive in the afternoon. And depart in the morning.

Being Moslem and Christian girls from good families, they have no other diversions.

Again paraphrasing from Casablanca on the peppers, "We must have been misinformed," since they did not exist in this town and the plantations outside had only wild coffee.

But a few days later, we did find the pepper sauce in Kota Kinabalu by following our noses. And, frankly, our noses almost fell off in the process.

Coming back to the capital, we had been told that on Saturday–only on Saturday–one section of the market would have the celebrated chili sauce. An expedition of illegal refugees from Indonesian Borneo was expected near the capital, and they would be carrying this, their only treasure, to sell.

That Saturday, we planned our strategy. The concrete market that leaned precariously on the port was massive. We ploughed through rambutans and dried beef, sticky rice, dry rice, green rice, brown rice. We sauntered through basket shops and bamboo shops and through the fish market and...and then we had it.

Our noses had it. It was a smell that severed our nostrils like a yakitori master severing a chicken. One hundred feet away, yet our eyes started to tear, our noses to run – and with the enthusiasm only a hot-pepper man can exercise – I started to run, too, with Andy close behind me.

There it was. A great barrel, which Poe would have called a maelstrom of steaming blood-red pepper juice, sizzling, smoking, stirred by an untainted lady in a ramshackle shawl and hat.

We approached, like Dante's hero approaching the River of Flames. Upon our miming request, she spooned out for us – in a large Hellmann's Real Mayonnaise jar – our real Kalimantan chili sauce, which we covered (lest it escape), then taped, triple-taped wrapped in zinc foil, and smuggled onto the plane and into an unsuspecting Hong Kong.

That sauce lasted us for eight long months. It took only one drop–a single bead of the brew–to light up any curry. The secret was not only the hottest jungle peppers in the world, but that when the peppers were crushed with mortar and pestle, they were crushed with a dull mortar and pestle. So the skin, the seeds (the seeds being the secret of the sizzling heat) remained virtually whole, while concoctions of garlic and bits of onion were added.

Never have any people had hotter, more satisfying peppers. The steam was demonic, the taste was of pitchforks rammed into the tongue, the eye ducts became reservoirs, the nasal passages opened like the Grand Canyon. Our satisfaction was complete.

And today, when I see and hear those Old Asian Hands talking of their spicy memories, I can only cry and laugh. When speaking of pepper sauce competitions, it's a jungle out there. But we, Andy and I, had been to the jungle. And our eyes, thinking of that wonderful moment of discovery, sparkle and weep together.

Recipe: Spicy Stuffed Eggplant

Alas, the best recipes of Borneo are based upon the Three Ugly Sisters of foods: sago, cassava, and tapioca. They may all be the same vegetable, as I have done no research on any of the stuff, though I have been forced to eat it at times. I can find no recipes worthy of mentioning here. But Borneo does have wonderful forest eggplants, which are tinier than our oblong eggplant. They are light green and white in colour, rounded, hard, and work well in jungle curries of all kinds. This is a semi-urban Malayan recipe, but the stuffing gives a decent equivalent of the original "hottest sauce in the world."

> 4 eggplants
> Cooking oil for shallow-fat frying
> Stuffing
> ½ c. dried prawns, washed and drained (try to get tiny prawns)
> 6 fresh red chilies (very fresh)
> 2 dried chilies
> ½ piece roasted blacan (a fish paste, at any Asian grocery)
> 2 cloves garlic
> 8 small onions
> Pinch of salt
> Sugar to taste

1. Cut the eggplant slantwise along the length into pieces of 1½ inch thickness. Make a deep slit along each piece.
2. Put some stuffing into the slits.
3. Heat cooking oil. When hot, very gently put in 4-5 pieces of eggplant at a time to fry. When one side is done, turn over gently to cook the other.
4. Remove and drain well. Serve hot.

Chapter Fourteen

From Soup to Notes: Two Musical Musings

A. Richard Wagner: "The Ring of the Nibbling"
Recipe: Medieval Venison Stew

It is not generally known, but the great composer Richard Wagner (1813-1883) loved absolutely everything Jewish. Outside of his light-hearted drolleries ("The Jews are the scourge of the earth, deserving to be condemned inside towers filled with rutabagas and rotting pigs."), Wagner had nothing but admiration for these people. Thus, his operatic paean to Jewish business practices ("Tristan? I Sold It!") and garment-sewing machinery ("The Master-Singers"). Later commentators were not so charitable to the composer, but he laughed off their criticism as "nothing but circumcisial evidence."

Above all, Wagner loved a good Jewish meal. The evening he tasted his first bagel, his eyes blazed with rapture. Wrapping his shoulder-length Aryan hair around the golden orb, he laughed as he christened the dish "bagels and locks."

"I shall," he declared to the congregation of Bayreuth natives who had crowded around the delicatessen to watch the Master eating, "commit my inspiration to writing the four greatest operas in history, my magnum tetralogy in honor of the bagel."

Thus, Wagner's "Ring of the Nibbling," for which a brief synopsis of each opera is hereby appended.

I. Das Golden Ring

The Prologue brings us to the Kingdom of Val-Chollah, with its turrets of golden breads, its vaults of pickled herrings, and streets piled high with market sellers advertising potato pancakes and exotic blintzes. Through the centre of the street is an aqueduct of Rhine wine, wherein the three Rhine Maidens – Spaetzel, Strudel, and Schnitzel – disport themselves with joy and laughter.

Their play is interrupted by the great giant Gorgonzola, king of the Cheeses, who insists that they show him their Golden Bagel – the great Ring of the Nibbling. In fear, the nymphs lead Gorgonzola to the Bagel Cave, where he seizes the delicacy and begins to munch as the maidens scream in terror.

The next scene starts with Bratwurst, King of the Gods, and his wife Fricassee, she who guards kitchenly virtue. They are awaiting their breakfast, but their servant, Fasching, warns them that the Golden Bagel has been stolen. In a rage (orchestra playing thirty-five minutes of raging music fortissimo), Bratwurst vows revenge. Fricassee, though, has already gone to give her body to the evil-smelling Gorgonzola in exchange for the treasure.

In the meantime, Latke and his consort Pancake secretly take the Golden Bagel from Gorgonzola and hide it in the mountain fastnesses of the Kingdom of Hofbrauhaus, whose denizens seize it and transform it magically into a loaf of white bread. Bratwurst mourns and vows to go in search of the Golden Bagel.

II. Der Swine's-Knuckle

To protect his wife, Bratwurst enlists the wiles of Piggyknuckle, the infamous dwarf. Piggyknuckle is not so easily deceived by Gorgonzola and Pancake, and he disguises himself at first as Hansel, then as Gretel. First, he asks to be married to himself, as an example of incestuous transsexual narcissism. Then, when Das Grosse Court rules against that, saying it isn't aa apt example of Civil Reichs, he pleads to be let into a Gingerbread House and baked in an oven. However, he has not reckoned on the equal wiles of Latke, who indeed bakes Piggyknuckle, transforming him into a demon who is ready to deceive his one-time employer, Bratwurst. Together, the demons of Gorgonzola come together and send him on a pilgrimage which, if he succeeds, will transform him back into a wily dwarf.

III. Schweinfleisch

The pilgrimage begins with a long trip down the river of Wein, Women, and Song. Schweinfleisch, the great hero who has been worshipped from afar by the Rhine Maidens, but actually is in love with the delicious Pumpernickel, goes into a ship and sets down with his crew, rowing the boat with a Magic Pole, nicknamed Frederic Chopin. They pass the Smelly Factories of Cheese, the Jolly Towns of Dumplings, and the Dangerous Fighters of Oktoberfest, led only by the knowledgeable Scout of Frankland, the Michelin Guide. At the foot of the river, they have been told that the Golden Bagel is to be found — but they cannot find it. As they search in vain, Latka, Pancake and their cohorts sing the dazzling Cheesecake Chorus in evil triumph.

IV. Das Eating and Der Nibbling

Where could the Golden Bagel be? Bratwurst and Fricassee fly down from their perches, guided by the nose of a Magic Dachshund, whose nose has detected it under the Riccotaburg (The Mount of Cheese). With the help of Schweinfleisch, they dig furiously to find it, but as they dig they are assailed by Flying Chives, Grunting Onions, and the infamous Gentile Strawberries. Just as they are about to find the Golden Bagel, two of the most mammoth giants of all, Catskill and Hammercher-Schlemmer, descend on a swing made of dangling Schraffts, and condemn all the people to a terrible life, devoted to pleasing Calories, Carbohydrates, and Sloth. As the Cream Cheese Mountain pours down on them, the Kingdom of Val-Chollah goes up in flames, all the people are consumed, and Bratwurst screams in mortal terror, "Vee Are Toast!"

Curtain

Recipe:
Medieval Venison Stew

Wagner's Tristan und Isolde is fine on the mushy-love stuff, but kind of weak when it comes to the manly sport of hunting. The original romance, Tristan, had a long section on how to hunt and (more important) how to cut open the deer when caught. Tristan is an expert at this, as any member of the nobility would be in those days, and, like Hamlet with the actors, teaches them of their own craft.

Obviously, they owe him much for his lesson, and this is chronicled eight hundred years later with Thomas Mann's Debts in Venison.

The opera ignores the killing but does have a few references to hunting at the beginning of Act II. But the particulars obviously don't fit into Wagner's game plan.

Enough. Here is a medieval recipe for Venison Stew, taken from an extraordinary book by Lorna J. Sass, To the King's Taste, published by the Metropolitan Museum of Art. It is made for 4-6 persons.

> 2 tbsp. bacon fat
> 1 medium onion, minced
> 2 lbs. venison, cut into 1½ inch cubes
> (beef or veal stewing meat may be substituted)
> ¼ c. flour
> 1½ c. boiling water or beef stock

1½ c. red wine
2 tsp. finely minced fresh ginger or 1 tsp. powdered ginger
1 tbsp. (or more) vinegar
½ c. currants
Salt
½ cup breadcrumbs (optional)
Fresh deer's blood, to taste, if available

1. Melt bacon fat in a large saucepan.
2. Sauté onion in fat until it is transparent.
3. Dredge venison cubes in flour.
4. Brown cubes in skillet, combining them with onions.
5. Combine water or stock, wine, ginger, vinegar, currants, salt to taste.
6. Stir to blend.
7. Pour liquid over meat.
8. Cover and simmer for about 2½ hours or until meat is tender.
9. Add breadcrumbs to thicken, if desired.
10. If blood is available, remove pot from flame a few moments before adding it, as it should not boil. The blood will thicken and flavor the sauce as well as darken the color.

B. Antonio Vivaldi: "Le Quattro Gelati"
Recipe:
Çikolata Tatlisi

Music critics assert that during his sixty-five productive years, the great composer-violinist Antonio Vivaldi wrote only the same concerto some six hundred times, for every instrument from violin to bassoon to mandolin. True, they all seemed to have the same sounds and structures, but as his colleagues used to say, shaking the canal waters off their tunics, shrugging their Venetian shoulders: "Hey, it's a living."

More than a living, though, was a series of four violin concertos based upon sonnets written by Vivaldi himself, and these have become perhaps the most popular concertos of all time. The title, as any schoolchild knows, is Le Quattro Gelati, translated as "The Four Ice Creams." (Certain references, such as to a "Schubert tune" may seem suspect, since Vivaldi died thirty-six years before Schubert was born, but Vivaldi was a very prescient artist.)

The Four Ice Creams

I. Vanilla

1. From the Madagascar forests.
    1. Introduction in low woodwinds.
2. Pods are plucked and peasants trill.
3. Balancing their precious treasures.
    3. Brass and winds in march tune.
4. Ready for a vanilla thrill.
5. The whiteness of the earth's beginnings.
    5. Strings in reverential counter-theme.
6. Simple, yes, but oh so clean.
    6. Orchestra continues this elegaic theme.
7. So pure in taste, like grassy meadows.
8. White stars are vanilla beans.
9. And would'st stain it with chocolate sin?
    9. Jaunty hints of march.
10. Of course! This happy cream's a harlequin!
    10. Full orchestra in original march theme.

II. Chocolate

1. Darkness in the Afric jungle.
   - 1. Slow, soft tom-toms. Theme in double bass.
2. Gently drop the cocoa beans.
3. Blending with the morning dew.
   - 3. Glissandi on the harp, a lowly oboe theme.
4. With whispers in the wind so mild.
5. Cocoa's crushed and hints of spices.
   - 5. Softly, strings pizzicato.
6. Cinnamon and sugar drop.
7. Like rays of sunlight in the black.
   - 7. Strings start to bring forth a melody, falling back.
8. Of chocolate's land, so dark, so wild.
9. Take the chocolate, one small spoon.
10. The magic of a Schubert tune.
    - 10. Above tom-toms, pastoral oboe theme.

III. Strawberry

1. The berries have returned, so festive.
   - 1. Fast scherzo movement. Jaunty strings.
2. Greeted by the songs of sparrows.
3. Fountains dance with drops of orange.
   - 3. Full orchestra repeating the theme.
4. Pistachio nuts like Cupid's arrows.
5. To the pastoral farmer's flutes.
   - 5. Interlude of flute duet.
6. The sparrows twirl into the air.
7. A cone! A cup! A bowlful merry.
   - 7. Repeat of original theme.
8. Berries here and berries there!

IV. Tutti-Frutti

1. Ecce gusti! Behold the flavors!
    1. Sudden introductory chords.
2. Peaches, lemons without end.
    2. Swirling very fast string theme.
3. Tiramisu, caramel, melon
4. Spellbound artist's blend.
    4. Theme turned into a fugue with each…
5. Mocha beans, vanilla pods.
    5. …instrument following.
6. Apples, rose-hips, lovely berry.
7. Pistachio and gaudy almond.
8. Mixed for dancing to make merry.
    8. Full orchestra turning original theme…
9. Smoothly scooped, spooned, never glott.
    9. As dance theme, ending with first chords.
10. The universe savoring such sweet gelati!

Recipe:
Çikolata Tatlisi

Don't even attempt to duplicate the luscious ice creams of Naples or Sicily. It can't be done. One variation comes from Turkey, a prime influence in south Italian cuisine. This recipe comes from Tarsus, where St. Paul apparently had his revelations. One would like to think it was from the heavenly chocolate "rush."

    1 tbsp. gelatin
    2 c. milk
    2 oz. unsweetened chocolate
    ¼ lb. ground sweet almonds
    1 c. whipped cream
    ¼ c. milk
    ½ c. sugar
    ¼ lb. cut-up marshmallows
    3 egg whites
    Slivers of milk chocolate

1. Dissolve the gelatin in ¼ c. milk.
2. Put 2 c. of milk, sugar, and unsweetened chocolate into a saucepan and heat. Beat very fast for 2 minutes, then remove from heat. Add gelatin and milk and continue beating until smooth and creamy. Remove from heat, chill until it begins to set.

3. Stir in the marshmallows and almonds and fold in the egg whites, stiffly beaten. Then fold in whipped cream and chill thoroughly.
4. Serve in tall sherbet glasses decorated with the slivers of milk chocolate.

CHAPTER FIFTEEN

CRAZY RHYTHMS IN THE SULTAN'S KITCHEN
Recipe:
The Omnipresent Satay

To the best of my knowledge, Yiddish is not spoken in the third sector of Borneo, the Islamic Republic of Brunei. Yet, the only word to describe the Bruneians is chutzpah. They are the most brazen, audacious, arrogant, self-confident go-it-aloners in all of Borneo, as they have every right to be.

Brunei, you see, never needed anybody else. Not only were they never colonized (sharing this honor only with Thailand, China, and Japan), but they were the ultimate colonizers. In the seventeenth century, those daring sailors came out of the Borneo rainforests and conquered territory, which today extends between southern Malaysia up to Manila in the Philippines. Like the Bugis people of Indonesia, they sailed — without compasses, without even nails in their grand schooners – throughout the whole South China Sea. They took no prisoners, established no culture, built no cities, but were feared and venerated.

The word Borneo itself is a Portuguese translation of Brunei, since these people dominated the whole giant island. In fact, the division of Borneo into sections (the Dutch took the south, Rajah Brooke took the west, and the British East India company governed Sabah in the east) was a mere pimple on the history of the territory. Brunei was dirt-poor at the beginning of the twentieth century, as is obvious by a visit to the palace of the present Sultan's grandfather. It looks (to be charitable) like a poorly constructed giant outhouse. The discovery of oil soon made them, on paper, the richest people in the world.

Visiting Brunei Town to write an official history for the Royal Family, I was astounded at the ironies. Due to Brunei's wealth, the people pay neither taxes nor school or hospital fees. It also means that Bruneians go out to the coast, make a few rupiahs and come back to their "water village" houses. They throw so much garbage from their porches that the water today is literally papier-mâché.

Brunei is where the "All-Night Market" ends at 7:00 P.M., where the world's largest mosque and the world's largest palace and the world's largest polo stables and the world's largest Churchill Museum exist side by side, guarded by kids in NY Yankees baseball caps.

When the country of Malaysia was formed in the 1960s, intended to comprise Malaya, Singapore, Sarawak, Sabah, and Brunei, the Bruneians simply laughed at the idea. They could survive on their own, they had only contempt for others, and they still believe that the world revolves around the Sultan of Brunei. Which, with his riches, it possibly does.

His royal palace has thousands of rooms. But below the

surface–literally–is an underground Bedlam, which I was soon to discover.

While some stories in this book are frivolous, for mere entertainment, the following has medicinal value, assisting in the prevention of lunacy and incipient madness. While I make no claims that it can actually replace Prozac or the Freudian couch, the remedy here is … er, more rhythmic.

It started when I met Dieter, a young Salzburg chef who had been seconded by the Sheraton Hotel to run the kitchens of the Sultan of Brunei. When invited to the sultanate for some official royal writing, I had made his acquaintance. And after getting a pass to the royal palace (accomplished by showing my Hong Kong Park'n'Shop supermarket credit card as identification), I was directed to the royal basement, wherein the royal kitchens were sited.

But the word "kitchens" is insufficient. That would be like calling Wagner's Ring Cycle a coupla tunes. The kitchens were made up of eight miles of corridors. Nothing less would do for the world's richest man. The first time I was taken on a tour I lost at least three inches around the waistline hiking around this culinary castle. My new Austrian friend described the atlas of objects.

"Here," he said like a Manhattan bus tour guide, "are three thousand golden goblets, five thousand silver goblets, twenty-five thousand forks, knives and spoons, all with the royal crest of the Sultan. Look, in this room are nearly two thousand ivory platters, with thirteen thousand Japanese-made porcelain plates embossed with a picture of the Sultan."

We came next to the larders, the refrigerators created in Valhallan mountain kingdoms for the Sultan. They were to shelter each day a thousand cartons of fresh eggs flown in from Singapore. Perhaps two dozen were used, and the rest were thrown away. Salt was stacked in mile-high towers. Five-gallon-high bottles of soy sauce and chili sauce towered over a quarter-mile-wide series of Thai fish-paste cans.

And the next time you find no turmeric at your Indian provisions store, blame the Sultan of Brunei. A three-hundred-foot mountain of turmeric lay in its own room, golden brown, covered with a Plexiglas pyramid.

His Majesty loves caviar, and stocked in one fridge were four dozen cans of the stuff.

"Okay, caviar, big deal," you say. Nay, this was not mere Beluga or Osetra. That stuff would be given to the royal cats. No, the Sultan of Brunei then had privy to the caviar of the Shah of Iran himself. For this was the rare yellow Beluga. No commoner can imagine the taste.

Gargantuan refrigerators were reserved for frozen mutton, Kobe beef, fresh salmon, Filipino bangus fish, coconuts grown in isolated Manila gardens for the Sultan, Seville oranges flown in from Seville. And when the Sultan's brother loaded his private plane with Swedish ladies, he filled up the cargo with Swedish black bread, cheeses, and Baltic herrings.

We finished the tour, and Dieter asked what I thought.

"Wow," said I, appropriately admiring. "You must be in hog heaven, you should forgive my apostasy."

Dieter forgave me. But he looked at me sadly as we strolled through the Room of Vessels, a flame-colored thoroughfare of copper and brass kettles.

"No," he said. "It's madness. It is not hog heaven."

I asked him to explain. So he did.

"At three in the morning, the phone will ring. An assistant secretary to the assistant secretary of the assistant secretary of the Sultan of Johore Bahru in west Malaysia will announce that his sultan is flying in with a party of five hundred. So I must please prepare breakfast for five hundred people. Or the next day, one of the royal wives will declare that she is giving a birthday party for two thousand children. Please arrange individual cakes for each child, with their name written in Belgian chocolate on each cake.

"Or without warning, a small Moslem-style banquet for fifty must be changed into a Chinese-style banquet for eight hundred, where they want fourteen courses and, of course, no pork or lard. Anywhere else, I could do the job and have a few drinks to keep up my spirits. Here, no drinking is allowed."

We stopped, and he sat down in his office, a tiny cubbyhole at the end of one of the corridors.

"So how," I asked, "do you keep from going mad?"

At his work-table, filled with diagrams, menus, seating plans, lists of infinite royal titles, he poured out his heart, his coffee, and his solution.

"You see, I do have a solution. Every month my wife and I have four days' break in Singapore. In Singapore, we have searched out places for dancing. All kinds of dancing. Tango and rock, rumbas and jitterbugging for middle-aged people, even Chinese dancing for traditional couples.

"So we go and we dance. We go to discos and dance. We go to old people's homes and waltz, we go to dark little bars and cuddle up and dance to Perry Como, and we go to tea halls and dance Mandarin style. Sometimes I sleep in my hotel for a few hours. But mainly we will go dancing and dancing and dancing some more. Then we return home, and we are sane again.

"For at least four weeks."

The phone in his office rang, and he lifted it groggily off the receiver, nodding at the commands, shrugging his shoulders at me. I didn't have the heart to inquire what new assignments he might have. His fingers and brain were on the wooden table, his feet were on the floor, but his heart, I knew, was beating in the unending dance halls of Singapore.

Recipe:
The Omnipresent Satay

Talk of food from Brunei to Singapore to Johore Bahru to the Beach of Red Ants on the Thai border, and the only ubiquitous food is satay. Grilled on the street, sizzled with royal aplomb in sultans' palaces, they are the center of every Malay restaurant, and Malay housewives all have their own recipe for the sauce. Simple as they seem, and quick as they are to cook – about ten minutes at most—they take many ingredients and several hours of preparation.

 1 lb. beef or chicken
 10 shallots
 3 stalks lemon grass
 1 thin slice ginger
 ½ tsp. ground coriander
 ½ tsp. ground aniseed
 1 tsp. ground cumin
 ½ c. sugar
 1 tsp. salt
 1 tsp. turmeric powder
 ½ c. grated coconut
 ½ c. oil

1. Cut the meat into thin pieces.
2. Grind shallots, lemon grass, ginger into a paste. Mix this paste with the ground spices, sugar, salt, and turmeric.
3. Marinate the meat in this mixture for at least 1 hour.
4. Thread the meat on to thin satay skewers. If not available, use tinyskewers, like miniature shishkebab skewers, or use forks.
5. Refrigerate this meat in the marinade overnight.
6. Use some fresh coconut milk or canned coconut milk to baste the meat while grilling.
7. Make a charcoal fire in a charcoal brazier. A wire toaster with an open top can do it. Light the fire and grill the meat, basting it with the coconut milk mixture.
8. Serve with satay sauce (see below), onion, and (if gentrified) some toast.

Satay Sauce

12-15 shallots
2 thin slices ginger
½ inch piece ginger
1 stalk lemon grass
1 lb. roasted peanuts
2 tbsp. tamarind
½ c. oil
1 tbsp. ground red chilies
10 tbsp. chopped palm sugar
1 tsp. salt

1. Grind shallots, ginger, and lemon grass.
2. Crush roasted peanuts with a mortar and pestle (or, if gentrified again, in a blender; boring but effective).
3. Extract ½ c. tamarind juice from 2 tbsp. tamarind.
4. Heat ½ c. oil and fry the ground chilies and other ground spices until the oil separates from the ingredients.

5. Add the crushed peanuts and mix. Then pour in chopped palm sugar, salt, and tamarind juice.
6. Stir the mixture and allow it to simmer with the oil rising to the top.

Chapter Sixteen

The Spirit Is Willing, but the Flesh Is Inedible
Recipe:
Tom Kha Thalay (Seafood Soup)

Thailand was an extended rest-stop. Altogether, nearly ten years. I had hitchhiked up from eastern Malaysia (my first visit to the turtles of Trengannau), through the smuggling town of Kota Baru, over the border to Thailand, then to the western part of the Isthmus of Kra so that I could go to Phuket Island. Outside of almost stepping on a cobra stretched out on the road, it was a delightful week, even more delightful when reaching Bangkok and the stay in a temple, which specialized in cremations, Wat Hualompong.

The second night sealed my fate. I had grown in love with Bangkok quickly, and was invited to an art exhibition, where the owner's wife asked me to teach at her school. With nothing else in mind, I taught for a few months, then joined the Bangkok Post as proofreader, and later as restaurant reviewer.

Those first years were delightful. Since nobody knew anything, we all had opportunities to bring our virginal talents to a climax.

That would have been impossible anywhere else. My restaurant reviews were great fun to write, since I could always summon up experts who would teach on the job. A Ceylonese restaurant? The entire sports section of the paper came from Sri Lanka, so we would all go out and I would learn. Arabic food? My still great friend Farouk el Hussein and his friends and I would do the whole thing (minus goat's eyes). Thai food had endless people vying to go out and teach me about the real thing.

But the best of the lot was one Ayumongkol Sonakul, who had come back from university in Dublin, so was in the mood for drinking more than dining. Still, when a magazine was conceived, he and I became the editors, and managed to turn S'nuk Magazine (the word means "fun") into a quite readable journal.

Little did readers know that we basically did the whole magazine in a day and night. Fierce procrastinators, fast writers, and in a no-man's-land of no competition, we simply took all of our stuff each Thursday for lunch to a restaurant called the Sorndaeng, and managed to get the stuff to the printers late that night so it would come out Friday morning.

In those days, a meal at the Sorndaeng was an experience more like a circus or Monty Python than a restaurant, and its program is worth repeating.

Then, Bangkokians with seven or eight hours to kill, a weakness for al fresco cafes, and a penchant for surprises would inevitably wind up here. Today, it caters to indoor tour groups. But a few years ago one could sit out on the verandah on the Avenue of Kings. There, one inevitably conversed with the throbbing cogs of this great metropolis. Squid vendors and chewing-gum-vending children, lottery ticket hucksters, and lichee-nut merchants all strolled by this verandah, leaning against the wall, making half-hearted efforts to sell, talk, and simply gaze into the night air.

There, one would see film stars, tycoons, hairdressers, students, and stonecutters, all passing by, sitting, enjoying the polluted air.

But for visiting farangs, the foreigners who spoke no Thai, the main motivation for Sorndaeng dining was they could never know—or even suggest—the result of their desires. The menu was printed in Thai and English, but the latter was something of a handicap, since no waiter could read Roman lettering at all. If they had, the experience would have been simply a good meal, not a quintessentially Thai experience.

To get down to the nitty-gritty, one never received what one ordered. I mean never. No matter how good a customer felt before sitting down at the Sorndaeng, one couldn't help leaving some hours later with a feeling of insecurity, nervousness, slight tics, spasms, and a Kierkegaardian feeling of fear and trembling, which sometimes took years to evaporate.

Some newcomers say the fault wasn't that of the waiters. Why should they speak English at all in Thailand? Were they taking revenge on some obscure wickedness done to them in years past? Or perhaps the Sorndaeng was a halfway house for a loony bin far up in the northern forests?

Explanations explain nothing. The real motivation for Sorndaeng was to keep customers on their toes and in a distinctly oriental sense to show there is more to reason than mere logic.

The following was a typical Sorndaeng experience, a single experience taken from multitudes of meals here. I would come with Ayumongkol. His outlook on the world was as Irish as mine was New York. As co-editors of S'nuk, we would repair to the

Sorndaeng circus together on publishing day to watch tourists attempting to work up a good lunch.

"Good afternoon, sir," would say the waiter, a charming man of antediluvian senility.

"And good afternoon to you," would say this farang victim. "Do you speak English?"

"Yes, sir, I understand. What do you want?"

"Well, let's start off with a plate of prawns with chili, beef in oyster sauce, rice, a bottle of Thai whiskey, and a few mangoes to finish off. All right?"

"Yes, I understand English," he would say.

"Heh-heh-heh," would say the farang. "I guess we will have prawns in chili, beef in oyster sauce, rice, whiskey, and mangoes. Now do you understand?"

"No."

"Oh."

"No. I speak English. But I don't understand."

"I see. You speak it. But you don't understand it."

"No. Yes. No."

"Oh." (Silence.)

"I get other waiter. He speak. He understand."

Aeons later, a head waiter would come in, fit to kill (but I anticipate myself). He would speak immaculate English, indeed. Anyhow, it was original English, as it contained neither vowels nor consonants. But it was spoken awfully quickly and with tremendous confidence. The main thing is that he believed that he understood what was being told him, and was darned quick and efficient at executing orders. (But I anticipate the execution order.)

So once again the tourists would try:

"Fried prawns. Beef. Rice, whiskey, and mangoes. Okay?"

"Okay, sir. Pork spleen, buffalo penis, earth grubs and Chinese tea."

"Not exactly. Now first, what is your name?"

"My name Daeng."

"Okay, Daeng, try it after me. Fried prawns in chili."

"Prawns chili."

"Beef in oyster sauce."

"Beef oyster."

"Rice and whiskey and mangoes."

"Rice 'n' whikee 'n' mangoes."

"Good. Now all together."

"Buffalo feet sautéed in garlic, noodle fried with peppermint, Burgundy wine, and melon. I sorry, sir, no have Burgundy."

"That's okay. I'll take it with whikee."

"An' you wan' buffalo feet with mangoes, sir?" (Waiters were always polite at the Sorndaeng. It gave the illusion of efficiency.)

"Sure. That's very kind." (Customers were always polite at the Sorndaeng. It gave the illusion of sanity.)

The waiter would go off for an hour, leaving the customer to his thoughts, which are unprintable. Then he would return with an apology.

"I sorry, sir. We all out of mouse-deer fingers in peanut butter sauce."

"No problem, Daeng, my friend. I will take the prawns with chili sauce instead."

Some minutes later, the waiter would return with fifteen cans of Diet Coke, four papaya, and one broiled cat topped with a whole three-foot round of feta cheese.

"Never mind the cat," says the knowing customer. "I'll take the papaya and Coke."

"What about cheese?"

"Well, actually, I only ordered half a cheese. But I'm willing to settle for a feta complete."

The waiter would feign distress, even distraughtness.

"But you only order the cat. Other for another table."

"True enough," would laugh the guest maniacally, handing the snarling beast to one of the curious chewing-gum children who would stick a wad of Wrigley's in the feline's ear. "But the whiskey looks good. Would you mind if I had some. With maybe some fruit?"

"Right away, sir," would say the waiter, skipping over to the refrigerator. He would literally dance back to the customer.

"Here, here," he would say with a victorious smile. "Look, I discover some chocolate soda to go with your basted elephant hide soufflé."

"That is splendid. Do you think I could have a knife and fork for the elephant?"

"Oh, I sorry," would say Daeng. "We closing now. Look, mistah, we keep elephant in icebox tonight for you. An' if ice melt, then we give you soup instead."

The customer would be so intrigued with the idea that he would immediately agree, possibly even suggesting that the waiter prepare the mastodon with his own personal recipe.

So the tourist would leave the Sorndaeng – never to return unless both St. Peter and the Devil throw him out of their own domains.

Today, alas, this experience has almost disappeared. But, like so many travel experiences which seemed hellish at the time, the Sorndaeng today is a dream. And – oh, lordy, give thanks for great blessings – Thai food, no matter how one calls it, is the food of heaven itself.

Spice Chronicles: *Exotic Tales of a Hungry Traveler*

Recipe:
Tom Kha Thalay (Seafood Soup)
(Serves 4)

This is my favorite seafood recipe, which is decidedly not from the Sorndaeng. It came from a now defunct restaurant in Pattaya Beach, Krua Suthep (Suthep's Kitchen). Suthep, now retired, was one of the most innovative chefs in the country, and I secured – after much friendly persuasion, like threatening to break his kneecaps – this extraordinary recipe for a traditional dish. It is, admittedly, complicated to make, and the ingredients are not readily available. But that makes its taste even rarer.

    4 c. coconut cream
    2 blades lemon grass, cut in 8 pieces each
    1 rhizome galangal (which is like ginger), cut into 20 thin pieces
    6 kaffir leaves
    8 crab legs raw, cleaned
    16 slices cuttlefish, raw
    20 mussels, washed, scrubbed, and steamed open
    12 fillets of sole, cut in 1-inch pieces, raw
    20 medium-size shrimp, raw, peeled
    2 oz. lemon juice
    2 oz. Thai fish sauce (nam pla), from Asian grocery stores

2 tbsp. sugar

4 chili peppers, fresh or deep fried, finely chopped

Cooking

1. Pour coconut cream into soup pot and bring to a boil.
2. Add lemon grass, galangal, kaffir leaves, and seafood.
3. After boiling for 5 minutes, add lemon juice, fish sauce, and sugar to taste.
4. Garnish soup with chopped chili peppers and serve.
5. Optional: Put rice on the side, as the soup can be consumed as a kind of sauce over the rice.

Chapter Seventeen

The Pizza Papers
Recipes:
Blasted Brownies/Pizza Rustica/Labna

I was once commissioned to write some pizza parodies for a Hong Kong restaurant. While they were never used, I kept some of them, which appear here.

A. Ernest Hemingway: "The Dough Also Rises"
(From CHAPTER 8: The running of the pizzas)

When the bus stopped in Pastalona, I needed a drink. I drank because a man does this when he does not wish to be afraid. Also, I was thirsty.

So I pulled the cork from the bottle with my fingers and allowed the wine to dribble on my manly shirt. And when that was soaked, I allowed the wine to dribble on my chest. Looking at myself in the window of a café, I saw many whom I wished to fight, but they did not wish to, for they were speaking of the Running of the Pizzas, to be held that afternoon in the streets. Even when I poured drops of red wine into the black hair of the girl who sold bullets from the sidewalk, and she cried, she would not fight me. I told her that the wine would dry sooner or later. She moved on and peddled her bullets at the next café.

My friend Scott sat at the table. He looked afraid. But Scott had witnessed the Running of the Pizzas in Pastalona many times.

"Hullo, Papa," Scott said. "Is it right," he asked, "to fear when the pizza runs?"

"No," I said. "Good pizza never sticks to its crust, just as a bear never sticks to its cave when the springtime arrives. In Pastalona, it is spring today. So the pizzas will run. Like the bears."

"Oh," he said, rubbing the stump of a leg he had broken at the Great Siege. "Goodbye, then. I will see you later."

I didn't see that old fire, the fire of wood-baked ovens, in his eyes. So I drank another drink. The sun was hot. Hot enough for the pizzas to run.

"Hullo, Papa," said Lady Zelda fFoxx-Terrier. "How well do you think the pizzas will run this afternoon?"

A mule hee-hawed. I drew from my leather wine bottle again. The sun grew even hotter.

"They have a word for pizza that runs well," I said. "The word is scappati. It means fleeting. Like a seagull chasing a large fish. That is the good way for pizzas to run."

"That is good," said Lady fFoxx-Terrier, "But Papa, how do they bake the pizza to make it scappati?"

I took another drink. The dry rum burned my tongue and

went to my mouth, down to my esophagus and stomach, then it was digested and continued to my kidneys and my bladder and then to the street.

"If the baker is a man of honor, then the pizza is a pizza which flees off the crust. That is a baker of respect. He is respected if the dough is sifted and kneaded thoroughly."

"All men of honor need something thoroughly," she said.

"Yes," but I did not smile. "For when the dough has risen, the pizza must have tomatoes and cheeses."

"Cheeses loves me," whispered Lady fFoxx-Terrier. "That I know."

I was tired of her jeu de mots, but did not tell her.

"James Joyce said that cheese was the corpse of milk," I told her.

"I don't read Joyce," she said. "Rejoycing is not in my character."

I wanted her to shut up, but could not tell her, so I told her about the running of the pizzas.

"After the cheese, the sauce must be generous. And the oven hot. And when the pizza is done and it is removed and the sauce drips over the edge of the crust like the bull's tongue when he is tired, and when it is brown like the Catalonian sun, and the tablecloth is sticky and your mouth is wet with perspiration. That is how the pizza will run."

"That is good, Papa," said Lady fFoxx-Terrier. "I think that I no longer fear pizza. And I will eat pizza in the piazza."

Softly, I told her that piazza pizzas were prized.

Then I crossed the square to where the pizzas were running on the sidewalk. I ran my index finger along the side of the gutter and licked off the cheese and tomatoes and olives. It was good. Very good. The people cheered and I returned the gesture and then returned to my hotel to think about these pizzas. With honor. With strength. With oregano. With dignity.

But not too heavy on the anchovies.

Recipe:
Blasted Brownies

No, I don't see Hemingway noshing on a pizza or eating brownies. He was a steak-and-pommes frites kinda guy, but would eat anything so long as a bottle of good whiskey or good wine was on the side. But Gertrude Stein – the progenitor of Alice B. Toklas cookies – was his style. So I put this together with a book given to me when I was in Kentucky to do stories on Bourbon whiskey. From The Book of Bourbon, by Gary Regan and Mardee Haidin Regan, comes this amazing dish.

> 6 oz. semi-sweet chocolate, chopped
> 2 oz. unsweetened chocolate, chopped
> 8 tbsp. (1 stick) melted butter
> ¾ c. sifted, unbleached all-purpose flour
> ¼ tsp. baking soda
> ¼ tsp. salt
> 2 large eggs
> 1½ tsp. vanilla extract
> ¾ c. sugar
> 6 tbsp. Kentucky Bourbon … no, make that 8 tbsp.
> ½ c. chopped pecans

1. Try that Bourbon. One tablespoon will do. Maybe two or three more just to make sure. Pass it around. Replenish.
2. Now, on to the broonies…er, brownies. In a small saucepan over moderately low heat or a heatproof bowl in a microwave

oven at medium power, heat the chocolate and butter until almost   melted. Remove and beat until smooth. Set it aside. Have a drink.

3. Preheat the over to 325 degrees. Butter an 8-inch square cake pan. Stir together the flour, baking soda, and salt.
4. In a bowl, with an electric mixer, beat the eggs until thick and pale. Add the vanilla, sugar, and half the Bourbon. No, make that all the Bourbon (you must have another bottle somewhere). Beat until well blended. Add the chocolate mixture and fold together. Fold in the pecans. Fold yourself up on a couch and go to sleep.
5. Scrape the batter into the pan and smooth the top. Bake for half an hour, or until a cake tester comes out clean and moist. Remove the pan to a wire rack and let it cool to room temperature.
6. Congratulate yourself. Have a drink.
7. Poke small holes in the brownies with a skewer and shprinkle…er, sprinkle the remaining liquor over the top, pushing it into the holes. If any drips on the floor, call the cat. Let it set for an hour.
8. Cut the brownies into small squares and serve.
9. Sleep.

B. Shakespeare: "Hamlet: The Trattoria Scene"

Shakespeare should have written about pizza, as so many of his plays were set in Italy. Here, though, a Danish prince instructs a group of visiting Italian pizzeria people how to make the best pizza that King Lira can buy.

(Enter HAMLET with POLONIUS and four or five BAKERS)

Hamlet: Welcome, good bakers, welcome all. What hast thou?
Polonius: Aye, what hast though for my master Hamlet?
First baker: We have all manner of pizza for thee, my liege.
Polonius (aside): Pizza? That dost bode well in these ill times
 For 'tis said that pizza cures madmen and their crimes.
 (To Hamlet) I think, m'lord, that a single pizza platter
 Perhaps so large as thy beneficence
 And sweet as my Ophelia's breast
 Would be most festive an addition
 In this, our troubled land.
Hamlet: Perhaps.

       But enough from thee and me, Polonius.
       Speak, my flour-powered bakers and relate
       What sorts of pizzas thou hast brought.
       Dost include tart anchovies and shrimp?
       Dost have atop its hemisphere tomatoes
       Off'ring poisoned kisses from the New World?

Second baker: Aye, m'lord, dost include both and more.

Polonius (aside): More? This pizza will, methinks ignite
       Amongst the meanest gentlefolk unlimited delight.

Hamlet: Hush, thou, old Polonius, let the bakers speak
       About their Roman festive flavors so unique.

Third baker: Since thou tak'st such interest in our dishes,
       Then, m'lord, thou shouldst be glad to hear
       How the pizza taste doth gird the universe
       With sheer variety.

Fourth baker: Aye, for those
       In ignorance are oft misled
       To think that pizza's solely yeast and sauce and bread.
       'Tis more, far more.

First baker: 'Tis peppers sizzling red and green
       And olives black as gypsies' eyes. Below the earth, unseen
       Lie its mushrooms. Yet the sun shines with radiant ease
       Upon its Mozzarella, Romano, Bel Paese.

Second baker: Nor can'st thou e'er forget the onions springing
       Midst the parsley. Fisherfolk bringing
       Tuna first, then butchers' succulent salamis.

Polonius: Salome? Why is that wicked wench
       Fit to sit about the bakers' bench?

Hamlet: Nay, Polonius, thou err, by God. They speak of meat.
       Now, meet, you bakers do excite our very senses
       E'en if sent from Papacy, to please a heretic's indulgences.
       I commend thee all.

Third baker: Then instruct us, sire,
  Our Pasta Noster in our own art.
Hamlet: Their art indeed. In lesser pizza chefs, their Kraft.
  (To bakers) First, thou must pierce the pizza so it sits
  Trippingly on the tongue.
First baker (to others): 'Tis good advice indeed.
Hamlet: Be not too tame in thy spices,
  But let your own discretion be your tutor:
  Suit the toppings to the crusts with this special
  Observance: that you o'erstep not the modesty
  Of pizza's nature. But let it rise
  And let taste be a mirror of the taster:
  Salt to the witty, clams to the calm,
  Peppers to hot-blooded and mild cheese
  To lovers supping as one.
  Nor cans't oregano e'er ignore:
  Oregano complements, nay adds that to pizza
  Which imagination addeth not.
  Nor should'st thou ever forget Chianti (as glass or carafe)
  Is oft employed to make the god of pizzas laugh:
  For wine and pizza have, like lovers, oft embraced.
First baker: Whither goeth this pizza master now?
Polonius: Hamlet hath become so inspired by his teaching
  That he to the oven goeth to practice what he's preaching.
Second baker: Aye, and look, for he brings forth his pizza here.
  (Hamlet passeth among them with his platter)
Polonius: Now cracks a noble crust. Good slice, sweet prince,
  From anchovies in Peru,
  To squid, mushrooms, surfeits and at times, hints:
  At first a slurp…and then adieu.

(Exeunt all to sounds of dishes clashing)

Recipe: Pizza Rustica

The question: Whether 'tis nobler in the mind to use an Elizabethan or an Italian pizza recipe? Pizza Rustica is the perfect compromise. The recipe itself comes from central-south Italy, but its origins (as are most of the southern Italian dishes) go back to Shakespearean (or medieval) times, when all kinds of beautiful ingredients were baked inside a "pizza" or pie. You'll never find this in restaurants, but homes around Abruzzi often spend a day making it. This serves 4-6 people. (I especially like this for the Mortadella sausage – a sausage that inspired one of Sophia Loren's most charming, and least seen, films, called, of course, Mortadella.)

First, make a pastry dough, kneading the following ingredients:

> 2¼ c. flour
> 2 egg yolks
> ½ c. butter
> 2 tbsp. iced water
> ¼ c. sugar
> Pinch of salt
> Wrap this in plastic and chill for at least 1 hour.

Here are the ingredients for the filler. Obviously, substitutions can be made.

5 oz. Prosciutto
4 oz. Mortadella
6 oz. Mozzarella
10 oz. Ricotta
4 tbsp. freshly grated Pecorino or Parmesan
½ tsp. ground cinnamon
2 eggs, lightly beaten
Salt and freshly ground black pepper

1. Cut the Prosciutto, Mortadella, and Mozzarella into strips and put in a bowl. Add the crumbled Ricotta, the grated cheese, cinnamon, eggs, and salt and pepper to taste.
2. Mix this well.
3. Roll out a third of the pastry to a thickness of about ½ inch and lay it on the base of a greased 8-inch cake pan.
4. Cut off another third of the pastry, roll it out in strips, and line the side of the pan.
5. Seal well where the side joins the base.
6. Pour the filling into the case, banging the dish once or twice on the work surface to force out any air bubbles.
7. Roll out the rest of the pastry and place over the filling. Press the edge tightly and seal with moistened fingers by pinching the edges together.
8. Place in an oven, preheated to 400 degrees, for 50 minutes until the top is golden.
9. When cool enough to handle, unmold the pizza and serve warm or at room temperature.

c. The Egyptian Book of the Dead

"Look thou, o servant of Osiris, yet yonder in the domain of the crocodile who ye shall see across the fiery path to mountains of the inland sea, thus shalt thy Priest whip and set his gangrenous breath upon thee if the wheat is not cultivateth and gathered into bales and tied together and then brought to thy storage place, there to be trampled upon and set forthwith aside until the great floods bring large beasts and beetles and bugs and then to be unpacked and with the glowing fires of Amakis, the wife of Khumun, who shall command thee to pour forth yeast upon the trampled wheat and to watch it rise forthwith with the Fourth Cataract and thence to hurl this trampled wheat and yeast into the air, yet above the Ladders of Heaven, o far above where the dead may climb to the spirit of Osiris, and then to let it drift down unto the oven in which it will burn with a great heat for several minutes until it steams and is indeed a noted gift for Serapis, who maketh the flowers of the field to bloom, and then atop this orb of wheat shalt thou place, o mighty one, all the peppers of the earth and the fish of the sea, ye shalt lay in the order of growth tomatoes and curd from which the herdsman shalt sacrifice his kine, and it shall have the scent of the Flowers of Punt, and then shalt it be offered to Osiris and Osiris shall get a whiff of this, thy heavenly orb, and he shalt offer it then to Horus the One-Eyed and Horus shall feel like the child Harpocrates, which he once had been and his sidelock shall be long, and his children, the pathfinders of the dead, shall stand atop a lotus and will ingest this thy holy orb with the great fungi which they call the magic mushroom and the kernel of the corn which indeed is the corn of rebirth as it doth sprout through the husk and thus to show the power of the once and always Osiris who doth return from his bed of serpents to refertilize the land and then shalt thou offer blessings and command thee and thy brethren and cistern, thy descendants and the descendants of thy descendants to pass into the world beyond odor and crowns and the waves of the Holy Sea and then to play upon the Sacred Oregano, to proclaim that this, this alone is isolated from all else as a food, as a pastime, as a snack, as a meal, and thou who did make it, though thou be a small herdsman, yet the heavens shall proclaim thee with thy great cake of cheese and tomatoes and all that thou hast harvested, equal to Osiris himself, and thou shalt be purified for thy creations through every dynasty throughout and beyond eternity."

Recipe: Labna

While ancient Egyptian recipes do exist, I choose to offer a dish that extends throughout what was the entire Egyptian kingdom at its height, up through Lebanon and Syria and Jordan. It was made from goat's milk, as the remaining Bedu prepare it today, giving it a sourish, pungent taste far different from cow's milk. The latter, though, does appeal to Westerners more, so the choice is yours. In older towns of Syria, a year's supply of labna is prepared at one time, with the cheesecloth of yogurt hanging from the ceiling of the attics. Every twenty-four hours the bag is opened and the yogurt is stirred as the whey oozes out, thickening part of the yogurt. Salt is added each day. When all the yogurt is uniformly thick, it is removed and – with wet fingers – a small amount at a time is scooped and rolled into a ball in the palm of the hand. Then it is dropped into a large glazed earthenware urn, half-filled with olive oil, and kept for use or storage.

> Here, though, is the basic recipe.
> 4 c. yogurt
> 1 tbsp. salt
> Olive oil
> Cheesecloth bag

1. Stir the salt into the yogurt, pour into the wet cheesecloth bag, tie the opening, and hang for 24 hours.
2. Remove the yogurt from the bag, put it in a jar, and sprinkle the top with olive oil. It can be used on pita bread, ordinary bread, or just as a side dish in which to dip celery or other vegetables.
3. Be certain to take a clean container and put it under the bag, so when the whey drops down it can be collected and used for cooking or even straight drinking.

Chapter Eighteen

Travels with My Ants
Recipe:
Mee Grob

The subject here is ants, but—as usual in Thailand—paradox is logic. In this case, the ants begin with elephants. Specifically, a story I was covering about the fate of Thai elephants. For that, a bit of background is needed.

The world thinks of Thai white elephants, which are not really white. Like witches, they have other characteristics, which prove their magical powers. As reincarnations of the Buddha, these elephants are treated with solitary reverence. True, as social animals, elephants enjoy each other's company, so such reverence may be misplaced. But at least they eat regularly and are worshipped.

What else could any animal want?

The history of ordinary Thai elephants, though, is not so endearing. In the eighteenth century, a Cambodian tribe called the Suwai brought their elephants into Siam to act as mercenaries. They were war elephants, and in those days, war elephants – as well as their drivers and handlers – were rare, well paid, and talented.

Until 1900, the war elephants and their Suwai keepers were in much demand. But when elephants were discarded for tanks, elephants changed professions. They became logging elephants. They could understand about thirty words – in the Suwai language – and they could go into the Thai jungles, gingerly stepping through the gnarled viney mountain paths, dragging huge tree trunks, delicately bringing them on to the roadways and rivers, loading them on to trucks and barges for the trips down to Bangkok and the sea.

By the 1970s, machines and conservation methods had made the elephants obsolete. So they came down another rung and joined the circus, doing tricks and racing and imitating their military ancestors in the Surin, Thailand, annual Elephant Roundup. But that was a four-day affair. A few elephants went to Pattaya beach, where they played elephant football, curtseyed, and bowed to the oohs and aahs of Chinese and Japanese tourists. It was humbling, yes. But it was a living.

The more fortunate ones live in the elephant conservation project under the protection of Richard Lair. They are free to roam about, or paint, or make music with instruments invented for their delight by renowned New York composer David Soldier. The recordings are delightful.

Fortunately, elephants have never been a food for man, though one restaurant used to serve game animals, and claimed to have the beast. Its menu (and this is true) consisted of a Thai hunting license, and the animals that one couldn't kill. The restaurant did. They had cobra, bats, and mouse deer, and claimed to have elephant meat, which had to be ordered forty-eight hours in advance. (These were the days when "conservation" referred to marmalades and jams, as in "Yes, Maude and I are making a pickle conserve.")

Others, alas, are unemployed. It was in search of these elephants that I came upon the ant restaurant described below.

Now the setting: Five of us – three airline executives, a photographer and me – were in eastern Thailand on the Cambodian border to do a story about the downfall of the Thai elephant. But these were the lucky elephants. The others, with their mats (the Suwai name for mahouts, the Hindi name for elephant-handlers) lolled about in eastern Thailand, in the poorest area of the country. Some of the elephants illegally hauled logs out of Cambodia, others were driven into Bangkok or Chiang Mai, "working the streets" with their mats, begging for money. Thais pay to run under an elephant's belly to promote fertility. Foreign tourists shell out money for elephant photo ops.

But about three hundred elephants stay on the border. And when the national airline decided something should be done to help them, I went out with a photographer to publicize their plight. This was difficult, since the Suwai people speak neither Thai nor Khmer, but their own language, which they shared with their animals. We were rarely allowed into their intimate conversations.

But at sundown we would see them passing through the river. Endless elephants and their mats going for a stroll, oblivious to us poor media folk. Sad, sad, a remnant of the past…

Which meant that we needed some happy news. In this case, the news of the Restaurant of the Red Ants, one of the eerier memories of dining.

I had read in an old book how Thais living on the eastern border, near Cambodia, used to relish red ants as a dinner or lunch treat, so we asked around the town of Buriram and discovered the world's only red ant restaurant. The name (for those who are madly salivating) is Satow Wan. The Lao and Cambodian people find the title ironic. Satow is the bitterest leaf in Thai food. Wan means sweet. Taking the bitter with the sweet, we introduce Thailand's only oxymoronic restaurant.

Satow Wan looks like any outdoor roadside restaurant, but the specialty is mot daeng, or red ants. Since this area has no lime or lemon, people use the ants for a sour, sometimes bitter flavor.

Be assured that these ants are always freshly hunted and–like lobster–not killed before the meal is made. Each morning the sous-chef of Satow Wan heads out to the farms where the ants live in great piles. He takes a shovel and throws the mound into the air. Like wheat from chaff, the ants separate from the dry dirt and are swept into bags. Some are delivered to Buriram market, where they sell for about eighty cents a kilogram. The rest are brought to the restaurant.

While a kilogram probably contains hundreds of thousands of ants, they are not wasted, since the menu is a sumptuous one. We began, for instance, with a piping-hot duck soup. This was virtually a full dinner. Everything edible in the duck is placed in a mild, boiling chicken stock. The liver, meat, and blood are tenderly simmered and stirred for several hours. In fact, since morning, the large cauldron had been gently boiling, with water tossed in every thirty minutes or so.

Just before serving, the chef deftly tossed in several thousand red ants, which immediately congealed into a cluster that could have been a dollop of strawberry jam. The soup was now poured from the cauldron into an ochre-colored clay tureen brought triumphantly to the outdoor table. The meat, having been simmered for hours, peeled off the bone, a bit bedraggled, almost soggy. Yet, the crisp ants had a sour tingle, something like kaffir lime. In fact, without this addition, the result would have been like a fricassee of duck, boiled to anonymity. The ants added the tang.

The Northeast is also known for lahp, a Laotian quasi-pâté of minced pork or beef with tiny and extremely hot prik khee nu, or "mouse-shit chilies." In this restaurant, they make the lahp from minced catfish, a specialty of the local streams. The peppers are larger, and thus milder than those of the Northeast. The taste is relatively bland, but hints of gamy fish, the occasional bone and—yes, hidden amid the pâté, piquant pieces of red ants peeking out from the dish.

The other soup is catfish, but this has a more interesting harmony of tastes. The catfish is in that neutral chicken broth, but the large, white meaty pieces (and errant bones) are cooked with the bitter satow leaves, while the delicate serving of red ants on top adds a soupçon of acid.

Satow Wan also serves a dish sadly missing from modern Thai cuisine: the jungle curry. This curry is probably the hottest in Southeast Asia, but is eaten only in the countryside. It is a brew made with marble-sized, pale forest eggplant; wild garlic; onions; and fermented peppers. The usual meat is buffalo, which one tears viciously with the teeth. The only mollifying influence is brown rice. (The brown is from the dirt, not the husk.) True to its reputation, the restaurant here adds some ants, but they serve the same function as parsley, giving hardly any taste but serving mainly as decoration.

For this is indeed an evil-tasting dish and needs no additives.

My photographer and I were probably the first farangs to eat here. But eastern Thais are insouciant about such visitors. We waited our turn with the traveling laborers, who, like Elizabethan artisans, leave their villages to find itinerant work. They missed the food of their homes, and would save for weeks to come here and spend a lordly $5.00 or so for a grand meal.

Yet, red ants are not merely for the hoi polloi. At the beginning of the twentieth century, red ant eggs were prized in the royal palace of Laos. Alan Davidson, editor of the Oxford Dictionary of Food, edited a Royal Lao Cookbook when he was British Ambassador to Laos, and speaks about a particular regal recipe for "sour ant salad." The eggs are gently steamed in a banana leaf over a slow-burning fire, and then covered with fish sauce.

Thailand is not alone in its love of ants. Medieval European surgeons used ants to cure rheumatism, and some feel that the formic acid might have had a salubrious effect. Chinese doctors even today crush them to improve blood circulation.

But on a menu? Some say it sounds distasteful. But Columbia University anthropologist Martin Harris once explained that ant-loathing is an unfounded prejudice. "Insects, like ants," he wrote in Good to Eat, "are excellent nutrition, being seventy-five percent protein. But because they come out at night, they are icons of fear and loathing. But a phobia of eating ants is as irrational as refraining from pork or beef."

True, educated Thais refrain from these all-ant dinners, as this writer found out when dragging some Bangkok businessmen to the restaurant. But finishing dinner, we all discovered, with enough beer and Thai whiskey, an inexplicable contentment in what could only be called a sumptuous Thai b-ant-quet.

Recipe: Mee Grob
(Serves 8)

It isn't necessary to give ant recipes here. Virtually any dish can be an "ant dish" by simply adding red ants. Instead, we go to the opposite ends, to the posh century-old Oriental Hotel, which has always been in the forefront of melding European and Thai recipes with great subtlety. This recipe for an ordinary Thai noodle dish was given to me fifteen years ago, and with a change of chefs it has probably been transmuted to something else. But this is still exceptional.

- 11 oz. rice vermicelli
- 2 oz. cooking oil
- 2 eggs, beaten
- 7 oz. lean pork, finely chopped
- 3½ oz. prawn meat, shelled and coarsely chopped
- ½ slice hard bean curd
- 1 tbsp. fermented beans
- 2 tbsp. tomato sauce
- ½ tbsp. lemon juice
- 1 tbsp. fish sauce (nam pla)
- 1¾ c. palm sugar

Garnish

    Sliced pickled garlic
    Bean sprouts
    Red bell peppers, diced
    Lemon slices
    Parsley

Cooking

1. Soak vermicelli in water until softened, strain, and allow to drain completely.
2. Fry in 1 tbsp. oil until crispy.
3. Heat 1 tbsp. oil in a pan and stir-fry (scramble) the eggs until golden brown and crispy. Strain off excess oil.
4. Heat 2 tbsp. oil in a pan over moderate heat, adding pork, prawns, bean curd, beans, tomato sauce, lemon juice, fish sauce, and palm sugar. Stir-fry until most of the mixture has evaporated.
5. Add the crispy vermicelli and mix well.
6. Serve on a silver platter lined with a doily and decorate the top with the garnishes.
7. (Both silver platter and ants are optional.)

CHAPTER NINETEEN

PICNIC ON THE GRASS: A LAOTIAN MEMORY
Recipe: Kai Yang
Laotian Grilled Chicken

Several of my stories for the Bangkok Post dealt with kai yang, Laotian chicken. I would write that it was "the most delicious chicken in the world." That was presumptuous but still, I believe, essentially true. Anyhow, it has never been disputed by those who taste these delicate, grilled, spicy, tender, sweet fowls, for which an approximate recipe is given below.

Grilled Laotian chicken, though, is not from Laos. It originates in the northeast part of Thailand, which once incorporated Laos. The best is served around Bangkok's boxing stadiums, since most Thai boxers come from the ethnic Lao area of the country.

Real Laotian food was very different, and almost impossible to get in Vientiane, the "administrative capital" across from the Thai border. In that strange town, three castes of Lao-domiciled foreigners lived in strained harmony during the American "secret war." First were the "official" Americans, comprising diplomats, CIA, and military. Second were journalists, making reputations between going to the "big" war, in Vietnam. Third were the pariahs: beatniks, hitchhikers, and local writers, who wanted to get a peripheral share of the action. As a writer for the Bangkok Post, I belonged to that untouchable caste.

Thus, my most memorable Laotian meal never included this chicken. It took place in Luang Prabang around 1975, as the wars of Indochina were coming to a close.

For a tiny country, Laos hadn't produced much in the way of material goods, but when it came to official capitals, Laos could beat the pants off any other nation. Vientiane was the "administrative capital" while Luang Prabang (LP) was the "royal capital." And a floating area in the north was the leftist Pathet Lao ("Lao Nation") capital.

At this time, the whole country was on the verge of collapse, with the rebels of the "third capital" ready to take over the "administrative capital." But Laos was still a fairy-tale land of sorts, with strange characters having happy opium apparitions believing it was still a wonderland, that the king was the beneficent ruler, and that the royal capital was the centre of the world. While it was indeed royal, LP consisted essentially of eight Buddhist temples, seventeen noodle shops, and one royal palace.

Just before the apocalypse, the ever-dreaming son of the prime minister – your traditional playboy prince – decided to make his dream come true. The prince (let's call him Panat, since he is still around today) decided that the survival of Laos depended on its becoming the most attractive tourist resort in all Southeast Asia.

Laos, he felt, had everything that every tourist could ever need, except for hotels, roads, seaside, peace, visual attractions, sports facilities, or viable transportation. Being prudent, Prince Panat invited three seasoned travel writers from Bangkok to be his guinea pigs in showing Laos at its best. I was happy to be chosen, so that I could again visit Vientiane's unfinished war memorial, the unfinished bridge, the unfinished library, and the latest movie in town, Chaplin's Modern Times, which had just reached the administrative capital.

LP, though, was new to all of us, so we were excited to fly to the town one night from Vientiane. True, Royal Air Laos was delayed for six hours, since nobody had paid for the gasoline, but finally somebody rushed out from the Ministry of Procrastination with the right amount of dollars.

After the thirty-minute flight, and five hours sleep, we happily woke at 6:00 A.M. to climb up the town center mountain for a thrilling visual sight. As the sun rose above the rice paddies, glittering over the two rivers that surround LP, monks came out in file from the temples. From a hundred feet up we could see long lines of saffron-clad men and boys walking the roads and paths, crisscrossing against each other, glowing like the sunrise itself.

Prince Panat hadn't arrived yet, but we walked down the mount, slurped some black, thick, sugary Lao coffee for breakfast, then visited the temples and finished with an unprepossessing lunch of noodles, rice, and fermented fish.

We were then commanded to rest until the Grand Picnic Dinner. For Prince Panat had cabled from London that he was about to serve the banquet to end all banquets.

At about 4:00 P.M., a truck picked us up, and we joined a dozen or so Lao teachers, poets, and obscure Luang Prabang lords, ladies, princelings, and courtiers, bumping to the outskirts of town, where the rivers met by what appeared to be a large gazebo.

Actually, this was a miniature pagoda, glowing in red and gold, next to which was a makeshift outdoor kitchen. Two dozen fires were burning in dug-out pits in the grass, each attended by three or four Lao chefs, with their wives and children.

Most were for cooking. But, in Lao fashion, half the fires were accidental, so the chefs spent half the time cooking, half the time trying to stamp out the ashes, which – since they were barefoot – became a tortured comedy. The Laotians, their feet burning, were laughing as hard as we were.

After that entertainment, we sat on the riverbank sipping our rao chao khao, a moonshine corn likker that had chunks of bee larvae (and a few bee corpses) marinated in it. When made badly, it goes down like a rusty razor blade. When made well (as this was), it goes down like over-sweet sherry, bad brandy, and a soupçon of new razor blades.

After this, we lolled about, drank more rao chao khao, and prepared for our grand banquet.

Now admittedly, my notes for the occasion, while legible for the first few courses, become increasingly scratchy as the moonshine began to inundate my brain. We started with an "ordinary" chicken and mushroom soup. Except that the chefs wanted to show us all of Laos's mushrooms. Here were Chinese jelly mushrooms, tree mushrooms, and an orange mushroom resembling one of Snow White's dwarfs.

They especially prized some dangerous-looking toadstools, but we were told that although they looked dangerous, they were actually harmless. Obviously, it would have been uncivil to doubt the axioms of Laotian mycology, so we chomped away with great glee.

The next dish was quail stew, a sort of Lancashire hot pot à la Mekhong. Like most Lao dishes, the quail had been fermented, but what would have been an acrid taste was drowned out by a marinade of lemon grass, chili, bamboo, basil, and long beans, along with some pungent veggies found only in Laos.

After this, the catfish arrived. One was big and bony, the other was tiny and meaty. Both catfish had been fried in pork fat until golden, then simmered in a Chinese wok with onions and peppers, huge amounts of fresh coconut milk and coconut meat, along with lime leaves. And mammoth piles of coriander.

For the first time, I understood the derivation of the word. Coriander comes from the Greek for "bedbug," since the stench was reputed to be insectivorous. But we had all been in enough bedbug hostels in our lives to use this stench as a memory jogger. The Laotian bedbug summons memories like the Proust madeleine.

Water buffalo is so important in the fields that only on special occasions is it consumed. This was special. So we had a stew of meat, skin, eggplants, peppers, sweet basil, lemon grass and–naturally–the penis of the bull, chopped in little pieces so we could all have our share from the clay cauldron.

"From soup to nuts," someone exclaimed. "If ya wanna see me," added another, "just gristle."

We all laughed. It was that kind of silly picnic.

As the moonshine glasses filled to overflowing (our chefs, their wives and children matched us, glass for glass), the alcohol dripped into the food and things began to get blurry. I do remember a rice vermicelli with peppers, then a fish-head with those orange mushrooms, and then I remember being slapped on the back …

This, though, was no ordinary slap. It smacked–literally –of royalty. In fact, Laotian royalty.

"Your Highness!" we all shouted.

Yes, as in the best fairy-tales, the prince had finally arrived. He had managed to fly in from London to land by the river in some wind-up plane he had snatched in Vientiane. The prince, though, was not alone. He was accompanied by Algie and Geoff, two of the cockiest cockney hack press agents he could find in London.

They looked at our now sloppy tables leaning awkwardly into the grass wet with drink, while mats of fish bones and sauces and peppers were sprinkled on the ground. They obviously thought this was a magic illusion of sorts, so avoided even looking at it. Instead, they launched into a totally irrelevant but obviously sincere megillah, telling us it was their duty to single-handedly "put Laos on the map."

Such charlatanry would have been amusing in a more humdrum setting. Here, though, we thought they were nuts. (As did they we.) So when one of our party offered them a dish – I believe it was a raw ginger flower wrapped in banana leaf with onions, plucked from one of the accidental charcoal fires, they ceased their blather and simply backed away. One of the cooks, feeling this dish was not regal enough for such honored guests, rushed over to present them with his specialty: a whole stingray (the Mekong River has the only freshwater stingrays in the world) delivered with a fresh raw phallus-shaped pepper on top.

They turned away, and asked me if some plain eggs were anywhere on the premises. I shouted their request out to the chef. Happy to please, he gave them some Lao poached eggs. In other words, eggs with a sour sauce of pork fat and ground black pepper.

Geoff and Algie took a walk over to the pagoda, huddling together, wondering what to do next.

Prince Panat pulled me aside and asked how I liked his press agents. Then, without waiting for an answer, he asked how I liked opium.

At that time, I did like opium. So Prince Panat said that we two would pull Algie and Geoff from the riverbank and we could have a few puffs. And then they would present their strategy to "put Laos on the map."

The two cockneys had recovered from their extreme culture shock. We piled into a jeep, and the pair started telling how they had plans to make the Laotian mountains "the Alps of Asia," they would give picnics ("but maybe with different food"), and tourists could go on an elephant roundup.

At that point, I didn't have the rational powers to tell them that "the land of a million elephants" had few wild elephants left (American bombings had taken care of that). Anyhow, we had then reached a hut that housed the opium den. The Chinese doorkeeper, first bowing to the prince and his most noble party, hustled away to his account books and comic books and cartons of cigarettes and tried to sweep the floor of the dingy room. Then he left us to retrieve the pipes and opium.

Geoff and Algie were nervous. They had probably had a few joints in their lives, but never a joint in a joint like this.

The Chinese man came back with four long bamboo pipes, and the little brazier over which the evil black balls were placed and started to melt.

Thomas De Quincy and Samuel Coleridge and William Burroughs have tried to describe the aroma of opium, but, like explaining Bach or Rubens, nothing comes close to the real thing. For as that too, too solid, raven-black flesh melts, thaws, and resolves itself into an ebony dew, so the aroma uncurls into the acrid air of the room with its burnished fragrance of an earth sweetened. If opium was a jewel, it would be amber, for its sweet aroma could attract insects like the sap of pine trees.

Not that this was said. Prince Panat and I knew that the occult mystery of inhaling opium was an utter hush. To inhale the smoke (harsher than its fragrance would have predicted) and then let the dreams have their own way.

But neither Algie nor Geoff was aware of this. They talked and talked away. About London and their birds and the trip and then…Then, by the third pipe, Algie was trying to speak. His last words, as I recall while sinking deeper and deeper into that sable-colored Elysium of opium, was something like: "The land of a million … no, a billion elephants. We will draw your elephants, Your Highness, then lacquer them with gold and grey clay, Your Highness, the wings will be painted with the green of your rain forest…"

He inhaled his last pipe and continued his Elizabethan soliloquy.

"We will fly through the elephant universe to the far reaches of the Laotian empire …"

Then he passed out. We lay on that hard wooden bed and our bodies became soft and we passed out, too. We all passed out, royalty and commoner alike. And slept the sleep of the weary, the drugged, and the pure.

The next morning I woke to reality. The Laotian monsoon (the mother of all rains), and headaches that pounded worse than the water on the roofs. And I was alone. Panat had woken the cockneys early, hustled them out to the buffalo field airport, and they had departed in their private plane.

The world was a blur, but I stumbled out of the God's-Little-Acre shack into the lanes of Luang Prabang. Somehow, I managed to find the hotel where my colleagues were staying. They had survived the toadstools and the whiskey. We had coffee, took a walk, and then returned to Vientiane and Bangkok. Three months later, Cambodia and Vietnam surrendered to their Communist insurgents and administered varying degrees of punishment to the American running dogs. Thoughts of making Laos the center of the universe were shelved, unceremoniously dumped on the back burner, while Prince Panat apparently went back to Paris.

Laos, initially, with the gentility of an old gentleman giving a seat to a lady, peacefully allowed the Pathet Lao to enter and rule. Until recently, few foreigners were allowed to enter. Today, they can cross over the bridge (now finished) and experience the same unfinished war monument, unfinished library, and movietheater.

Both opium and marijuana are illegal. The Luang Prabang palace has not been demolished, but the king, spending his last days gardening, has departed this mortal coil. And so far as I can fathom, groups of foreign tourists are forbidden from having grand drunken banquets by the side of the river. But the town is still charming, low-key, frozen in time.

And I long to return to that Luang Prabang of yesteryear, my own Isle of Innisfree nestling among the mystical Asian mountains of an opium dream.

Recipe:
Kai Yang
Laotian Grilled Chicken

3 lb. whole chicken, split in quarters
10 garlic cloves, finely chopped
3 tbsp. black peppercorns, coarsely crushed
2 tbsp. soya sauce or Thai Siracha sauce (the latter is very hot and garlicky)
1 tbsp. sugar
2 tbsp. cheap Thai whiskey, like Mekhong, or Laotian Hill Tribe moonshine (if available and no police are in sight)
1 tsp. salt

Sauce

1 c. white vinegar
½ c. sugar
3 garlic cloves, coarsely chopped
2-3 fresh red chilies, pounded well but preserving the seeds (seeds actually have all the "heat")
Pinch of salt

1. Mix the chicken with ingredients in a bowl and leave to marinate for up to 4 hours.
2. If possible, barbecue this outside over charcoal for 30 minutes, rolling on a spit. Alternatively, in a 350-degree oven, roast for 40 minutes, turning halfway through.
3. For sauce: Mix the ingredients and boil over low heat until it becomes very thick, almost viscous.
4. Serve with the chicken and glutinous rice. Chicken should be eaten with the hands, dipped manually into the sauce to get full flavor.
5. Serves four, conservatively. But make more since second helpings are inevitable.6.

CHAPTER TWENTY

SNACKING AWAY IN DOWNTOWN MANDALAY
Recipe:
Ginthoke (The Ginger Mix)

Traveling to Burma for fun is always tinged with guilt. The equivalent would be trips to the "old" pre-Mandela South Africa, or drinking Chilean red wine during the Pinochet era. I had allayed my guilt by taking two illegal trips to the country. Thus, my single legal "guilt trip" to Burma was alleviated by two unauthorized trips. One was in the Golden Triangle, illegally crossing the bridge to see where the opium merchants hung out. (It looked like any Thai provincial hotel.) The next was over the Three Pagodas Pass, where the Burmese had just slaughtered an entire village of Karen. This was later documented, but I never felt pride in that journey.

The legal journey was to Mandalay, on a holiday of sorts.

Rudyard Kipling's "road to Mandalay" suffers from various misconceptions. First, the "road" is actually the Irawaddy River. Second, if he saw "the old Moulmein pagoda looking eastward to the sea," he would have been dixlexic, as Moulmein, a thousand miles south of Mandalay, looks wester. Third, Kipling never reached Mandalay—or even Rangoon. He was too busy and, like most British colonialists, he thought Burma was a crazy country.

At that time, it was. Unlike Thailand, which graciously welcomed foreigners, Burma could have been named the Kingdom of Xenophobia. Its kings moved their capitals almost monthly. A dream, a fortune-teller, or maybe a bad case of indigestion, and the kings would take their slaves, retainers, wives, elephants, monkeys, soothsayers, ministers, and chums, and move somewhere else. Thus, around Mandalay are literally dozens of almost unpronounceable names – Thabyedaung, Myanaung, Amarapura, etc. – which were capitals for a few weeks.

Besides that, the country was very dangerous. The king, during Victorian times, was a decided Anglophobe. Hearing that a "mere woman" was ruling England, he thought he would show her who was boss. He decided to build the world's largest pagoda. Or at least the tallest pagoda. And he personally designed a six-hundred-foot-high pagoda on an island near Mandalay.

"When Queen Victoria sees this pagoda, she will not come near to invade us, for this will be a monument to our greatness," he told his courtiers.

The king was a king, not a structural engineer, so the pagoda inevitably collapsed, and its ruins still lie there. Today this desolate island stands only as a monument to folly, incompetence, and a situation all too well known in other countries: the paranoia of patriotism.

Which brings up the original subject about snacking it big time in Mandalay.

Ask any Burmese where the best food in the country may be, and the response will be quick. He will dart away. This is because Burmese are not supposed to speak to foreigners.

But ask in theory where the best food will be, and Mandalay will be the answer. It took a while to realize this, for the food I had eaten previously was greasy, tasteless, with the red chilies so pulverizing to the mouth and so acrid to the nose that neither flavor nor aroma were possible.

I had already planned to write yet another best-selling diet book here: "The Burmese Curry Guide To Losing Weight Fast! Eat as much as you want, whenever you want, wherever you want, and lose twenty pounds in five days. The explanation? Nobody wants any of the damned stuff."

That was before Mandalay. And a conversation with a professor of political science named U Maung, who encountered me on the ferry traveling from the old deserted pagoda island.

U Maung was not shy, and was quick to realize that my proclivities led to the stomach rather than his politics, and that I had been disappointed in his food. Glancing at the sun (neither of us wore a watch), he mentioned casually that when the ferry docked it would be "snacking time in Mandalay," and that we would survey true Burmese food. "Give me two hours of your time," he said, "and you will never regret it."

How could I refuse? And so we docked and strolled over to the now defunct Zegyo market, originally laid out in 1903 by the Italian Count Caldrari.

Italian architecture is a hallmark of Southeast Asia. Many of Thailand's temples and large buildings are Italian, the Great Mosque of Brunei was of Italian design (Anthony Burgess wrote lovingly of this in his first novel). And the Zegyo market. Before it burned to the ground around 1995, Zegyo extended over five or six avenues. At night, it was a smuggler's paradise, with all the illegal goods of the capitalist world shipped into the country. Without them, the Burmese Path to Socialism would have been as muddy as the Burmese Road to Mandalay.

During the day, though, tribal people came flooding into the market with their meagre but colorful wares. Mainly baskets, cigars (oh, those huge cheroots!), makeup, iridescent sarongs, umbrellas, parasols, lacquerware, Buddhist scriptures, and a variety of hats.

They also had food. But the main restaurants were anything but appetizing. One had to have a guide to find the best food, which was always hidden behind columns, crates, corridors, and traditional Burmese anarchy.

"We begin," said U Maung, "with the flower stall. The famous flower stall Pan Dan, for the most famous dish in Burma." Threading our way through little alleys, down tiny streets, behind countless counters, we saw a lovely old lady surrounded by her trade – the trade of making mohinga. A simple dish of noodles with fish, perhaps. But the filleted fish was the tender butterfish, and we could choose broad flat noodles or round noodles. On this came a world of spices. Dried chilies, ground-up shrimps and shrimp paste, minced onions, garlic, minced ginger, a pinch of turmeric, some lemon grass powder, limes, coriander leaves, peanuts, and stench.

Stench? No, this was more that mere stench. It was as if Lucifer, when leaving heaven for hell, had given the Almighty an almighty barrage of farts, and that each fart had filled the universe with fermented fish and rotting pickles, with onions that had been buried in the ground and garlic that had suddenly sprouted to become six feet high.

"Um, yum," said I.

"And that," said U Maung, "is the best ngapi in the world."

Well, I had always thought that nappies were what you gave

to babies, but no, this was the fish sauce, a fish sauce that would make Thai fish sauce seem like a chocolate mousse from New York's Jean-George.

Very smelly. And a smelly beginning to a true moveable feast. That is, we moved, and the feast was spread before us.

It was quite international, in a provincial way. We had a smelly herring curry – herring, the consummate New York fish, here a real hilsa herring from the Andaman Sea. It was wrapped in a sour leaf, a leaf so sour that it was like – wait for it – Sixth Avenue Delicatessen herring in sour cream. (Okay, an exaggeration.) We then had a vegetarian dish. A mixture of fermented cabbage, fermented seaweed, fermented onions, and fermented bean sprouts.

Fermented heaven!

My favorite dish was actually a Burmese aperitif. It was a pile consisting of pickled tea leaves, peanuts, and sesame seeds, all crunchy, all faintly sour but absolutely delicious. Some soups, some prawns (finger-licking good), different curries, and finally, in one last aisle, they tried to sic those terrible gelatin sweets on us. I pushed them away, and we went to another cubicle, here to be greeted with orange-hard Thai papaya (not those mushy Caribbean paw-paws) with bananas, and with other fruits for which the names are far away.

We left the market then, since U Maung had to go to his family. Besides, walking with a foreigner was always dangerous. So we parted, and later I went to Pagan, the thirteenth-century capital for which even Marco Polo had wonderful words. And there I took a bike and went to the countryside, and sat out in a garden and drank Burmese toddy, from the palm trees, and fell asleep…

When I awoke, the bike was waiting, the sun was going down, and I wheeled my way through the temples and courtyards to the sleep of the weary and innocent.

Recipe:
Ginthoke (The Ginger Mix)

Pickled tea leaves are very difficult to find in the United States, but Burmese restaurants will certainly have them. This, though, is another appetizer found in every Burmese market. I learned the recipe with great difficulty not in Mandalay, but back in Rangoon (now known as Yangon) in the famed Strand Hotel. The hotel has been tarted up recently, but when I was there it was tiny, chummy, and had a famed "lost-and-found" glass case with everything from an Eton hat to a yo-yo, and what looked like a jellybean. It may have been an insect. While the kitchen didn't serve Burmese food (they specialized in tiffin, a British colonial repast), I went drinking with the chefs one night, and they feasted on this marvelous mixture.

Ingredients:

    4 oz. fresh ginger, as tender and soft as possible**

    About 5 tbsp. of lemon juice, from fresh lemons

    About 2 tbsp. of peanut oil (not an ordinary vegetable oil, I was warned)

    1 tsp. sesame oil

    12 garlic cloves

    Some sesame seeds

    Salt

**It is vitally important that the ginger be as young as possible. Ask your market to reserve ginger that has translucent skin with pink roots. Don't use any part of the ginger that seems hard. Burmese chefs, always practical, may take off the unused parts of the ginger and make a preserve, which they sometimes add in cooking curries. They told me they used cooking sherry for this preserve.

Preparation:
1. Scrape off the skin of the ginger and cut as finely as possible into little slivers.
2. Take the lemon juice and marinate the ginger for up to 2 hours. The color should turn pinkish.
3. Take the two oils, peanut and sesame, and heat them in a small frying pan.
4. Add the pink ginger and fry it very slowly. (Nothing in Burma is very fast, including cooking.) It should turn the color of the Shwe Dagon Pagoda steeples, radiant gold.
5. When this happens, take it out immediately before it burns, and put it on absorbent paper, where the ginger will turn crisp.
6. Now take the sesame seeds and heat them slowly without oil (like coffee beans) until they turn golden. Take them out to cool.
7. Take the ginger (make certain no oil or lemon juice remains) and put it in a bowl, adding the golden sesame seeds. Mix them together gently, put on a banana leaf (oh, okay, put them in a bowl), and serve with drinks.

Chapter Twenty-One

The Day of Swine and Hoses
Recipes:
Ayam Rica Rica (Spicy Chicken)
Rendang Beef

Political/economic journalists acknowledge that Indonesia is a mass of frustrations. Itineraries are created in order to be broken, ships are built to be wrecked, government organizations are invented to confuse governments, timetables are minced into a solar/nocturnal Cuisinart to be minced. The most dire poverty is amidst some of nature's most sumptuous riches.

I was always aware of this each time I would fly into Jakarta or Bali's capital, Denpassar. At the same time, the history of these exotic islands made the fabulist in me drool with pleasure. Here, giant dragons loll under ancient trees. The religion, theoretically Islamic, is a joyously eclectic blend of Allah, the Virgin Mary, Buddha, Vishnu, and the Holy Mountains of the pre-Islamic adat religion. Volcanoes glow and spit hot orange syrup. Music and dance reverberate through endless moonlights, their influence extending to the music of Britten, Ravel, and Debussy. Ceremonious feasts make the Master Chef of Olympus look like a Burger King french fry fryer.

While trips have taken me to Komodo, Sumbawa, Java, Bali, Lombok, and Flores, Sulawesi offered me a rather strange search of food. True, the Toraja people of South Sulawesi, with their massive funerals, are oft written about. My story was quite different. For down by the port in Sulawesi's capital, Ujung Pandang, is the largest restaurant in the world. And two hundred forty miles north is the biggest, noisiest, most hysterical kitchen in the ... in the universe. Let us take them one at a time. They are both astonishing.

First, the restaurant. Ujung Pandang is a sprawling port town inhabited by the Makassarese people. Surrounding them, all along the coast of southern Sulawesi, are the Bugis people, possibly the world's greatest sailors. They are fierce Moslem believers themselves. But being wanderers, crews of Odysseuses to a man, they know that there is a world outside of Islam, and give grudging respect to others. Or, to be more unsentimental, they don't give a damn.

The capital has two distinct ports.

The port of the Bugis people is outside the main drag. The waters here are like a sailing inner city, packed cheek to jowl (sorry, port to stern) with ancient schooners, short-masted carracks, Elizabethan galleons, merchantmen, frigates, quadremes, and virtually every sea-going vessel since the raft was invented. The ships' chandler shops adjacent to the port display hand-written signs showing daily destinations. They include names that are not on any map today, nor any map of Joseph Conrad's time (he loved the Bugis, just as he despised Indonesian landlubbers). These ships go everywhere in the Pacific and South Seas. Everywhere!

I have never sailed with the Bugis, but others who do sail with them find the experience filthy, exciting, disgusting, frightening, and exhilarating.

The second port fronts the town itself. It is international and adheres to vaguely international rules. But at night, this littoral of the town comes alive. Actually, around 6:00 P.M., the outdoor food stalls along the seafront are put up for the night's entertainment. It is gargantuan.

    Along the sidewalk and across the portside street are literally thousands of curry carts, shishkebab carts, juice carts, fruit carts, sweets carts, lamb-grilling, beef-broiling, fish-boiling, shank-braising, soup-simmering, chicken-frying, and ice-creaming carts. Altogether about five miles of carts. You buy your food, lean against the jetty, and enjoy nighttime palavers with diminutive Papuans, boisterous Zamboangans, Moslem guerrilla Tawi-Tawis, ex-cannibal Trobrianders, fleshy Samoans, shy Trukers, jolly Cebus (who talk about their killing of Magellan as if it were yesterday), and the whole thesaurus of Indonesians, Javanese, Sumatrans, Lombokis, and Sumbawans. Endless languages, cultures, and mores of the eastern world.

    The meals go on until past midnight. Then the men drift back to their ships or the dreary amusement parks and brothels in the town. The food is as delicious as it is eclectic, and the talk, for sheer knowledge of the world's mysteries, can beat the hell out of the Algonquin Club or the Oxford Union.

    As they would say on New York's West Side, if they knew of Ujung Pandang, "Why, practically everybody shows up here!"

    That is the ebullient restaurant of the capital. The kitchen, though, is far into the remote mountains, and it must be the largest in the universe – as well as the most sinister. For this is the gateway to the kitchens of the famed Toraja highland funeral ceremony.

Now the Torajans shun the capital and stay far from the coast. They live up in the mountains, about six hours from the capital. They practice their own form of Christianity, but like most Indonesians their religion derives from adat. Adat is the original Indonesian religion, predating "established" beliefs but influencing them the way Greek and Celtic legends are reincarnated in our Western beliefs.

To the Torajans, death is anything but morbid, since the afterlife has as much fun and jollity as this life. The deceased are considered alive until the big sacrificial ceremony. And that can be held up to two years later, when enough funds are amassed to hold the ceremony. Since that duration is used for preparing the funeral, the body lies around the house, semi-mummified.

The body stench is masked by a bouillabaisse of forest herbs and soaps. When asked about the mummy, sitting at the table or resting on the ground, the occupant explains that the body is "sick" or "almost sick" or "almost dead." It's like a dotty old uncle who has come to live. You have to move him around when sweeping up the house, but otherwise he's no problem at all.

Once the family has enough rupiah, the money is used to build a funeral area, which is also known as the "kitchen." Actually the kitchen is a large oval piece of ground that resembles a Spanish corrida. Up to five thousand people – friends, guests, relatives, anybody who wants to drop in to the funeral feast – crowd into the circular bamboo stands that run around an open area. About a half-mile in circumference, it serves as mortuary, display grounds, music hall, cabaret, and dining facilities for the grand holiday.

This is how it works. First, you hire traditional funeral engineers to build the bamboo stand. A few months later, invitations are sent out. Verbal invitations like: "Oh, remember my brother Shakli, who died last year? Well, we're giving him a grand send-off today. Why not drop by? It should be fun. Bring your friends.

"And by the way, this is a B.Y.O.B. affair, if you know what I mean."

B.Y.O.B. means "Bring Your Own Beast."

When going to a funeral, you are expected to visit the market and offer a sacrificial animal or two. Most buy a pig. Rich Torajans may offer a buffalo.

By 5:00 A.M. the morning of the great funeral, guests stand in line with their animals, waiting to get into the stands. As the day goes on, the clamor of moos, oinks, squeals, singing, rattling tambourines, smashing drums, and joyous screaming is deafening. So are the aromas of feces, blood, offal, urine, putrefying corpses, both human and beast. A Paris parfumerie it ain't.

Once guests pile into the arena, they become part of an enormous abattoir cum food-processing plant. As each animal is taken by hand (or paw), the shaman – literally the master of ceremonies – screams out his thanks. Then he screams to the rest of the crowd that Mr. Shakli and his esteemed family have offered a big pig or a huge buffalo in order to show their respect for the body. Everybody in the stands shouts out deafening approval, and the pig, about to join the din with a great squeal, is silenced when an assistant shaman bashes it over the head with a six-foot-long frying pan.

As the pig lies motionless on the ground, a sword is drawn and plunged. So quick is it that the pig, already senseless from the frying-pan knockout punch, doesn't even know what's happening. Or if it does, it might be happy to be going to hog heaven. We mortals don't comprehend these things.

Anyhow, once the sword is extracted, and the blood goes flying, a dozen people rush into the ring to extract the offal and skin the animals. For convenience sake, let's call them sow-chefs.

Hardly has the blood spurted in the air but the sow-chefs take the body of the pig to the side of the corrida where a stewing vat is bubbling under a big fire. The vat, a cooking utensil probably stolen from the sculleries of Mount Olympus, could retain a dozen pig corpses, and the water would melt an Antarctic iceberg. So the pig quickly disintegrates, stirred around by official boiling people. At this point, the strainer-men approach. These are men who carry butterfly nets. That is, if butterflies were the size of 747 jets, these would be butterfly nets.

The strainer-men strain out the meat and skin from the bubbling vats and pour it into huge tureens, which in turn are hoisted on to official broad-shouldered mourners. These mourners now take the tureens into the bamboo stands. Here, each guest has brought some clay bowls, taking wooden spoons from trousers, holding the bowls to accept the meat of the sacrificed pig. But even as they eat, more and more pigs are taken into the arena ready to be noisily sacrificed and consecrated.

Immediately after each sacrifice, with clockwork precision not found anywhere else in Indonesia, the authoritative cleaners enter the stadium, busy with long hoses gushing out brown water, turning the mess of liver, intestines and blood into slurry, slush, and finally reddish brown water that floats to the edge of the ground, seeping into the dirt. For now the ground is clean enough to allow in the next esteemed family.

Say what you will, but a Toraja funeral ceremony is a very nice place to which one can be invited. But it is not a Versailles state dinner.

I had only a vague idea of the Torajan ceremony, and being invited, thought myself honored. This was understandable, since Torajans have little else to entertain them. Anyhow, I asked my guide what kind of gift I should offer.

"Oh," he said, "since you're a foreigner, they'll be thrilled just to have you at all. Nobody expects much, so you can just bring a carton of cigarettes. Foreign cigarettes are best."

Well, as an ardent anti-smoker, I reasoned that as Toraja people don't really "die," cigarettes can't really kill. I bought a carton of Marlboro Lights (okay, cigarettes don't kill, but why take a chance?), feeling suitably generous. Accompanied by my guide (his "gift" was the foreigner, me), I got in the noisy line of animals and merrymakers from the district.

Would I be the only alien to this most alien ceremony?

Not quite. In fact, just in front of me were six very jolly Germans. So jolly were they that they had gone to the market, and they had brought their own swine to the ceremony. How wunderbar! How native! How schwein-respecting!!!!

The Frankfurt sextet had bought the swine, picked it up, tied a log to the paws of the screaming creature, then triumphantly hoisted it on their broad shoulders and jostled their way into the arena. While I politely took my bench seat in the lower stands, they paraded in their animal and laid it at the feet of the somewhat nonplussed shaman. Then the German foreign guests marched back to the lower stands one row in front of me.

This was the portion of the ceremony when the shaman, his head-feathers dancing in the wind, shouts out which family contributed what. So when it came time to describe the foreigners' contributions, he was literally beside himself.

(Actually, he was beside the writhing pig, but you know what I mean.)

As he shouted, my guide translated the words of this Torajan Demosthenes for me.

"Here…here in our very presence are German people. They are from Germany. Which is near to Holland." (The Indonesians still have grudging admiration for the old colonizers.) "They are heroes for Torajan people. Because they respect Torajan people. They know that we have respect for our families. The German people understand our traditions.

"And in our honor they have carried a pig. Not an ordinary pig but a pig of immaculate quality. This pig will feed far more people than any normal pig. And the Toraja people should cheer our German friends wildly. For not only is it very big, it is a very lucky pig."

("No," I whispered to my translator, as the pig glared in horror at its hovering, sword-wielding executioner, "that damned pig is very unlucky." "Shhhh," he said.)

Then the Torajans did cheer. Led by the shaman, egged on by the sow-chefs, echoed by the strainer-people and official boilers – and, of course, augmented by the damned pig – the stands screeched louder and louder and louder, until the whole arena was on its feet.

That was when the Germans broke the rules. They rose from their seats in the stands and marched, then trotted, then ran on to these killing fields like first place winners at the 1936 Olympics. They stood beside the writhing pig, taking pictures of themselves, posing with the jubilant shaman and his exhilarated minions, and the crowd went into near hysterics. This, I thought, again discourteously, was what the Nuremberg rallies must have sounded like.

Well, the pig was duly sacrificed (see details above), and the band (did I tell you that they had fifty or sixty Juilliard dropouts blowing horns and banging drums?) played music and banged and sang…

And now the crowd suddenly hushed. Because now, said the shaman, this ceremony would be blessed. Blessed with yet another foreigner.

The shaman, finished with the prancing Germans, looked straight through the arena into my eyes and pointed. The crowd followed the pointing fingers to my destination in noisy expectation. What, they wondered, could possibly be more imposing, more moving, than a German pig?

The shaman shouted out his question to my guide, who shouted something back.

I didn't understand the words of my translator. But somewhere in the sentence, I heard the word "Marlboro" talktalktalktalk Marlboro Lights talktalktalktalk. I knew – and the shaman knew and the sow-chefs knew – that he wasn't referring to British nobility.

The shaman looked at me, looked at the ground, then shrugged his shoulders. Then he shouted out the news to the multitudes.

"The other foreigner," he proclaimed, "has brought a carton of cigarettes."

The arena was silent.

"Foreign Marlboro cigarettes," he shouted, hoping this would put icing on the cake.

For a moment, a hush fell over the crowd. And then, bless their modified Christian charity, they politely clapped. I smiled. I waved with the enthusiastic wave Queen Elizabeth gives from her car. More precisely, I gave a microwave.

What was I thinking at that time? I was thinking back to the old Jimmy Cagney movies. Specifically, Cagney prison movies, where one guy bangs his cup against the cell bars, followed slowly by others until the whole prison is rife with banging.

And I hoped against hope that the polite clapping would have increased into a grand crescendo, and people would have realized that, yes, the Germans brought a whole pig. But this foreigner needed no beast to sacrifice. This foreigner had brought his heart, his soul, his...his modest sincerity.

Toraja, alas, is not an old James Cagney prison movie. It is reality. Well, a kind of reality.

Instead of polite clapping, the Torajan eyes thought the same thing. "Cheap Charlie." "Lousy miser." "Jew-boy." "Stingy."

The family of the deceased, bless their hearts, did have a genuine nobility. They came through the stands and happily took the carton of cigarettes and thanked me. Shaking my hand, smiling, telling my translator that I was a kind man. They were kind, civil, polite. To the stares of the multitude, they opened a pack, lit up a Marlboro, shook my hand, and marched back to open ground near the boiling cauldron, waving their cigarettes triumphantly like that smoke-loving comic, Denis Leary.

I still think of them with charity.

The stands, like Romans already exhausted with the last sacrifice, were turning to the next, and we were soon forgotten. I tried to make light of the incident.

"Listen," I explained, "this pig thing isn't really so great. I mean, what about Torajans who are veggies? Shouldn't vegans get an even break? And cigarettes are quiet, too. Maybe next time I'll bring some string beans or potatoes to fry…"

My translator looked at me like I was crazy, but I assured him it was a reasonable idea. I also thought that, since sacrifices would be continuing far into the night and the next day, it was time to leave. I said my farewells to the multitudes (who seemed not to care, as a heifer was now on the chopping block), strolled through the shouting people, and took a stroll in the Torajan hills.

Recipe:
Ayam Rica Rica (Spicy Chicken)

The Toraja Highlands separates South Sulawesi, home of the Bugis seafarers, from the more sedate North Sulawesi people. They are predominantly Christian, hardly adventurous, but do have the world's largest snake in their jungles. This dish was given to me by Benny Widyono, a long-time United Nations official from Indonesia, who is not only one of the savviest people at that organization, but a terrific cook as well. This first recipe is the most traditional of North Sulawesi.

> 1 two-pound chicken, cut into pieces
> Salt
> Limejuice
> Bunch of large red chilies
> Ginger
> 1 large onion
> Vegetable oil

1. Rub the chicken with salt and limejuice and let stand for 2 hours.
2. Put the onion, red chilies, ginger, and more salt in a blender and blend them coarsely.
3. Grill the chicken until half done.
4. Rub the chili mixture into the pieces of chicken and grill until done.
   To be eaten with white rice. Enjoy!

Version Two

Ms. Unggu, the Indonesian United Nations chef, has a variation on this recipe. The first part of the foregoing is correct. Namely, that the chicken should be rubbed in salt and limejuice. But Ms. Unggu insists that the spice mixture should include salt, red chilies, ginger, lemon grass, pandan leaf (available at Asian grocery stores, though sometimes in powdered form), garlic, and onions. This mixture, after going through the blender, should be sautéed in oil. Only then should you baste the chicken with this mixture.

> 1 chicken, cut into pieces
> 1 c. water
> 6 tbsp. oil
> Salt
> Sugar to taste
> Limejuice

Spices for blending

> 1 large onion or 4 shallots
> 5 cloves garlic
> 1 bunch large red chilies
> 1 pandan leaf (available at Thai or Chinese grocery stores)
> 1 stalk lemon grass
> 1 piece ginger
> 1 tomato

Cooking

1. Rub chicken with salt and limejuice; let stand for 2 hours or so.
2. Meanwhile, blend spices coarsely, sauté in the oil, add the water, sugar; set aside when the wonderful aroma comes out clearly.
3. Dip chicken pieces in this mixture; continue grilling until done.
4. Pour remaining spice mixture and serve with hot steaming rice.

Selamat makan!

Recipe:
Rendang Beef

Since this chapter may put you off pork forever, let us proceed to one dish common throughout Indonesia. Whatever city or town one is in, the Sumatran restaurants are ubiquitous, for good reason. This food is spicy (unlike the usually mild recipes of Java), but the spices never overcome the food, the recipes are imaginative, and the dishes are displayed in the windows. One can't go wrong here. The most common dish is Rendang Beef, which can be fiercely hot, as it should be. This recipe could be modified for more temperate households.

    1½ katties (about 3.3 lb.) beef, cut into large pieces
    2 coconuts, grated
    1 tbsp. vegetable oil
    Fresh juice of one lime
    Salt to taste

First, pound together the following ingredients:
    10 dried chilies
    10 black peppercorns
    1 tiny bit of ginger and a piece of fresh turmeric
    5 cloves garlic, 10 small onions, 4 stalks candlenut, and 4 stalks lemon grass

1. Squeeze out the juice from a coconut and add water.
2. Now heat oil in a wok-like frying pan over slow heat until it is slightly smoking.
3. Add the pounded ingredients and fry them until you can smell the fragrance.
4. Add meat and salt and fry for another few minutes.
5. Add more coconut, a little at a time, waiting for the liquid to be absorbed. Cook until tender.
6. Put in more coconut, and simmer over very low heat until the curry is dry. Stir constantly to prevent boiling.
7. Add limejuice and cook for another 2 minutes.
8. Serve hot with yellow or plain rice.

Chapter Twenty-Two

The Monastic Tryptych

In writing a history of Macao, I loved describing the Laurel-and-Hardy religious riots of the seventeenth century. Not Catholics against Moslems or Buddhists against Christians. But the inevitable Easter convulsions, when Dominicans and Augustinians trooped down the main street to each other over the head with big crosses and portraits of their various saints.

Three of the holiest orders of the Catholic Church used food as symbol, metaphor and, yes, nutrient. But each of the religions used its own disciplines and philosophies to see food as a different element of the Eternal Verity.

A. St. Francis at Eventide
Recipe:
Greens and Beans

Then did Francis – yes, that Francis of Assisi – tiptoe into the church that he had built with his own hands, made with wattles and clay and simple things. He climbed to the pulpit and addressed the multitudes, who today consisted not only of the poor and helpless, but those who had great wealth in the vineyards of Italy and abroad and were looking for an answer. One of the companions had whispered that these men should look "for salvation, not salivation."

But St. Francis was more forthcoming.

"How do my followers prepare the meal for evening or afternoon? They prepare it in the way that my followers believe in the sanctity of life, yes, even for the meanest things, which grow in the dust."

He then lifted a pot upon the pulpit, and with it the ingredients for his meal.

"The simple garlic," he said, extending the roots to the rapt congregation. "How gently we feel its bulb and see the white skin grown slightly gray with age. It shakes in my hand, fearful of its fate. Yet, how carefully we peel it, taking care to never cut the skin, so not a single utterance of pain does it feel.

"And now we see the leaves of garlic not fall but dance their way into this receptacle. Dancing through the air."

The congregation smiled.

"Our Savior asked in the Gospel of Luke whether we had the

faith of a mustard seed. And here we have mustard greens. Together, a community, a bunch, a congregation. Gently we peel it and tenderly place it in the placid waters with his brother Sir Garlic.

"And with it, we remember our own creation by A Supreme Bean."

And as the morning went on Francis took lemon juice, juice that smiled with its tender tang, then olive oil, the oil Minerva in the ancient days called the most valuable treasure of all mankind.

"And finally," said Francis, "the pea. Consider its roundness, consider it nestling like an infant within its mother pod. What heavenly inspiration did create this vegetable?

"Our ancestors wrote in secret caves the Dead Pea Scrolls. But I do proclaim that in its roundness, it doth live as a universe…"

St. Francis finished his sermon, and though the congregation was now fast asleep they could hear the mild bubbling of the water, their noses could catch the wafted scent of the fresh aroma. And Francis was pleased, and with a ladle made of clay he spooned his creation to all those who believed that all of life breathed and multiplied.

Greens and Beans

1 tbsp. olive oil
1 tbsp. garlic
2 bunches fresh greens (mustard or turnip will do), washed well, drained, and chopped
1 tbsp. fresh lemon juice
Salt and pepper
1 can black-eyed peas

1. In a deep pot, heat oil over medium high heat. Add garlic and cook, stirring, for about 1 minute. Add the greens and cook until wilted. Cover pot, reduce the heat, and let greens simmer in their own juices (the pot likker) for at least 10 minutes.

2. Uncover the pot. Stir in the lemon juice, add salt and pepper to taste. Stir in the black-eyed peas. Leave pot on heat until peas are warmed. Remove and serve immediately as a side dish

b. Pére Gorgonzola Blesses A Lobster
Recipe:
Lobster Salad with Grilled Vidalia Onions

The darkness all around, yet now flambeaux on the walls were lit by slaves from Abyssinia, their own ebony making them near invisible, shadows against shadows, as the flickering lights played on the mosaics picturing hell on the floor of the chamber.

They were always around these places, thought one onlooker. "Abyssinia," he wrote, "in all the old familiar places."

Then did the Dominicans march in: Pére Gorgonzola, stern, glowering; Abbot Canard-Sauvage, his eyes and countenance blacker than a cassock; the pockmarked acolyte, Mousseline, juggling quill and parchment. And then the legions of monks and inquisitors. The Dies Irae squeaked and creaked on a tiny pipe organ secluded in the corner of the room.

They stopped. Pére Gorgonzola, crotchety and infirm, leaned to the cruel acolyte, Mousseline, and the two laughed together at some secret jape. The others began to laugh, but suddenly stopped.

"You wonder why we are here without a disbeliever? A heretic?" Abbot Canard-Sauvage called, and the walls resounded with his sandpaper voice.

"Because of this!" He pulled the lobster from beneath his skirt. The lobster dangled from the gnarled fingers of the old saint, but could not curl up to bite those dangerous fingers.

"And this!" And with that he pulled, as if by magic, a cauldron six cubits by six cubits, the water boiling madly as if incited by the waves and flames of Hell itself.

"Behold!" he said. "Behold this crustacean, created even before man himself. Behold the lobster, which in its infancy knows no pain, fears no spirit, is an affront to the Kingdom of Heaven itself."

The lobster had ceased writhing, but now lay still, then extended one claw up to the cauldron, withdrawing it immediately upon feeling the steam.

"And now behold how we deal with this maritime aquatic apostate.

"First...the DOWSING!" With a scream of delight, Pére Gorgonzola plunged the lobster into the cauldron. The lobster thrashed, moaned, lifted one claw from the steam, but it was gone.

A voice came from the back. "Shouldn't you slowly raise the flame rather than bring it into the hot waters?"

Pére Gorgonzola inhaled, but kept his temper.

"Heretic," he glowered. "That is the treatment for believers who have made a false judgment. It is not the treatment for the lower animals."

They were not done yet. As the Abyssinians cowered in fear, Pére Gorgonzola motioned to Mousseline, who reached into his bag and withdrew more articles of torture. First, the chilies. Then the onions; enough onions so one would scream with agony upon peeling them.

Even more. "You like babies?" he roared to the multitude. "Well, try these babies on for size."

And with that, he threw a clump of quivering baby greens into the cauldron.

Silence, as the lamps flickered.

"Have you…have you no mercy?" whispered the same voice from the back of the room.

Pére Gorgonzola glared back. Perhaps another time, another place, that whispery voice would be screaming in agony. At this time, though, the saint was finished.

"Of course I am a merciful man," he said. "Look for yourself. Look how it turns dark, dark as the slaves here in this room."

Yes, they hadn't called the Pére the Black Fryer for nothing. He might have been cruel, he might have led his followers through endless autos-da-fé. But now he softened. Almost in a whisper, he beckoned to Mousseline.

"Maybe you would like a little chicken soup? As my mama used to say, it's good for what ails you."

Pére Gorgonzola tossed the chicken broth into the mixture, spluttered his loud Satanic laugh, and marched from the chamber.

Spice Chronicles: *Exotic Tales of a Hungry Traveler*

Recipe:
Lobster Salad with Grilled Vidalia Onions

2 small dried chipotle chilies
1 ten-ounce pkg. frozen spinach, defrosted
¾ c. chicken broth
Salt to taste
1 large clove garlic, peeled
2 Vidalia onions, cut into ½ inch slices
4 lobster tails, grilled, with meat removed from shells and sliced
4 c. mixed baby greens

1. Pour boiling water over chipotles. Let soak for about 10 minutes. Drain water. Stem and seed chilies.
2. Place chilies, spinach, broth, salt, and garlic into a blender. Purée until smooth. Set aside
3. Place onion slices on hot grill; cook, turning occasionally, until slices are soft and translucent.
4. Place 1 c. greens on each of four plates. Top with sliced onion, and top the onion with sliced lobster tail. Drizzle corn-chipotle dressing over all.

c. Jesuits in the New World
Recipe:
Sweet Potato Buns

"Now, class, come to order," said kindly Father Sean O'Regano to the Indian braves kneeling on the ground in the shape of a mezzaluna. The father smiled to see his children, the children of our Heavenly Father, waiting for his instructions. Back in Dublin, his fellow students at Trinity College would hardly have believed how he could be looked upon with such adoration in this, the untamed wilderness of the New World.

Father O'Regano had always felt that the Lord's work would take him to the most uncivilized territories. And Kentucky in 1791 was just what he was looking for. Carrying only the King James version of the New Testament, a change of cassock ("Gotta look good in the 'hood," he would jest), various currencies, and a seemingly unending bottle of the King Jameson version of Irish whiskey, he had come to Maryland for training, then trekked alone out through West Virginia, Tennessee, and finally Kentucky. Saved not only by his faith, but his goodwill toward men, his compass, his faith, and his Jesuitical logic.

And why did he take such a dangerous journey? He was asked this innumerable times, but always replied the same way.

"Oh, to preach the Gospel," he would laugh. "Have a few drinks and a few jokes. And teach these people the correct way to make Kentucky Burgoo."

The father had heard of this exotic dish, created by other missionaries, trappers, and Indians since Kentucky had become a territory. While he had never tasted the dish, he had seen many a chronicle of those passing through Kentucky trying it. Each recipe was different, each method of cooking separate from the others.

Burgoo, he knew, was as varied as the wild ingredients of its making, field and forest inhabitants, feral cats, and undomesticated wolves, along with rodents of many varieties.

Yet, he was fascinated by the mixture.

"In fact," as he told his monsignor before setting off for the New World, "I see Burgoo as a kind of symbol of Our Lord."

"Why, how do you see that?" asked his astonished mentor.

"When I first heard that they would put twelve water-animals, as well as the slightly fermented hardened milk of their kine, I said to myself, 'Hmm, we can call this dish Cheeses and the Twelve Opossums.'"

The monsignor did not know whether Father O'Regano was serious or making a pun. But he let it go. At any rate, it was too late now.

Here, in the circle of Indians, Father O'Regano would put his Jesuitical training to work. Now the Burgoo would no longer be made with emotion and passion, but with strict Jesuitical rules and regulations.

"So," he told his students, "please follow me, and follow my instructions exactly. First, we take the oil. We measure out exactly three-seventeenths of a tablespoon of oil."

The Indians, who knew little English, understood the miming of the good Father, and were easily able to calibrate his teachings.

"Next, the special onions. I dedicate these onions to the Virgin Mary, and hereby call them Our Lady of Shallot. We shall take 2.7 tablespoons of white shallots, and .062 red shallots. The parsley shall be chopped into pieces. Half of the two tablespoons of parsley shall be chopped into pieces as follows. You shall divide the first quarter of your parsley into pieces of 3.2 grams each. Or, if you wish, into .007314 grams."

The Redskins had been sharpening their knives just for this occasion and they were meticulous in their cutting.

"The flour, however, will be separated into drams. I would say 17.62 drams each."

"Excuse-um," said Fred Mousse, their leader, "but we learn-um not dram but karat. How many karat?"

The father did a quick calculation. "I would say about 156.0894 karats."

"Thank-um," said Fred Mousse, cutting his flour portion. As the day went on, each ingredient was cut into exact portions and poured into the basin over the fire, cooking merrily.

That night, to celebrate the "perfect Burgoo," Father O'Regano celebrated a very special Mass, and the throng dug in. So much food did they have that night, he recalled, that they were unable even to wear the clothes they had on.

"So," he said, "I gave them each a waistband, which they could expand or contract as they wished. And in each waistband I put a miniature copy of the New Testament."

Even to this day, Father O'Regano's waistband is known, from Kentucky to Alabama, as the very first Bible Belt.

Recipe: Sweet Potato Buns

The Jesuits were astonished to find that the "natives" actually ate well, with sweet potatoes one of the great staples of the native American. These buns come from an old Creole recipe and go back to the early eighteenth century.

>   3 tbsp. lukewarm water
>   1 packet dry yeast
>   1 pinch of sugar
>   1 can yams (1 lb. 4 oz. size), rinsed and patted dry
>   1 c. sifted flour
>   4 tbsp. butter, at room temperature
>   Additional flour for dusting

1. Preheat oven to 400 degrees.
2. Dissolve yeast in water. Add sugar; then set aside to rise.
3. Mash yams in a bowl; add the yeast mixture and half the flour.
4. Work the mixture together with your hands, then add the second half of the flour and mix in.
5. Place the mixture in a bowl dusted with flour; cover and set aside in a warm place until it has risen.
6. Remove dough to a lightly floured board and knead in butter.

CHAPTER TWENTY-THREE

THE TEN COMMANDMENTS OF CHINESE FOOD
Recipe:
Almond-Flavored "Bean Curd"

After a decade of travels in Southeast Asia, I was offered a cushy job in Hong Kong. An English-language paper, South China Morning Post, had signed a contract with a television station to publish a weekly magazine, and they wanted me as editor. The problem was that nobody told me about the connection with the television station, and so in my ignorance, I publicized both stations, leading to the dissolution of the former contract and an independent magazine.

Needless to say, the veddy veddy British Suits who controlled the South China Morning Post harrumphed and heeeed and hawed about "that insufferable American" who had been hired. I, on the other hand, expanded the magazine into the "TV and Entertainment Times" (which shows you what I thought of local television; it definitely was not entertainment!) and, of course, added a restaurant review section.

The first restaurant reviews, in fact, weren't tied to advertising, and thus had integrity. Obviously, I learned much about Chinese food while editor. Even when leaving to pursue a free-lance career, I was going to, and writing about, Chinese restaurants. In the process, I published, for the Cathay Pacific Airlines Magazine, the following story.

Hebrew wanderers in the Sinai Desert, and Chinese chefs of the Chow Dynasty had different definitions for the phrase "eating out." The Hebrews of 1500 BCE tediously gleaned globules of manna from the bitter tamarisk plant, chewed on barely singed quail, and were chased away when trying to barbecue a fatted calf.

On the other hand, the Chinese of the same period were gleefully inventing intricate dishes in cavernous kitchens, eating on candlelit verandahs. Their gourmets not only published cookbooks, but composed poems glorifying "tasty sauces and pickles for roast meat," "beans growing fat and tall," and "blessed wine to make men brothers."

Now use your imagination. Think of Moses taking the wrong turn. Instead of entering the Land of Judah, he and his people would wander into the Far East. Instead of climbing Mount Sinai, he would ascend Mount Sin-o, and enter (perhaps bewildered) Dong's Tasty Dumpling Emporium. After encountering the God of the Kitchen, Moses and his chef would schmooze about dumplings, chicken soup, and wine. After a long meal, he would waddle down the mountain bearing two tablets, upon which were written a totally different set of Commandments from what we know today.

A few millennia later, some lusty Mongolian shepherds, stopping off for a goblet of fermented mare's milk in a Gobi singles-cave, might find these Ten Commandments of Chinese food, and the document would be translated and published.

Needless to say, the rules then are the rules today, since good food (like good fellowship) is eternal.

I. I AM THE LORD THY HOST. THOU SHALT NOT GIVE ANY ORDERS BEFORE ME

Traditionally, the Chinese banquet host followed age-old precautions and rituals. He would send his most faithful servants in advance to order the meal. Seated with his back to the door, so as to be the first to suffer assassin treachery, he would wear the gaudiest robe and bring the finest vintage rice wine to the table. Today's host of the Chinese banquet will sit at the head of the table and will be offered the first cut of the meat or vegetables. He should—with time and willingness—go to the restaurant a day in advance to order a meal fit for his guests and his budget, taking the suggestion of the chef or restaurant manager, leaving nothing to chance.

But, if ordering with his guests, he must follow an authoritative commandment: Chinese restaurants are not democratic.

Since all dishes are shared, monopolies on favorites are forbidden. Instead, the Host selects the entire dinner after assaying various rejections ("No pork, I'm kosher"; "Eel? You kiddin'??"; "No vegetables, I'm carnivorous") and preferences (inevitably, "Order lotsa onion cakes"). After this preliminary data, he will hush the multitudes and order a well-balanced meal appropriate for all.

II. THOU SHALT NOT WORSHIP FALSE SAUCES OR CONDIMENTS

Don't be seduced by those tiny saucers of black, red, green, or brown sauces on the table. Cooking is finished when it leaves the kitchen. Pouring additional sauces rarely compliments the dish and never compliments the chef. A few exceptions. For the Cantonese, soy sauce goes back five thousand years so can be used sparingly as a salt substitute. Northern food can take a few drops of sesame or chili oil. The slight acidity of sweet-salty plum sauce makes it appropriate with fatty roast meats. Essential with Peking Duck is hoisin sauce, made with soybeans, red beans, garlic, and sugar. Sichuan dishes can be as hot as possible with pepper sauce. Hot mustard is a recent innovation. Best to let the food be taken on its own terms without an excess of anything.

III. THOU SHALT TAKE THE WORDS "CHINESE FOOD" BUT IN VAIN

The phrase "Chinese food," like "European food," is an indication, not a description. Embracing ten million square kilometers with climates from sub-tropical to sub-arctic, the only commonalities are chopsticks and minced food. The Southern School (Cantonese) was the first international Chinese food, and the rich fertile land brings fish, meat, vegetables, fruit. The food is always fresh, rice is the staple. The West (Szechuan and Hunan) has hot spicy dishes, while Eastern (Shanghai food) is a little oily and, as a New York-style metropolis, is a combination of all Central European cuisines. This commandment basically says, "Know thy restaurant's style before dining." Ordering, say, Peking Duck in a Cantonese restaurant is tantamount to ordering Swedish meatballs in a pizzeria.

IV. MANY CHEFS AND SOUS-CHEFS SHALT LABOR FOR THEE AND DO ALL THE WORK FOR THY BANQUET DISHES, SO REMEMBER TO EAT THEM SLOWLY

How absurd to schedule a Chinese dinner as the prelude for more entertainment. Two traditional banquets—the Chinese "Han" and Mongolian "Han"—would last for at least three days, offering thirty-four varieties of meat, fifty or sixty plates of cakes and pastries and eighteen plates of fresh fruit. Chefs in those days were granted full Imperial honors, while today, Hong Kong chefs are lured to different restaurants with financial incentives over which a star basketball player would drool.

V. HONOR THY FATHER AND MOTHER OF THE KITCHEN

The da sa fu is the Great Person of the Kitchen (almost always male, but more and more frequently female) and has been revered since the Tang Dynasty. (Only during the Cultural Revolution did political cadres replace chefs, with stomach-turning results.) Should you have the honor to know a Chinese chef personally, take it as a brush with greatness, always acknowledge the suggestions, and bow to age-old authority.

VI. THOU SHALT NOT KILL A WELL-BALANCED MEAL

Individual Chinese banquet dishes are like phrases in a Mozart sonata. Their tastes are memorable on their own. But they are part of a more substantial structure, in this case the feast itself. Like dissonance and consonance in music, each ingredient has a yang (or masculine or hot) aspect, and yin (or feminine or cool) aspect. Yang dishes are more "outgoing" and aggressive, like beef, chicken, garlic, ginger, green peppers, red peppers, and wine. Yin includes most vegetables and fruits, as well as pork (the somnolent pig is the only yin animal). Actually, every ingredient and combination is listed in an ancient pharmacopoeia, the Pen T'sao. The banquet should be built upon these contrasts. Should you order yang dishes together instead of separating them with yin turnips, soya beans, and mustard greens, you will upset the all-important balances. As in great music, inspirational oddities are always welcomed, but a constant violation of "natural" laws kills the architectural beauty of a banquet and its consequent appreciation. While you may order the dishes, the chef (or your knowledgeable head waiter) should decide how to bring each course.

VII. THOU SHALT NOT OMIT A POULTRY

Peking Duck is the grandest Chinese dish, but the plethora of fowl in a Chinese dinner should never be underestimated. No good recipe book will have less than fifty chicken recipes (with Beggar's Chicken the oxymoronic king of chicken dishes). A few not-nice facts. Pigeon should be served with the head. Quail in China is bought live and killed on the spot. If turkey were served in the north (which it isn't), it would be called Peking Tom. Anyhow, salted, broiled, glazed, roasted, barbecued, or boiled, treat yourself to as many bird dishes as possible. Fair is fowl…

VIII. THOU SHALT NOT "STEEL"

William Mark, writer of the authoritative "The Chinese Gourmet," opines that forks and spoons were used thousands of years ago, but were disposed of as impractical. (For ethical reasons, Knives are never used.) Both wooden and plastic chopsticks are environmentally questionable, but are superior to metal. In fact, the only metal used outside the kitchen was for testing poisonous substances. A drop of poison on an iron chopstick was supposed to sizzle and turn it brownish. The best crockery is porcelain from Wan Li, Chiaching, and Cheng Hua, but it is so expensive that using it takes away from the joy of eating. ("Whoops! Sorry! I dropped the plate!") Chieng Lung Imperial kiln is elegant enough. A good restaurant will use a variety of sizes for all the dishes. Kitchen woks may be made from aluminum, copper, or stainless steel, but the best chefs will insist on a cast-iron wok. Other utensils are usually made from bamboo or wood, the only exception being the all-purpose cleaver, made from steel.

IX. THOU SHALT NOT BEAR-PAWS WITNESS

"Rare" animals and fish were, for some godawful reason, chosen to be particularly appetizing, and usually for the wrong reason. Today, we know—or should—know that these exotic choices are either endangered or extinct. If the former, resist. Resist wildcat, turtle, and other friends of the field and forest. Resist shark fin, not only for its rarity (sharks in the South China Sea are almost fished out) but also for the cruelty in how they are caught: The fins are torn off, and they are pushed in the sea to drown. On the other hand, exotica like eel, bird's nest, and seaweed are not only plentiful but also delicious. Be not afraid.

X. THOU NEED NOT COVET THY NEIGHBOR'S RICE…

…or fish or shrimp or pak choi. Chinese don't understand why westerners don't share their dishes with the community. When platters are hogged (so to speak) to one person, it takes away the joy of the table. Individualism should exist in business, not during the communal joy of eating. True, one should not take the final morsel on the platter, but this custom goes back seven hundred years. During the Tang Dynasty, the kitchen would take the ingredients from the unfinished platters and create, on the spot, a dish that had been unknown before, eaten once, and never repeated. (Though, to the less philosophical, this is chop suey!) Yes, banquets are dictatorial affairs. But these are benign dictatorships. As the old Chinese maxim goes, "Friendship is not eternal, but will endure as long as your feast."

Recipe:
Almond-Flavored "Bean Curd"

Only in the north are Chinese desserts memorable. Tianjin is the home of the sweet dumpling and the hot sugar-coated fruit dipped in ice-water. But this southern-style dessert is an exception, an inspiration by William Mark, who created the recipes for The Chinese Gourmet.

The genius of this dessert is that it is especially for those who, like myself, find bean curd as delicious as blackboard chalk. This is not bean curd at all. It serves 6-8, the minimum for any decent banquet.

> 3 c. water
> 3 tbsp. powdered agar agar (seaweed gum found in Chinese grocery)
> ½ c. sugar
> c. sweetened condensed milk
> 1½ tsp. almond extract (essence)
> 12 oz, canned fruit salad. But it's advisable, if possible, to use fresh lychee, mandarin oranges, tangerines, or other soft fruit

1. Bring water to a boil in a large pan and add agar agar and sugar.
2. Lower heat and cook for 5 minutes, stirring occasionally.
3. Add condensed milk and almond extract, stirring to mix well.
4. Pour mixture into shallow cake pan, let cool. Refrigerate until set, about 1 hour.
5. Chill the fruit at the same time.
6. When set, cut the "bean curd" into ½ inch cubes and place in serving bowls.
7. Cover with the fruit and serve.

CHAPTER TWENTY-FOUR

THE FRENCH, HONG KONG, AND CHINESE BANQUET ROADSHOW
Recipe:
Hou Tin Ngarp with Pancakes

Working with the Hong Kong Tourist Association was a mixed blessing, since it had an extremely colonial attitude, and insisted on making Hong Kong look like Victorian England, albeit with the "very polite and hospitable Chinese." (Note to HKTA: The Cantonese are feisty, opinionated, exasperating, funny, absurd, conscientious, and very much themselves. "Polite" and "hospitable" are meaningless.)

Several years ago, the Hong Kong Tourist Association went into battle mode. They had learned that several estimable French chefs were going on a dining tour of China – and they would not be stopping off at Hong Kong. Having just come out of their Cultural Revolution, where food was simple to nonexistent, China hardly had interesting restaurants, whereas Hong Kong, a veddy proper British Crown Colony, had made damned certain that the food was top rate (and a lot better than back in Blighty). With Chinese master gourmet William Mark, I was asked to help rectify matters. This is the story of that campaign.

I. WHEREIN A NOTE OF AMITY IS CONVEYED FROM VERSAILLES TO AN ASIAN COLONY; AND WHEREIN THIS NOTE CREATES SUSPICION AND CONFUSION IN THE COLONIAL POWER, GIVING RISE TO AN UNDECLARED WAR.

When Monsieur Claude Jolly, the most estimable gourmet journalist in that self-proclaimed centre of the world of gustatory delights, Paris, appraised a dish for his journal, L'Express, his culinary world swallowed. So when he decided, in his most infinite Gallic wisdom, that it was appropriate that the master chefs of France pay an official visit to the master chefs of the People's Republic of China, his declarations had all the weight of a Papal Bull (or a Versailles state banquet boeuf). M. Jolly prepared himself with the same finesse as he would prepare a Timbale de Poulet Rouen Voisin. First, he made diplomatic approaches to the Chinese Embassy, which were initially rejected since China recognized no cuisine save its own.

After a whisper in the ear of the Chinese Ambassador that the cuisine of France had a…er, perhaps peripheral interest for barbarians, he reluctantly accepted receiving a quartet of French chefs for a two-week visit.

The chefs were truly les plus fameux of France. Alain Chapel of Chez La Mere Charles. Michel Guerard, founder of the Cuisine Minceur movement. Pierre Troisgros of le grand Troisgros Restaurant. And portly Alain Senderens, soon to be the cynosure of France, granted a third Michelin star.

Along with this group would come Remi Krug, scion of the champagne dynasty–carrying with him an unopened case of 1971 champagne to China.

At this point, an informal note was sent to this writer (a notable gourmet journalist himself, specializing in popcorn avec beurre, pizza des fromages, and Trois Mouquatieres, the eminent chocolat bar. However, M. Jolly did not know my limitations, so he informed him (oh, hell, moi … er, me) that he would be taking his entourage to China for some grande dining. And if I didn't mind, would I possibly prepare a light repast for the entourage on their route.

That is, if any decent food was available in this British colony.

The note was innocent enough, as are most diplomatic notes. The outcome, though, created the First (and only) French-Hong Kong War of the Twentieth Century.

Hong Kong, you see, took its chefs and restaurants almost as seriously as it took its accountants and banks. And when the Hong Kong Tourist Association (HKTA) learned of this informal note, they sized it up as an insult to the flag.

"If they want to stuff their bellies," said one executive, "then they can stuff their bloody bellies."

Like most British civil servants of that time, he was ex-military. And his upper lip was quivering, both with indignation and mustard.

"Do those frogs really think they're getting Chinese food in China? Ha! We'll give them food coming out of their damned ears by the time we're through."

WELCOME BANQUET

I. A Quartet of Nuts
    Chestnuts baked in suga
    Apricots baked in salt
    Fish-flavored coated peanuts
    Deep-fried walnuts

II. A Quartet of Cold Cuts
    Honeycombed tripe with peppery sauce, Szechuan style
    Spicy duck tongue, Shanghai style
    Roast suckling pig, Cantonese style
    Poached chicken, Peking style

III. A Quartet of Entrees
    Coquilles St-Jacques sautéed, Cantonese style
    Shelled shrimp, sautéed Peking style
    "Kung pau" diced chicken, sautéed Szechuan style
    Pig's tripe and kidney sautéed with coriander, Peking style

IV. An Octet of Main Courses
    Sharks fin soup, Cantonese style
    Roast Yuen Long duckling, Peking style
    Braised sea cucumber, Shanghai style
    Abalone stuffed with diced black mushrooms and bamboo shoots, Cantonese style
    Bird's nest with Yunnan ham, Cantonese style
    Double-boiled pigeon
    Black mushroom clear soup, Cantonese style
    Steamed sliced fillet of garoupa with ham and black mushrooms, Cantonese style

V. An Octet of Hors d'oeuvres

    Pressed air-dried duck
    Duck liver sausages
    Pork sausages
    Salted fish
    Béan sprouts, chives, and shredded sautéed ham
    Air-dried pork
    Chinese greens, sautéed
    Preserved cabbage with dried shrimp

VI. A Quartet of Seasonal Fruits

    Tientsin pears
    Mandarin oranges
    Water chestnuts
    Papaya

II. WHEREIN HONG KONG INSPECTS ITS STOCKS AND STRATAGEMS AND RESOLVES THAT ITS PAUCITY OF POPULATION SHOULD IN NO WAY PRECLUDE THE KIND OF DECISIVE VICTORY THAT WOULD HAVE DELIGHTED LORD NELSON HIMSELF.

The public relations force of HKTA was put into motion. They immediately cabled their Paris office: "INFORM M. JOLLY DO NOT RPT DO NOT WORRY. ALL STOPS PULLED FOR LUNCHES AND DINNERS IN HK."

Now HKTA went into battle mode, with a plan both transparent and scrutable.

"An elementary Chinese banquet for the Frogs," said an executive who wouldn't know egg roll from sea slug. "We'll put all the chefs into one kitchen and see what they can deliver. Who could argue with that?"

As a matter of fact, Confucius could argue with that. As Confucius actually did say: "Celestial harmony is limited to the heavens." Celestial harmony in a Chinese kitchen stops where the region stops. Thus, a contingency nightmare was created. The battle might commence when the Chiu Chow chef accidentally dropped a pot of black soy sauce on the floor as he was lowering the goose into the soy mixture. The Cantonese chef, preparing to chop the head of a Heavenly Fish, would slip on the soy sauce, and the Heavenly Fish-head would fly into the ropy mass of the Peking noodle-maker, himself tangling up the Szechuan chef who, to defend himself, would rub the eyes of his colleagues with peppercorns and garlic.

HKTA heard this scenario and scrapped Plan Number One.

They then enlisted a true professional to their ranks. This was Ms. Annie Woo, who was (and is) not only an encyclopedia of Chinese cuisines, she is an experienced, and tough, adjudicator and negotiator. She assured the British HKTA people that problems would be solved, and that the menu would be a classic.

Ms. Woo has the mind of a Mandarin scholar, but the tenacity of a Fukien fishwife. Her words were taken with sighs of relief.

Other plans were discussed. Said one exec: "Why don't we take the best dishes of the visiting Frogs and duplicate them with our Chinese chefs?" That was dismissed as silly. Then it was proposed that Lok Yu, the most important teahouse for more than a century, give a Grand Breakfast for the visiting Frogs.

But that was deemed immediately absurd, since Lok Yu had no affection whatsoever for gweilos, or Foreign Devils. Quite the opposite. They took inordinate pride in the fact that when a sitting Governor of Hong Kong actually came in for lunch, they made him sit in a corner next to the kitchen, laughing and pointing as he nibbled his shrimp in pastry.

Lok Yu was out. They would have one lunch and one banquet. And no monkey brains.

What they hadn't reckoned on was the monkey wrench. For now Monsieur Jolly had sent another note informing the HKTA that…er, outside of the dinner…er, would it be possible for yet another lunch to be served. Since the French would have yet one more day in Hong Kong.

Would it? The HKTA rushed to the fray, enlisting one William Mark, a portly, ever-smiling chef and writer, whose knowledge of his legendary cuisine was up to that of Ms. Woo's. He would be dispatched to prepare lunch. Willie and I took our plans to the HKTA the next day – and they were horrified. For we had the audacity, the brazen insolence to suggest that(a) we should take the French chefs to a Chinese market, and (b) we should take them to the rural New Territories for an auberge chinois-style lunch.

"The French will think that we're peasants," raged the British executive.

After some deliberation, and tenacity on our parts, we insisted. The French would learn that Chinese food wasn't manufactured in Chinese sweatshops, but that it actually grew on trees.

PIGEON LUNCHEON

I. Pigeon in Two Styles
24-day-old virgin pigeon, half roasted in ten Chinese herbs, half cooked in soy sauce with herbs

II. Pigeon Egg in Taro Nest
Pigeon eggs are unique in that the longer they are boiled, the softer they become. They are also more transparent and tasty. This calls for pigeon eggs to be placed in a crispy taro nest atop fresh green broccoli.

III. Pigeon Giblets
Quick-fried giblets spiced, with moderately hot Chinese chilies and spices.

IV. Bean Curd in Oyster Sauce
New Territories' bean curd was often presented as a gift to the Emperor of China. Here, the bean curd is doused with oyster sauce, made from the large Hiroshima-type oysters found in the port of Lau Fau Shan.

V. Double-Boiled Pigeon Soup
A clean, nourishing consommé made with boiled pigeon bones as well as pigeon meat and Chinese herbs.

VI. Fried Rice
Shatin was known as the Emperor's Rice Bowl. Fried rice here is spiced with Chinese sausages, seafood, and fowl.

III. WHEREIN THE PLANS ARE LAID OUT IN DETAIL; AND HOW A DISGRUNTLED COMMANDER RESOLVES TO TAKE THINGS IN HIS OWN DOVE-WHITE HANDS; AND WHEREIN THE DOVE OF PEACE IS BROILED AND PLACED IN A LIGHTLY CURRIED MARINADE.

Came the first official meeting of the Great Chinese Banquet. Annie Woo had laid it out in detail. Suckling pig, beggar's chicken, pan-fried glutinous rice from the Cantonese. Szechuan folks would donate bean curd and prawns in chili sauce. Mongolians would donate hot pots etc., etc.

A Brit exec asked about bear's paws, but that led to problems, since even then bear's paws were considered taboo by conservationists. Ms. Woo gave in on the subject, but nobody liked the idea.

(Actually, once it was served, I discovered that the French chefs were quite intrigued with the idea of bear. While wolfing down the dish, Monsieur Chapel was asked how he could eat an endangered species. He appeared confused by the question.)

"Ah," he said between gulps. "It is endangered, you say? By whom? By the hunter? By the trapper? By the chef? And how do they catch this bête noire? And how do they cook it? It is very delicious, so I am not very concerned about either their conservation or your conversation.")
So much for gourmets and ingredients....

A French banquet was also arranged for the chef, at a private club. Few of HK's French restaurants were interested in showing off in front of their countrymen. It would be, in Shakespeare's words, "a fly to little boys. They would kill us for their sport."

The final problem was the lunch set up in the rural town of Shatin. Shatin is famed for its pigeons, and Willie Mark felt that an all-pigeon luncheon should be offered. The Brits hummed and hawed and harrumphed, but finally gave in.

But Willie Mark had another surprise. "Tell me," he said to me one day. "What will those chefs do upon arrival? Are they expected to nibble on a ham-and-cheese sandwich and go to sleep? I know it's a long trip from Europe to Hong Kong, but I was thinking … I was thinking of preparing something extraordinary. The minute they land, they will be seated down to a thirty-six-course opening banquet."

Willie was adamant. He would work on the menu that very night.

The HKTA British generals were nonplussed that the "natives" were revolting on their own, but they had other thoughts on their minds. Should it be black tie or simple suits? Who would be invited? Perhaps they could find Nancy Kwan, and perhaps she could wear the same cheongsam that she wore in The World of Suzie Wong. (As Nancy Kwan was, at that moment, preparing for a stage play in London's West End, this was unlikely.)

Finally, the big Saturday afternoon arrived, and Hong Kong's (then) four million were told that This Is War. Hong Kong would be polite, respectful, and ready to do culinary battle.

Hong Kong was, to say the least, 99.9999 percent ignorant of the battle, with the other .0001 percent yawning.

IV: HOW THE BATTLE DID BEGIN AND COMMENCE IN FAVOR OF THE HKTA FORCES BEFORE THE ENEMY BECAME AWARE THAT A WAR WAS RAGING.

It did not go without fault, but the two Chinese banquets, one pigeon luncheon, and one French feast kept the grand party well occupied. They savored, sniffed, tasted, and acted the way any artists do upon encountering new stimuli. Frequently, with extreme pleasure, often with astonishment, sometimes with critical distance and–rarely–with stern judgment.

The opening banquet was indeed too much for the weary travelers, but the meal was happily ecumenical. Ham was flown down from Yunnan (yes, pigs do fly) to go with the Thai bird's-nest prepared in Cantonese style. The duck liver sausages were bathed in a piquant Swatow sauce. The Szechuan chicken was diced and sautéed with garlic and dainty red peppers.

The braised sea cucumber was as dull as sea cucumber always is. But I described it to the French as worthy of another kind of Michelin star. "I mean, it looks and tastes like a Michelin rubber tire," I explained.

But after the dessert–pears from Tientsin, oranges and water chestnuts from Canton, and papaya from the Philippines –they went to sleep.

The following breakfast was a disaster. The aforesaid Lok Yu had pulled a practical joke. They informed us of a special breakfast comprising forty-five dim sum – not one of which materialized. The Chinese families in the restaurant were shocked to see a troupe of bleary-eyed Frenchmen parading in. Tables were set up in a corner, insults were traded, and tea was consumed. It was a tragedy worthy of a Racine.

Next was a trip to the market, where the vendors were shocked to see their produce picked, plucked, pinched, fondled, and stroked. "Crazy gweilo," was the usual comment. "Tainted produce."

That evening was the French banquet, with which the chefs were not impressed. But they simply refrained from comment. Burps, belches, and bleeps were enough.

No rest for the weary. The next morning they went to New Territories–and their pigeon lunch was spoken of in France for the next year. The famed pigeon restaurant served two thousand pigeons a day and more than a million pigeons a year, with twenty-four different dishes ranging from satay to sweet pigeon egg.

The French were entranced. Eating al fresco, they used fingers as much as forks or chopsticks, and felt that this, truly, was a carte of great pride.

The Grand Chinese Banquet that night had caused most worry. Whether the regional chefs would go batting each other with woks and cudgels, whether the French would turn up their sophisticated noses…

Yet it worked out. Spontaneous noises and applause for some dishes, oohs and ahs and surreptitious asides to ask for secret recipes.

Before the meal, the art of killing snakes was demonstrated, but the following parade of dishes achieved the correct appreciation. Details are boring, but notes of that night speak of yellow fish "virtually leaping from the plate," "Mongolian hot pot with a dozen colors and aromas…date cakes with the delicacy of a Mozart string quartet…"

The talk was only of food. Where the Peking duck comes from (Peking, natch), how they stuff the chicken…

The French chefs beamed; the HKTA generals beamed; the Chinese chefs beamed; the chicken, ducks, and cows who gave their lives that this colony might live, beamed.

The beams held up the ceiling.

V: WHEREIN THE ENEMY WAS VANQUISHED; AND HOW THE ENEMY DID VISIT THEIR CONQUERORS AND INQUIRE OF HOW THEY WERE CONQUERED.

The victory celebrations were premature, though M. Jolly's speech was suitably effusive. "I wonder," he enthused, "why we go to China at all!"

Yet, politics in this case took precedence over reality. French journalists on the tour were biased from the beginning – possibly because the French have a knee-jerk reaction when they hear the word "culture." And the Cultural Revolution was thought of then as a good thing. The result was a flurry of stories in Paris praising the People's Republic of China, and giving slight, patronizing mention to Hong Kong.

Still, Hong Kong was happy enough in the end. The military precision, the strategy, the recognition that even natives have their purpose, gave proof to the old British adage that an army marches on its stomach.

Or was that a French adage? It doesn't matter. The major adage comes from a Sung Dynasty writer who described a feast held at that time: "For an emperor to achieve dignity, his food must spread over ten cubits square."

THE CHINESE BANQUET MENU

I. Hors d'oeuvres (Chiu Chow)
Mashed shrimp, deep-fried into the shape of a ball
Braised goose in white vinegar
Steamed crab cakes and braised steamed whelk

II. Suckling Pig (Cantonese)
The size is ruled at 6-7¼ lbs. After washing, the pig is fried for 6-7 hours, then roasted over charcoal. Like Peking Duck, the skin is the most delicate portion, and the dish is judged entirely by the cutting and texture of the outer layer.

III. Bear's Paw
(Censored. At this time, the bear was not noted as being endangered, nor, like shark, was its savage killing documented.)

IV. Monk Jumping Over the Wall (Fukien)
Some two hundred years ago, an apprentice monk would sneak outside his monastery and put delicacies he found into an earthen pot to simmer. The chief abbot, at first curious but not daring to break his vow of vegetarianism, finally found the aroma so irresistible that he leapt over the wall to try the soup. While this winter soup has several variations, traditionally the ingredients must include abalone, chicken broth, medicinal herbs, spices, along with chicken kidney, mushrooms, and ham.

V. Pan-Fried King Prawns in Chili Sauce (Szechuan)
From the mountain streams come these prawns, which are fried in chili sauce with a profusion of peppers, sliced garlic, native salt, anise, and other spices.

VI. Peking Duck (Peking)

Often served in three courses (meat, skin, and soup), only the skin is esteemed. The duck is Long Island duckling, but is force fed, then roasted over an open fire stove, finally presented for inspection before the skin is cut. Added to the skin is a special sauce prepared from sugar, soya beans, and other spices, cooked over a period of 10 hours.

VII. Beggar's Chicken (Hangzhou)

The origin of the dish goes back to the sixteenth century, when a beggar stole a chicken and, without any utensils, was forced to cook it. First, he gathered lotus leaves, wrapping the chicken. Then he used mud from the lotus pond for the outer layer. When the mud-wrapped chicken was well cooked over an open fire, the mud was knocked off and the chicken filled with a fragrant flavor from the leaves. Nowadays, a special mud is also used, but the stuffing has pickled Chinese cabbage, mushrooms, and onions.

VIII. Braised Bean Curd (Szechuan)

Shirred bean curd cooked in chilies, a dish dating back to the sixteenth century

IX. Steamed Fresh Fish (Cantonese)

Steamed 15-20 minutes on a bamboo support in the Chinese wok and kept moist with a bit of chicken fat on the outside. A favorite of Mencius, a student of Confucius.

X. Mongolian Hot Pot (Mongolian)

During the hard Mongolian winters, mutton is the main dish, but always served with eight or ten different sauces. Peanut, sesame, spicy chili, wine sauce, bean, and coriander, depending on the imagination of the chef.

XI. Pekinese Handmade Noodles (Peking)

The Empress Dowager at the end of the nineteenth century discovered these noodles. Outside her palace she heard the noise of a noodle vendor. He was ordered into the palace to demonstrate, and the Empress warned that if his noodles didn't justify the disturbance he was making, an unspecified catastrophe would befall him. He lived, since the technique is so interesting

XII. Pan-Fried Glutinous Rice (Fung Shing)

"Sticky" rice is a Chinese winter specialty. When prepared for a banquet, glutinous rice is fried with sausages and mushrooms like a Chinese paella.

XIII. Double-Boiled Siamese Bird's-Nest (Chiu Chow)

Bird's-nest can be sweetened with honey or lotus nuts, but is usually double-boiled with coconut milk. Medicinally, it is known for being good for the complexion and lungs. The nests themselves are gathered on an island near Phuket in south Thailand

XIV. Chinese Petits Fours (Mixed)

Cantonese Peony Delights
Chiu Chow Crystal Buns
Pekingese Mashed Date Biscuits
Szechuan Deep-fried Fresh Milk Fritters

WINES:

Mao Tai
The traditional aperitif
Hwa Tiao
A rice-distilled wine, served lukewarm like sherry
Tung Hua (German Hock)
Originally brought to China in the nineteenth century by Lutheran missionaries and today, distilled in Shantung province.

TEAS:

Narcissus
Gentle and fragrant, with the aroma of flowers
Iron Buddha
Chiu Chow tea, stronger than coffee, always served in thimble-sized glasses.

Recipe:
Hou Tin Ngarp — Roast Peking Duck

A reality check. With the Seventh Commandment, "Thou Shalt Not Omit A Poultry," the Chinese simply acknowledged that chickens and ducks and geese were more than bird-brained adjuncts to the world. They could be made for the grandest of banquets. But the Mongolians weren't so finicky in their recipes. Traveling around to conquer the world, they would catch wild ducks in their traps, and roast them over a fire that night while telling tales of rape and pillage. They would have so many tales that the fire would go on too long and the duck become barbecued to a golden brown. Taken off the fire, it would be ripped apart by the happy warriors along with endless bottles of fermented yak milk. (See "Where Shepherds Yell By Night.") When the Mongols took over Peking in the seventeenth century, they "tarted up" the fowl with all the accompaniments we know today. The luxury of the skin (served only to honored guests), the meat (to the less honored), and the soup (from the bones, served to the hired help). The type of duck is similar to Long Island duckling, with white feathers and a long wide back.

The following recipe was given to me by William Mark, my co-author on The Chinese Gourmet, published by Weldon Russell in Australia. It is suitable for the home, but few will be able to master the carving in great restaurants. Within five minutes of bringing the bird to the table sizzling from the oven, it must be carved into a hundred slices, each slice with some skin, each piece of skin with some meat. It is eaten in chewy crepes with a slice of scallion and a sweet-salt sauce for dipping.

1 duck, about 6 lbs., with head attached

12-16 c. of boiling water

½ c. aromatic or cider vinegar

1 c. water

5 tbsp. honey

¼ c. hoisin sauce (available in any Chinese grocery store)

1 tbsp. sesame oil

48 pcs. scallion, white part only, 2 inches long

48 sticks cucumber

36 Chinese pancakes (see below)

1. Clean the duck inside and out and pat dry.
2. Close the cavity of the duck with a skewer. Cut off the wing tips. Make a cut in the neck and insert a tube, like a bicycle pump tube, and pull the skin from the meat at the same time, to inflate the duck skin. Tie a piece of string tightly beneath the opening on the neck.
3. Place the duck on a rack in the sink. Pour a quarter of the boiling water over the duck. Turn over and pour another quarter of the boiling water. Wait for 5 seconds. Repeat the process, then rinse with cold water. Pat dry.
4. Mix the vinegar, water, and honey in a bowl and brush the mixture over the duck. Tie another piece of string around the neck and hang the duck to dry in a well ventilated place for 10 hours or more.
5. Preheat the oven to 400 degrees. Place the duck, breast side up, on a rack over a roasting pan. Reduce the heat to 350 degrees. Turn the duck at 15-minute intervals and cook for 1 hour.
6. Carve off the crispy skin, then carve the meat into thin slivers and place on a warm serving platter.
7. To serve, spread one teaspoon of the hoisin sauce to the middle of the pancake. Add some skin and meat and a piece of scallion. Fold the pancakes into an envelope and eat – with the fingers.

Pancakes

Willy's own restaurant prepared the Peking duck pancakes with this recipe. They are not confined for Peking duck, but can be used for minced beef or gooey fish-flavored Szechuan eggplant. NOTE: This recipe is for 4-6 people, for easy handling and kneading. For the Peking duck, do two batches!

> 2 c. all-purpose plain flour
> 1/3 c. boiling water
> 1/3 c. cold water

1. Sift the flour in a bowl, make a well in the center; add the boiling water and mix. Add the cold water a little at a time and stir to mix. Knead for 5 minutes. Cover and set aside for 25 minutes.
2. Roll the dough into a long sausage shape. Divide into 12 equal pieces. Roll out each piece on a floured board to form a thin pancake. Heat a wok or frying pan. Cook the pancakes on both sides until lightly browned.
3. Cover with a cloth until ready to serve.

CHAPTER TWENTY-FIVE

"MacBeth: The Chinese Restaurant Scene"
Recipe:
Scottish Honey Mead

A CT III
SCENE IV – Yang Kee Cantonese Emporium

Enter MACBETH and LADY MACBETH

Lady M: But m'lord, a restaurant from Cathay?
    So far away, with such rude country foods.
Macb: Tis no distance at all from Scotland to Asia
    There be restaurants of this type more than thrice
    As much on thy plate as are grains of rice.
Lady M: Yet thou must have special reasons to attend.
Macb: 'Tis to get away from Duncan I do come.
Lady M (aside): Chill, pick my teeth!

(to Macb): Yes m'lord, we must rid ourselves of that pan-faced villain.
Macb: Not King Duncan. I meant, my buxom glutton, I must avoid dunkin' doughnuts.
   For I mightily tire of Western foods.
   What is hamburger but pâté of dead cow?
   What be potatoes but sickening roots
   Still reeking of the loam?

Enter TWO WAITERS

1st Waiter: Now look, we come to show the Peking Duck,
   Roasted for hours, skin a-sizzle like the blazing sun.
2nd Waiter: Beggar's Chicken, too, cleaved apart like a traitor's head. To reveal aromas fit for Cleopatra herself.
Lady M (aside): That wretched queen; when I the throne have chaired,
   I will not with most fowl poultry be compared.
Macb: Be so bold, then, to explain quick-frying.
   Who doth practice this quintessential art?
1st Waiter: Everyone can practice
   With correct equipment and most serious mind.
Lady M: Thou mean'st, of course, all wok and no play?
Macb: Un-pun thee,
   Harridan. Back thy quick-frying, waiters, and pay no heed
   To the pismire tongue of that blushless virago.
2nd Waiter: Quick-frying means that if it were done,
   When 'tis done, 'twere well it were done quickly.
Macb: And can'st thou also explain sweet-and-sour chicken?
   For philosophers and knaves alike only blur these sauces
   When they try to tell their contrary tales.

1st Waiter: Why, begging thy pardon,
    'Tis very simple indeed. Sweet-and-sour means, by thy
    grace. That fair is fowl. And fowl is fair.
Lady M (aside): A vile mixture which only artless tourists share.
Macb: Now, thou detestable maw, do not talk but eat of this.
    But say, why dost thou stare so at thy Chinese cutlery?
Lady M: Is this a dagger I see before me,
    The handle to my hand?
1st Waiter: Nay, nay, nay.
    These are chopsticks. Come, can thou clutch them?
Macb: Infirm of purpose, my coming queen, be not lost
    So poorly of thy thoughts. What art thou so distracted?
Voices (off): Double, double, toil and trouble.
Lady M: List, m'lord, what are those weird sounds, which sound
    almost like voices?
Voices (off): Fire burn, and cauldron bubble.
2nd Waiter: Fear not, m'lady. They are but the chefs
    Preparing our Double-Boiled Shark Fin Soup.
Lady M: But then,
    I still do feel queasy. For what, pray tell me,
    What is this dish lotus-shaped?
Macb: Why 'tis lotus indeed. Yet m'lady
    Though it looks like the innocent flower,
    It be the serpent under't.
Lady M: Doth thou mean a light snake before dinner?
Macb: Hush, thou witch, thou penurious punster. Waiter,
    Please do not give us so much of this dish.
1st Waiter: Methought I heard a voice cry, 'Heap no more!'
Lady M: What be this sauce here which is dark as passion
    Yet black as hell?
2nd Waiter: That, m'lady, is wond'rous soy sauce,
    But be careful and do not spill e'en a single drop.

Lady M: Ohhhh!
    (Spills sauce) Out damned spot, out I say.
Macb: A little water clears us of this deed.
    Never mind, we are done. Now good digestion,
    Wait on appetite, and health on both.
1st Waiter: Here is thy bill, m'lord.
Macb: Hold, waiter. For whom does this bill toll?
    Doth it toll for me? For when it addeth,
    These numbers seem more than our meagre food.
1st Waiter: The bill doth indeed toll for thee.
Macb: Alas,
    To borrow and to borrow and to borrow,
    Or creep from this petty place today. Out, out
    Chief Vandal. This restaurant has but poor chefs,
    That boil and fry their foods upon their stoves,
    And then are stirred no more.
Lady M: It is a meal
    Set out for two idiots, full of pounds and ounces
    Signifying nothing.
Macb: Say not, though, that our food is worthless.
    No matter what the bill, one is never fleeced:
    Each single bite of Chinese food
    Is worthy of the most imperial feast.

    (exeunt all to sounds of clattering dishes)

Spice Chronicles: *Exotic Tales of a Hungry Traveler*

Recipe:
Scottish Honey Mead

While William Shakespeare may not have indulged in Chinese food, he certainly knew his drinks, and outside of wine and ale he could well have indulged in a bit of old mead. If so, he would have carried on a great tradition, since mead appeared in Homer, Plutarch, and countless times in Chaucer. Today, the closest to Homeric mead is found in Ethiopia, where honey mead is common (and has been manufactured in America).

Shakespeare's mead refers only to a meadow, but Lady Macbeth knew what it was to have a few drops too many.

"That which hath made them drunk," she says, referring to her royal prey, "hath made me bold."

No doubt she might have had a few libations after the murders! And she might have had the following Scots mead, which I discovered on the Scottish isle of Arran while doing a story about a new whisky distillery. It is simple but potent.

> 1 lb. fresh honey
> 1 gal. of water
> ¾ oz. dried hops
> 1 oz. yeast

1. Put hops and honey into a pan with water, bring to a boil and gently simmer for an hour.
2. Pour this into a crock, and when the liquor is lukewarm add the yeast, little by little into it.

3. Leave for 3 or 4 days, then strain into a barrel but do not make the bunghole too tight with a stopper.
4. Store for a year, then draw off the liquor and put into a bottle.

Chapter Twenty-Six

The Dog Who Cried "Woof"!
Recipes:
Howl Wheat/Smaller Collar Diet Bone

When co-writing The Chinese Gourmet with William Mark, an Australian editor named Katherine requested a chapter on some of China's more "exotic" foods, and I happily contributed well-chosen words on sea cucumbers, porcupines, anteaters and – horrors! – dog. She screamed back on the phone that dog was not to be mentioned, that any allusion to canine was definitely verboten, and that when she said "exotic" she did not mean man's best friend.

I replied that perhaps she did not realize that canned dog meat was already being processed, and that should she, Katherine, ever sample its contents, she might consider writing an interesting food review.

Entitled, perhaps, Kate On A Hot Tinned Woof.

Katherine never spoke to me again, though whether due to the play on words or the subject I will never know.

Thus, I am of two minds about publishing this piece. But since I published much of the information in the Asian Wall Street Journal, it has the imprimatur of respect. Still, while this article is absolutely true, it is not fit for more delicate minds. As for myself, the owner of Coco, a South Carolinian Boykin Spaniel who decided to live in Manhattan, I close my eyes and immediately turn over the next pages without reading them. To all readers, you have been warned.

Like opium, dogmeat eating in Hong Kong is, thankfully, dying out; but since it is illegal, Hong Kong has a euphemism for the subject. Like the New Guinea "long pig" for humans, Hong Kong speaks heung yok or "fragrant meat" for canines.

I always tried to explain to Chuppie (Chinese yuppie) friends that they had no business eating dogmeat, but the only way I could get to them was by speaking about business itself.

"Don't you understand," I would ask, "that the first business contract ever signed was between man and dog? Dog (the party of the first part) would guard cave. Man (the party of the second part) would provide bones." But they laughed at the concept.

The truth is that most young people in "modern" Hong Kong do not eat dog, preferring McDonald's. But in southern China – as well as in Laos, the hill regions of the Philippines, Korea, and parts of Central and South America – dogmeat is a popular treat.

My knowledge of South American canine-eating is secondhand, so will not be brought up (so to speak) here. But Hong Kong and China have a fascinating history of the subject. In fact, it is so ingrained for its historical as well as culinary and medicinal experience that dogmeat was used, quite recently, as a political club to beat the British colonial masters.

The genesis for that was a letter written to the editor of the South China Morning Post by a British civil servant. He had said that dog eaters in the (then) British Crown Colony should be "strung up, castrated, and beaten to a veritable pulp." (Or perhaps he meant, "beaten to a veritable pup." The meaning, either way, is clear.) To which a Chinese respondent, while denying he ever actually ate the stuff, wrote that, "dogmeat is a natural part of the traditional Chinese diet, dignified by ancient custom ... objectively as wholesome as pork or duck. The dogmeat business is yet another example of the unthinking, unfeeling arrogance of the European in Asia."

In theory, the question of whether to eat or not to eat was a moot point, since it is illegal to catch or kill or possess the meat, according to an ordinance passed in 1950. But enforcement has been spotty, punishment is lax, and the law is widely ignored. Yes, Hong Kong young people shun the animal, but across the waters in Macao dogmeat is a widely-enjoyed treat.

The history of dogmeat is anything but spotty. I found a reference in 500 BC, when birth control of a sort was being practiced in China. One emperor, who wanted more warriors for his army, offered to give "a succulent puppy" to any woman bearing a boy-child. And a century later, no less a philosopher than Mencius, who studied with Confucius, praised dogmeat as a medicine for "liver, malaria, or jaundice."

China's first recipe books were written long before Mrs. Beeton's–about two millennia before–and during the Han Dynasty a recipe was given for making the most out of dog. One favorite involved wrapping the liver of a dog in a thin casing of its own fat, then roasting it. "A crackling finish can be achieved by searing it at the last minute on the flame."

On to more modern times. First, the urban legend, which is not true. The story goes that a Swiss couple (why Swiss?) bring their pure-bred Dalmatian into Hong Kong, carry it to a Chinese restaurant, mime to the waiter that the dog should be taken to the kitchen, and while they (the Swiss) have a candlelit wine-and-caviar meal, the pooch should be fed with kitchen scraps.

Apparently comprehending, the waiter smiles, takes the dog to the kitchen, and some time later returns with a huge tureen which, upon opening, turns out to be Schatzi (or whatever the dog is called).

Well, the holes in this story would make Swiss cheese blush. First, dogs aren't allowed in Hong Kong without a quarantine period of a few months. Second, virtually every Hong Kong restaurant has English-speaking waiters. Third, animals aren't allowed in restaurants etc., etc., etc.

The most important thing is that no self-respecting heung yok restaurant would ever conceive of roasting a pure-bred Dalmatian. In China these days, special dog farms – yes, yes, this is repugnant—are the only way to raise dogs fit for the frying pan.

On the other hand, a story about the politics of dogmeat is absolutely authentic.

The great Chinese revolutionary, Dr. Sun Yat-sen, was fighting to free his people from the northern Manchus, who had ruled for several hundred years. The Manchus looked down on southerners with undisguised contempt – at everything from their "wily" business practices to their cuisine. "Why ... why, those southern Barbarians," they would say, "go so far as to eat dogmeat."

That was an insult to any revolutionary. So, at the beginning of any political meeting, Dr. Sun Yat-sen and his followers would take an officially designated revolutionary dog and roast it, eating the meat as a show of force against the Manchu warriors.

Much, possibly, as Chinese letter writers in pre-Chinese Hong Kong would write using dog as a symbol for their deep-seated dislike of the long-nosed devils.

As I write these words, my Boykin spaniel, who answers (sometimes) to the name of Coco, is glaring at me, reading – with enormous difficulty – these baleful words on his species. Usually as amiable as a twenty-three-pound hunter can be, I fear Coco may soon finally see the gist of the theme. And he won't be happy.

So, to finish off this bit of dogmatic research, a little 1880's joke from Punch magazine.

It was apparently the British who first expressed loathing for dogmeat consumption. But Punch, even in Victorian days, was able to show the humor of the situation. A poem published by the magazine related the tale of an Englishman facing his first meal in China, without knowledge of the ingredients – or the language.

Finally, he recognizes what he believes is duck. And the rhyme continues:

"Still cautious grown, but to be sure
His brain he set to rack.
At length he turned to one behind,
And pointing, cried 'Quack Quack?'
The Chinese gravely shook his head,
Next made a reverent bow;
And then expressed what dish it was
By uttering 'Bow-wow-wow.'"

Down, Coco, down. Down, Coco!

Recipes:
Howl Wheat/ Smaller Collar Diet Bone

To make amends for that terrible (if informative) piece, may I offer two recipes for dogs. They are provided by Michele Bledsoe of Jackson, Wyoming. She is a lovely lady who produces imaginative wonderful books of recipes not only for dogs but for those other animals...er, cats. Here are two from The Doggy Bone Cookbook, which can be ordered from her at PO Box 8004, Jackson Hole, WY 832002.

Howl Wheat

>   4 c. whole wheat
>   ½ c. wheat germ
>   ¼ c. cornmeal
>   c. corn oil
>   1½ c. water
>   2 tbsp. parsley (hopefully fresh, but otherwise dried)

1. Preheat oven to 350 degrees.
2. Combine flour, wheat germ, cornmeal, and parsley.
3. Add water and oil to dry ingredients. Knead for 2-3 minutes.
4. Roll dough to ¼ inch thickness and cut with cookie cutter.
5. Bake at 350 degrees on an ungreased cookie sheet for 30 minutes or until edges start to brown.

Makes 2½ dozen.

Smaller Collar Diet Bone (for the dog that needs to lose a few pounds)

2 beef bouillon cubes
1 c. warm water
¼ c. skim milk
1 tbsp. margarine
½ c. shredded reduced-fat cheddar cheese
3½ c. whole wheat flour

1. Preheat oven to 350 degrees.
2. Dissolve bouillon cubes in warm water.
3. Mix shredded cheddar cheese with flour.
4. Add skim milk, margarine, and beef broth.
5. Knead dough until firm and roll to ¼ inch thickness.
6. Stamp out with cookie cutter and place on an ungreased cookie sheet.
7. Bake at 350 degrees for 30 minutes.

Makes 2½ dozen.

Chapter Twenty-Seven

Graham Greene: "Our Man in Macao"
Recipe:
Suspiros (Sighs)

An editor who should have known better asked me once to write about Graham Greene in Macao. I told him that the author skirted that minuscule area. Orson Welles and W.H. Auden gave Macao some literary fame. But Greene was more interested in more substantial territories like Vietnam, Thailand, and Singapore. So he requested that I rectify Greene's geographical sin of omission by writing about Macanese food as if Greene had actually been there. It seemed a weird assignment, but a dollar is a dollar in anybody's currency.

"Green wine," sniffed the eminent Father, sniffing the cork impassively. He wiped his black beard of the green bubbles, which had attached themselves, and fondled the gift carafe of Portuguese vinho verde, then laid it on its side with a slight nuance of contempt. "Call me an apostate. But I prefer my brandy," he sniffed. Taking a snifter of Bagaceira, he sniffed the harsh purgatorial fumes reverently and snuffed out the candle, shuffling into the night air on to the four-hundred-year-old Praia Grande.

Like other monsignors in this, the tiny spit of land intended to bring the blessings of the Church to the pagans of the East, His Eminence Father Fernando was not an anchorite. After fifty-five years in the colony, he welcomed equally the cynical scholar, the Taoist monk, and even the White Russian and Thai jeunes filles de la rue who paraded outside his Spartan chambers.

His Eminence could sniff the brandy and talk of the loveliness of the human body. The girls would drink milk and bring him gifts of Portuguese chocolate eclairs or dainty Chinese rolls filled with crushed dates and chestnuts. They kvetched about sin, he prayed for them. They studied the portraits of saints on his walls. He imagined them dancing and looked carefully at their ankles, pretending to study the blue-and-white Portuguese tiles on the floor.

Macao priests don't fret about sin. So many churches, so many denominations, so little time for the spirit. Churches abounded in Macao, though they rarely opened their doors. Sinners would have to atone in the adjacent noodle shops or sip beers in a contiguous cathedral.

Once, long ago, he had left his cloisters to visit the Dominican church for a Sunday Mass, but the gates were tightly shut. Knocking, then pounding at the gates ("Pace!" he thought, "I feel like Martin Luther"), he finally saw a teenage girl wearing her Mickey Mouse shirt and a pair of shorts. She looked curiously at the priest, and he asked when the service would start.

"But Father," said the girl, "today is Sunday. How could you expect us to open the church on a holiday?"

That evening, he had conversed with a grand visitor from Lisbon, a very great monsignor both in the Senado and the Church. The great Power had refused to dine in a tavern, preferring watery bean soup and dry sausages to the spicier Macao specials.

Father Fernando had tried to explain his love for the special cuisine of the territory. "The duck," he had said, "is like the heart of our Savior, bathed in blood, pulsing with excitement."

The Bishop shrugged and lapped up more beans.

"And as the Catholic Church must embrace the whole world," continued His Eminence, "so Macao cooking is most catholic cooking. The coriander from Guangdong province, the pigeons cooked in Portuguese wine. The Macao stew with chunks of pork and Chinese cabbage leaves..."

The Archbishop poured himself more water.

"...Like spirit and matter, we combine the sea and the land. Our crabs are stuffed with ham and cheeses..."

"Jesus?" burped the Archbishop with nonchalant interest.

"No...er, cheeses. We have peppercorns from the Indian colony of Goa..."

"Ah," belched the Archbishop. "Goa." He was dreaming about the days of the Goan Inquisition, where Dominican priests routinely rounded up heretics who had taken shelter in the Franciscan church, and burned them with a fierce blaze.

"Those were the days," he said to Father Fernando, who was puzzled.

"What I mean," said the Archbishop to the priest, who was now beginning to feel like a cog in the large wheel of the Church, "is that long ago, in those days, we had history. Today, by Jesuitical definition, history does not exist."

Father Fernando was not convinced. He served the dessert, pudim, the gelatin-and-chocolate sweet so beloved by Portuguese, put the Power to bed, and walked into the night.

History, thought Father Fernando, was not eloquent in this backwater of Asia. But it was quietly elegant. He walked along the Praia Grande then, for the solitude of the sea. Macao, he thought, had been founded by a Chinese goddess of the sea and named for that selfsame mythical lady. He walked through the night, and that morning, as the mist lifted and the hopeful fishermen let their stake-nets down into the water, he imagined the Portuguese colonists of four centuries past, strolling on this same waterfront.

"They had their Mozambique slaves, their Malaccan cooks, their gardeners from the Catholic spice island of Flores. We were the Rome of the Orient, and people flocked to us, as penitents congregated at Rome's Basilica."

As the morning wore on, he sniffed the air. It was redolent of olive oil and vinegar, more pungent than the censers of the churches that lined the streets here.

"Take this," the Savior had said, offering the wafer. "It is my body." But to Father Fernando, no transubstantiation was necessary. Fresh Portuguese bread was body and health together.

"Take this," said the Savior, offering wine. "It is my blood." Father Fernando smiled, a bit foolishly perhaps. "Well," he thought, "I hope that our Savior was not offering Portuguese wine .That does need a bit of transubstantiation."

He chuckled to himself, knowing that he was passing only the ghosts of his history on the shadowy streets of Macao. "Perhaps our Savior should have offered His jailers some of that wine. They could have used it as the vinegar in His wounds."

Meditating on the Last Supper, the priest queried a theological point. "We had His body and His blood. But what about His soul?"

His Eminence giggled at that. "I suppose He would have had to come here for that. Macao sole is a welcome dish for a Last or First Supper."

He laughed to himself at the silly play on words. He had long ago forgotten sin.

Along the way, His Eminence saw live chickens being thrown off the trucks from Chinese farms along the border, and recalled their own changes. The chickens of Macao were marinated – "baptized," he once described them – in a juice of peppercorns, garlic, and other spices.

He began to think of his guest, that Eminent Power of Lisbon, that man of no appetite, who had sat up only when he confused cheeses for Jesus. Foolish mistake. Then again, the Church had been founded on a pun.

"Thou art Peter – the Rock. Upon thee shall I build my church."

Perhaps he would stop into the hotel for lunch. Sometimes they would import goat's cheese from the hills of northern Portugal. It was a gratification in which His Eminence rarely indulged. After all, he rarely had those extra patacas, the Macanese currency, to pay at this hotel. Those indulgences were for businessmen, the Pharisees of the community, along with their Chinese counterparts. The Chinese, he thought, were Oriental Calvinists. They honestly – or dishonestly – believed that money and success were proof that the fates had smiled upon them.

His Eminence stopped for a coffee and a chat at the local outdoor restaurant. "We are decaying," he thought. "Without love, without fame, without material possessions, perhaps without spirit. The warren of alleys and walks to deserted forts, locked-and-chained churches, quiet wine drinkers and professors with their rimless glasses peering through the daily Macao Tribuna…

"We are a superfluity on the real world. Perhaps even," he sighed, "a godless people."

His eyes became wet for a second. Then he smiled. For even as he thought "godless," he saw that all around him the people were indulging in God. They had it in their plates, on their forks, in their mouths, their stomachs, the Word of God, the scent of God, the…"

His Eminence stopped his meditation and gave a bitter laugh.

"Oh," he said. "Perhaps I was thinking of cod, not God. Yes, I most certainly was. Not that cod is less holy than God."

He thought again of the name given to the island four hundred years before: The City in the Name of the Glory of God.

His Eminence mused uselessly on a useless life in this hybrid backwater, a shadowy isthmus and two tiny islands, which embraced neither God nor Buddha, which languidly lunched on bread and rice. Macao was for neither sybarite nor priest. More for the likes of Job than Mammon. And as he thought of that luncheon gift he had promised himself, he recalled the words of Job reprimanding God with lactose outrage: "Hast thou not poured me out as milk and curdled me like cheese?"

His Eminence sighed and walked back to his room. He decided to abstain from that cheese in the grand hotel. A simpler meal, crackers and Portuguese vinho verde: Graham and Green. His own Eucharist.

Father Fernando listened to the waters lapping on the shore and looked hopelessly at the steeples of the churches. They were silent now, as every day. The church carillons had been hushed for decades, but the temple bells were ringing. He uncorked the wine and poured himself a Portuguese brandy. It was as fiery and golden as a sunrise in Sinai.

Recipe:
Suspiros (Sighs)

This is a dish brought to Macau from Goa, and is originally Portuguese. The name brings memories of Portuguese fado music, which is sad, mournful, a bit on the pathetic side, but very pretty.

> 3 egg whites
> 1 c. sugar, powdered fine
> 1 grated lemon rind (or imported Thai or Filipino lime)
> ½ tsp. fresh lemon juice
> 1 c. sliced blanched almonds (in Goa always fresh, in Macau usually canned)

Beat egg whites until stiff. Fold in the sugar, lemon rind, lemon juice, and sliced almonds. Mix well. Drop by teaspoons on a cookie sheet covered with a greased paper and bake until done.

CHAPTER TWENTY-EIGHT

YANGTZE NOODLE'S DANDY (BUT ENOUGH'S ENOUGH ALREADY!)
Recipe:
Congee with Dried Beef

Those old jokes about being hungry immediately after "eating Chinese" are spurious urban legends. After plowing through a hundred Chinese restaurants in twenty-one days, trust me, hunger is not a problem. The problem is trying to stay sane.

What prompted a normal American writer to attempt this dim sum triathlon? Neither gluttony nor sadism. It was an assignment to write the first book about eating out in the People's Republic of China, an almost unheard-of feat in 1979.

In those days, for a "gweilo" to enter a Chinese restaurant was almost impossible. At the tail end of the Cultural Revolution, one would either be turned away or quickly ushered to an upstairs room with the sign "Welcome, Foreign Friends, to Our Special Dining Room." Which meant an empty cubicle, overpriced, hastily prepared dishes for a foreign guest (i.e., sandwiches of a sort), nasty service, and even nastier food. But I decided to try the impossible and write Eating Out in China. My publisher made arrangements from Hong Kong with his Chinese counterparts, and permission was pending.

Of course they wanted to see whether my writing was acceptable, so I was assigned a "test" journey. After that, they insisted I cover the hundred restaurants printed up within one month of getting into China, and gave me one guide per city. True, those guides had little information on what I wanted, and were rarely enthusiastic on this eating orgy. Nonetheless, within three weeks I had returned, the book was written, and we came out almost in time. The following excerpts are from a diary written between (burp!) meals.

April 5:

Before commencing this journey into the unknown, a Chinese official in Hong Kong tells me to travel to Guangzhou (Canton) with an Official Tour Group. We will take in a pottery factory, a lecture about Mao, and a taro-growing commune. Naturally, I am very excited, especially by the taro, which is one step up from tapioca. Nonetheless, I reluctantly separate from the group in order to begin the Great Restaurant Hunt. Friends in Hong Kong had recommended several places, and with a Chinese friend I manage to sample steamed chicken and boneless duck, lamb brain in a Moslem restaurant, and duck kidneys with pig intestines. In the second restaurant, I make the first of many great discoveries. Here, I find an ancient recipe where the fish skin is peeled away and meat removed from the bone. Next, the skin is dressed on the fish bone, and the meat covers the skin. I can think of nothing more silly, but after all, they were ancients. At this point, our Official Guide has discovered us eating in a place not suitable for foreigners. We are given a lecture for deserting the Official Tour Group.

April 6:

Can this be only the second day? I seem to have gone through five thousand years of eating. But at 6:00 A.M., Guangzhou is awake, people are tai-chiing in the park, looking at me with astonishment, and then following me to the market where I survey the snails, worms, and other friends of the soil. For lunch, I snack at pork cutlets, followed by a python cat-chicken soup. I tell my guide: "Oh, I've always enjoyed a light snake before dinner," but he merely looks upon me without curiosity. Anyhow, I never liked cats. At the snake restaurant, of course, they tell me that over one hundred and fifty snakes are served each night. "And they are all wild. Not domestic." The menu lists "Braised guinea pig whole," "Shredded python thick soup," and "Wildcat fried with fresh greenstops." Difficult to ingest, but somebody has to do it.

April 7:

The last day of the inspection tour begins easy. A crabfin-sharkfin consommé and ten varieties of noodles at Shaho village, known for its beer and noodles. Later, we wind up at Chou En-lai's favorite pigeon restaurant. They have run out of pigeon (or did the birds desert in an avian coo d'état?), so instead are given eight incarnations of bean curd. At night, we are taken to meet some visiting New Yorkers. We share a banquet of sweet-and-sour pork, egg rolls, and the usual takeaway that they could get near their own Manhattan apartments. However, it doesn't taste exactly the way it does back home. Their comments consist of "What's this? Ugh!"

and "What's that? Oy!" I am about to say: "I agree, this isn't so great. You should have had the cat soup with us yesterday," but my companion hushes me.

This had been the test journey. From April to June, I am in America, waiting for a "private" visa, my Chinese counterpart reading the nice descriptions of our restaurants and approving them. In one San Francisco place, I note profoundly: "Frankly, American food could easily have been as good as Chinese if only more Americans were Chinese." The visa comes through. The diary continues.

June 7:
Now I return to Beijing, which S.J. Perelman called "a city built by giants for giants." Others on the plane go out to the Great Wall, but I wallow inside a Shandung kitchen, watching chefs steaming crispy chicken, gazing at the master of the spring rolls. At a restaurant serving nothing except lamb dishes, I have lamb soup, lamb with eggs, lamb in red sauce, and lamb in white sauce. I tell my Official Guide: "This isn't the kind of place you'd send somebody with an allergy to lamb." A Cultural Revolution stalwart, he is officially unamused. That night I write: "I got plenty of mutton, and mutton's plenty for me." Then I dream up a recipe for Mongolian sheep eyes: "First, boil eyes, stuff with lamb forcemeat, lightly fry until inedible. Then eat." It is the first of many dreams to come.

June 8:
I develop the hopscotch plan for tasting. Going out early to three kitchens, telling chefs to prepare three great dishes for two hours from then, returning, eating, and taking notes, then going on to the next. The same method for dinners. An arduous plan. But the rules are (a) only a spoonful of rice and (b) no liquor. I try my first Yunnan restaurant. (Actually, Bangkok once had a

Yunnan restaurant, but it was a front for opium smugglers. They never had food, but we'd go in to sniff the place out.) Again, they want to force me into a private room "for foreign guests." I insist on sitting with the drugged-up Yunnanese, eating egg soup with pungent smoked fish. They are very jolly people and keep offering me terrible things to eat. Then we go to another place to have scallops, mushrooms, and bean sprouts.

June 10:

    Begin with Mongolian hot pot in a restaurant under the street. Then to another underground restaurant, this from Hunan, Mao Tse-tung's home province. Large catacomb, silent people sitting alone, quietly. Very salty, very large portions. I am dragged off to Fang Shan, where the Politburo enjoyed what I managed to stick down. Pork fried with flour, egg, soy, and ginger. A sort of fatback sandwich. Back to the hotel, only to be woken for Sick Duck. This is Peking duck served at a famous restaurant near the hospital. Thus the name. "Is it true," I ask my guide, "that on Thanksgiving Day they serve turkey and call it Peeking Tom?" Her official position is to be not officially amused. But in my heart I believe she considers me the most diverting jester in Tiananmen Square that day.

June 16:

The first of the nightmares. That morning I had been served Szechuan duck, fried bird head (actually a veggie dish), and some sweets from Shandong province. But the nightmare was bad: An orange disc shining from afar. Oozing yellow. Reminiscent of that Italian dish called…But no, no, no! It couldn't be pizza. It must have been something I ate.

June 22:
I love Shanghai. True, these people have talked themselves into believing that they are the most civilized people in China, and that gets to be a bore. But the restaurants are fine. Veggie dishes looking like animals, chicken breast wrapped in oil, fried crisp duck with a coating of pepper, rice wine, soy, and oregano. Oregano? No, obviously an olfactory illusion. But things are getting desperate.

June 24:
The nightmares are increasing. The pizza (for that disc is most certainly a pizza) becomes larger each evening. It is almost family size. I wake up in a sweat, the anchovies having formed a sneering, snickering smile, taunting me to come out and eat it. The time is only 9:00 P.M., and I walk the streets of Shanghai, gorging myself in an all-night dumpling shop. Sesame cakes, small balls of steamed dough with minced pork. Attempt sleep, but wake up crying. The pizza has…it has attacked me.

June 26:
The pizza obsession is a disease, but I must soldier on. The next stop is Suzhou, where Marco Polo found rest and recreation. But did Marco Polo attempt the famous chattering squirrel-fish? Did he crack open the Shanghai crabs? Did he dawdle over the smooth Taiju Lake green soup and cut open the cabbage heart? Was there a Suzhou Hotel with its peacock-shaped eel? Its cold collation with designs and colors like a Seurat painting? Of course not! Marco Polo didn't need to eat Chinese. He carried his own pizza with him. I'm sure of it.

June 27:
Everything Marco Polo said about Hangzhou is true. But did he imagine Italy while he supped? I sip the Dragon Well tea and think

of Orvieto wine. Cut the West Lake fish and imagine marlin off Capri, sample crisp silver carp with ginger and imagine pasta with green peppers and mushrooms. The bean curd skin is as delicate as phyllo pastry–but not half so floury as a thick crust of Milanese pizza!

June 28:
No sleep tonight at all. I have been to one hundred and three Chinese restaurants in the past three weeks. Some for a snack, some for a meal. All I conceive now is pizza, pizza, PIZZA!!!! Alone and frantic, I roam over the bridges of West Lake. Each eel is an anchovy, each lake vegetable is a globe tomato, each water-lily is a pizza tray. Like an illusion, I run into that great futurist, the now late Buckminster Fuller, who is visiting Hangzhou. I had interviewed him before, and he recognizes me. As he continues measuring water in the lake, he greets me and I greet him. "You look distraught," he says. "Would you like something to eat?" Aaaaaagh!

June 30:
Today I board the plane for Hong Kong. Home and pizza. Friends and pizza. Television and pizza. I begin to froth in anticipation. I swoon and faint. My seatmates stare in horror as I utter the words "Easy on the anchovies" over and over, like a sad mantra. They look in dismay then, typically, forget about the whole thing and go to sleep. Perchance to dream.

A final note: Astonishingly, upon reaching Hong Kong, I forgot the whole opium-style series of dreams. In fact, I sat down to a beefsteak and didn't eat pizza for many weeks. The book was published, the publisher turned to other things and never promoted it, but I didn't care. For I still love pasta and Peking duck in equal measure. Unlike Chinese fairy tales, I have no morals for this tale (though will save a few morels for my steak), and offer this final quatrain:

> Guangzhou shrimp and Shanghai eel,
> Hangzhou chickens baked in clay.
> What wondrous truths these tastes reveal.
> Life can be both wok and play!

Recipe:
Congee with Dried Beef

After a long hard day of sampling, the simplest breakfast was always the best. Here is simple traditional congee, which can be made with a variety of meats and vegetables, serving 6-8.

Rice

    1½ c. short-grain rice
    1 tsp. salt
    1 tbsp. groundnut (peanut) oil
    10 c. water
    5 c.s chicken broth (stock)
    3-4 slices ginger
    1 piece dried orange peel
    1 lb. rump steak, ground
    2 tbsp. chopped scallion

Marinade

    1 tbsp. light soy sauce
    1 tbsp. Chinese rice wine
    1 tsp. salt
    1 tsp. sugar
    1 tsp. sesame oil
    2 tbsp. water
    1 tbsp. cornstarch

1. In a large bowl, mix the rice with the salt and oil. Add water to cover about half an inch above the rice and soak for 1 hour.
2. Place water, broth, ginger, and orange peel in a large pan and bring to a boil. Add the rice and cook over high heat for 15 minutes.
3. Cover the pan lightly and simmer over low heat for 2 hours.
4. For the marinade, mix all the ingredients in a bowl. Marinate the beef for 15 minutes. Stir the mixture with a fork for 5 minutes.
5. Using a teaspoon, scoop the beef into balls and set aside on a lightly greased platter.
6. Add the beef to the rice and bring to a boil.
7. Divide the mixture among soup bowls, add the scallions, and serve.

Chapter Twenty-Nine

Where Shepherds Yell by Night
Recipe:
Lamb from the Forbidden City

That wonderful chorus from Handel's Messiah begins "For we like sheep." Dear Georg Frederich didn't know the half of it. Somewhere in the northern desert of China are people who not only "like" sheep, they positively idolize the damned things.

I hadn't known about that, since few trips were made to China after writing Eating Out In China. Some years ago, the most fascinating town in China was Tianjin, a.k.a. Tientsin. It had been an "international" town until the Second World War, and even after a disastrous earthquake in the 1980s it still preserves districts—between the belching industrial towers—reflecting its cosmopolitan past. Here were a few streets of Georgian England, the bulbous towers of a Russian Orthodox church, a verdant French quarter and, of course, the factories and huge electrical generators. Little remains as testimony to its semi-colonial past. But Tianjin does have the never-ending heritage of its food.

Culinary-wise, Tianjin is hardly as well known as Shanghai or Canton, or nearby Peking. But the town is justly proud of being the home of the dumpling. Yes, the same food as "Mama;s little baby loves dumpings, dumplings." Every Chinese dumpling, fried, steamed, or boiled, comes originally from the four-hundred-year-old Tianjin tradition.

The town is also famous for its cabbages and pears, both bearing the name of the city. Equally renowned are the desserts: caramelized fruit and wild cranberries growing in the countryside. On the streets, merchants sell the cranberries on a stick along with apples and pears covered with oozing boiled sugar.

Tianjin also has grapes, but these are for wine, as this is one of the few areas where wine is not made from rice or sorghum.

Mesmerizing as these facts may be, Inner Mongolian shepherds take little interest in the history of culinary Tianjin. They have better things to think about. Like selling their sheep. We will get to that later. First, though, one must understand that when Inner Mongolian shepherds thought about food in Tianjin a decade ago, they thought about the Tianjin Food Palace.

For those readers who don't happen to be Inner Mongolian shepherds, the Food Palace was a conglomeration of restaurants reflecting all China's heritage. It had been created by the ambitious mayor of Tianjin in 1985, and was an instantaneous failure. In an outlying part of the city, it didn't attract tourists (the town didn't have any) or residents (who didn't want to taste any food other than their own). But as the first foreigner on the three-stop Tianjin subway line, I was told by passengers that the Tianjin Food Palace was a combination of the Pyramids, the Louvre, and the Empire

State Building, with a special je ne sais quoi of its own. Naturally, I had to go.

Well, the place was an obvious fraud. Claptrap restaurants that had started off clean but were soon covered with the soot of the town. One after the other, the empty rooms stood like Xian's plaster soldiers, lined up, ready to serve. The waiters were bored or sleeping, the enormous menus actually were a façade for the two or three dishes available that evening. (While no customers were ever around, the waiters would say that they were "sold out" of whatever I wanted.)

The one exception was the Mongolian restaurant. Mongolians hardly ever entered Tianjin itself. But since the Food Palace was on the outskirts, they found it homey. And their own restaurant, behind the others, overlooking a large empty yard, was where the Mongol shepherds celebrated in style.

Who were these shepherds? Most of us grow up with different pictures of shepherds. Some of us believe that shepherds are peaceful old men looking for a star while tending their sheep by night. To others, they are seraphic Greek boys playing sweet flutes and lyres. Or nymphs and cherubs gamboling with lambs. Or dour Scots red-bearded patriarchs accompanied by collies.

That could all be true. But the shepherds of the Mongolian Gobi Desert break the mold. Mongolian shepherds are loud, fierce, drunken, wacky. Their laughter roars over the desert and hills. They cheer and drink and burp and dance. If sheep can't go to sleep, they probably imagine Mongolian shepherds leaping into ditches. If sheep have nightmares, they probably dream of inebriated Mongolian shepherds.

About four times a year, though, these rambunctious Mongolian shepherds come down to Tianjin to sell their sheep. They do this in the suburbs near the Food Palace by a market that I have never seen. But once their sheep are sold and they have a few hundred yuan to call their own, the shepherds come into the big city to celebrate. In 1985, they didn't make it past the Food Palace, where they knew that a welcome awaited them from other equally raucous shepherds.

To reiterate, these were not the soulful, wandering shepherds of Virgillian pastoral poetry. As they stumbled through the dark labyrinth of corridors, bumping into the walls, looking into each deserted restaurant for their own place, they would blunder and topple through the maze. For already they had started drinking inside their open-air Huei Restaurant – Huei means Islamic, though nothing is teetotal about these Moslems. While a drink list was available, they always had their leather casks of fermented buffalo milk to get them to the Food Palace. Later, they would order up some Han or Chinese beer to show they had real money in their pockets.

Then these shepherds would dash into the open-air kitchen to order up massive quantities of – what else? – mutton.

Huei Restaurant was actually a café. A few tables, the steam pouring out of the kitchen, and shepherds sitting around, shmoozing. (The Mongolian Shmooze or the Gobi Kibbitz is best practiced by newly rich shepherds.) They would be wearing their woolen cloaks, with newly-bought tee-shirts and waiting patiently, loudly for their meals. When these appeared, the café would burst with liveliness.

What was I doing there? Some of the shepherds climbing the steps, singing and stumbling, saw me wandering alone down those dank corridors, so naturally they asked me to join them. The found it unreasonable that anybody should eat dinner alone, even if that person spoke not a word of Mongolian and only a smattering of Mandarin. So I was the unlikely witness to their revels.

Actually, nobody could eat anything, since the room had neither tables nor chairs. Soon, though, huge tables appeared and a few rickety bamboo chairs. The rest of us leaned against the wall or simply sat on the floor.

Next to arrive were bare-wooded platters about six feet in circumference. We stood up as the four boys brought them in and set them on the equally gigantic tables. The platter had an indentation about three inches down, and after the boys laid it on the table, they rushed out to get a full plank of sizzling mutton. This plank was poured on to the platter, along with bulbs of spring onions, carrots of Olympian dimensions, whole black and red peppers, covered with bubbling juices.

With a communal sigh of satisfaction, the shepherds dug in. They dug in with fingers, tin forks (which usually broke), sometimes chopsticks. Without much discrimination, they dipped the mutton pieces into chili sauce, soy sauce, peanut sauce, brown sauce with pieces of black splotch or green sauce of vinegar, lemon, and pieces of green splotch. They downed it with gusto and laughter and sometimes a story.

Fortunately, while I understood not a word of it, good bawdy tales are as universal as food. So I imagined hilarious gems about "the traveling sheep salesman and the mutton merchant's daughter," laughing with all the rest, devoid of inhibition.

That lack of inhibition, I confess, was a decision of my own. It was decided by my third helping of gaoliang. Gaoliang is a thick sorghum schnapps, a brew that resembles jellied vodka spiked with hornets. Once the shepherds proved they had beer money, they went on to their true love, gaoliang, which arrived in ornate clay vessels that were quickly downed, thrown on to the floor, and more vessels ordered.

Ditto for the mutton, which was endlessly delivered from this magical kitchen. The shepherds shouted louder, attempted to sing, poured the sorghum liquor over each other, disposed of the eating implements by either breaking them or throwing them out into the yard, with their fingers becoming the utensil of choice. What the hell, thought I, the fingers could be no greasier than the crockery.

Now the party began to gather pace and the shepherds began to dance. Oh, that's an exaggeration. They didn't actually dance. They stood up and clasped each other around the waist and tried a few decorous steps, like cripples helping each other across the street. A few steps to the right, another few to the left. A line soon stretched across the room, and I was the only one left sitting and clapping out the rhythm. There was no music, only what they made themselves by slapping their own thick-coated shoulders and stamping and dredging out some nonsense rhymes.

After a few minutes, most of them sat down, exhausted. One wrinkled old man was left. He shuffled and double-shuffled, and helplessly hopped to one side of the wall, then fell down and got up and wobbled around and sat down in hysterical laughter at the wooden table as the air grew blue with cigarette smoke, and more bottles of gaoliang were opened, and more dancing was essayed, and then we all swayed around the room.

We expected this gentle bacchanalia to continue forever. But Chinese law must be obeyed. At 10:00 P.M., the lights went out, either by law or by chronic Chinese brown-outs. Candles appeared from dark crevices in the wall and, like the finale of a ballet, each cigarette was lowered to the wick, glowed, and the flames lit the hall. They flickered for a few minutes, then, as if the tallow had been hastily piled up in some tiny village and sold in the big city, they just as quickly were extinguished and lit again. And as the matches gave out, so did we.

The old song could have gone, "Mongol shepherds don't sleep tight until, uh, eleven at night," so soon they were ready to slumber. In the shadows they did mime tricks (as if we didn't have enough, one of them did a shadow of a sheep's head), and they crouched down in their cloaks and the older ones went to sleep under the benches. The younger ones paid the overpadded bill without thinking or counting or caring. Then they dragged their elders out of the restaurant, over the corridors to the silent cobblestoned streets below.

The trucks were waiting here, and the engines hemmed and hawed and against better judgment motors began to turn over, and as we all clambered on and rolled out, the glimmer of the city faded and we reached the gates leading to the northern plains.

They gestured for me to come with them up to the Gobi desert to tend sheep with them, and I was tempted but resisted. At the gates, I left the trucks, and we bade goodbye, and they rolled up north, shouting to the air, happy to return to their huts and homes and sheep and wives. Far, oh so far, from any dot on any map.

And I stood and waved and watched them leave the soot and fumes of Tianjin before turning back. And I imagined them waving back to me as their clankety rusty trucks evaporated into what Walt Whitman called, with the mystery of a poet, "the teeming spiritual darkness."

Recipe:
Lamb from the Forbidden City

An original recipe from Baltimore's Ding How Restaurant, located in fashionable Fells Point, one of the better Chinese restaurants on the East Coast. Henry Chen's recipe isn't exactly Tianjin authentic, but the taste, rather sweetish and delicious, would make even tradition-bound Mongolian shepherds happy.

> 1 lb. lamb, clean, peel off fat and slice very, very thin
> ½ onion, chopped
> Green onion, chopped
> 4 tbsp. soy sauce
> 3 tbsp. plum sauce
> ½ c. chicken broth
> 3 tbsp. Chinese cooking wine
> 1 tsp. vinegar

1. Put 5 tbsp. vegetable oil into heated wok.
2. Stir-fry sliced lamb for 3 minutes, drain oil from lamb.
3. Remove lamb and reheat the wok. Add 1 tbsp. vegetable oil.
4. Stir-fry all the onions together and pour in all other ingredients except vinegar.
5. Stir for 1 minute and remove everything from wok.
6. Heat the wok once more, pour vinegar all around the wok until it evaporates.
7. Put everything back into the wok and stir-fry for 1 minute.

This will be served with rice in most restaurants. But in North China, wheat rolls or thin bread may be used to scoop up the lamb dish.

Chapter Thirty

Of Cabbages And Kims: An Epic Romance Of Korea's National Vegetable
Recipe: Pukpuui T'ongbaech'u Kimch'I
(Northern Style Kimchi)

For many years, visits to South Korea were anticipated with special pleasure, mainly for its lusty, funny, high-spirited citizens. Another motive was a pirate music shop, where I could pick up operas, symphonies, and collections of piano works for a few dollars. The third was the food, which is limited but delicious. Fourth was that I could gaze longingly on the mountains north of Seoul and imagine what was on the other side. Then, thanks to a "window" in the tourist business of North Korea, I could finally enter. Many adventures ensued during the visit of a few weeks. And food was certainly among the most enlightening.

During our visit, I must point out, we had no inkling of the famine in the countryside. We did see farmers traipsing through the highways or digging in the fields. Their implements were basic, the ground seemed fallow, but the tough Koreans, with their heavy sweaters, ruddy cheeks, and sparkle in their eyes, hardly seemed to be starving. Two years later, the truth came out, so I hesitate to write this. But equally, I cannot resist. Please ignore this story if you are so inclined.

The Talented Dragon Investment Corporation is situated in central Macao. Despite its cryptic name, Talented Dragon (as its friends called it) had the responsibility of opening the world's most hermetic country to the outside world.

Briefly, until 1993, North Korea, run by Great Leader Kim Il-sung and his lesser leader buddies, was a country forbidden to everyone except cadres, comrades, and compatriots from countries unknown to the rest of the world. So if you were President of the United States, you would quickly be told that you were an imperialist, colonialist, scumbag exploiter of the people. On the other hand, if you came from the Socialist Democratic People's Republic of Western Mauritanian Rebels, you would get a grand parade down the center of Pyongyang. Which – considering that there are no cars in the center of Pyongyang – was not really that important.

With the Pyongyang Times usually leading its news section with "Great Leader Shakes Hands With Appreciative Sierra Leone Assistant Foreign Secretary," I had little chance of entering. Then I heard about Talented Dragon Investment Corporation. Luck was mine.

North Korea, needing hard currency to survive, decided to open to foreign tourists, who would bring in aforesaid currency. Thus, after studying maps and charts, they opted to open up a pair of tourist agencies. One was to be based in Dresden, East Germany. The other was to be in Hong Kong.

Well, Dresden went down the drain, as East Germany became part of reunited Germany. The North Koreans didn't trust reunited Germany. They believed Hong Kong was part of China then, but Hong Kong, always politically cautious, refused the tempting offer to become the tourist mecca of the People's Democratic Socialist Republic of Korea, a.k.a. the Commies.

Where could North Korea go? First, they looked on a map and found that just next door to Hong Kong was the oppressed state of Macao, an imperialistic colony. The colonizers were the Portuguese, so the people of Macao would greatly welcome the Liberators of the Whole World, North Korea.

Well, the Macanese are hospitable folk so they said, in effect, "Why not?" "C'mon in," they said. "Just don't tell anybody you're here." Which is why the North Korean Tourist Bureau hid behind the name Talented Dragon Investment Corporation.

When I discovered Talented Dragon (working for the Macao Tourist Board, I had access to all kinds of esoteric knowledge), my life was made. Within twenty minutes, I had a visa for North Korea with promises that anything I wanted to do, I could do. So I made a list of the most doable things.

First, I took an easy one. I said that I wished to go backstage at the North Korea Circus to see how they trained the acrobats. That was okayed.

Then I took a chance and said I wanted to attend a town council meeting so I could meet the man who designed the 26,510 statues of Kim Il-sung. In my mind, I imagined listening to the minutes of the meeting:

First Counselor: "Hey, comrade guys, I got this great idea for the new park. Why don't we put up a statue right in the middle?"

Second Counselor: "Well, it sounds okay. But what statue could we use?"

Third Counselor: "Ya know, those Kim Il-sung statues are pretty darned popular…"

(Buzz of agreement)

Second Counselor: "They sure are. I've never heard anybody complain."

(More buzzing of agreement)

First Counselor: "Man, that idea is so crazy, it just might work."

I didn't tell this reverie to the North Korean visa officer, but he seemed to okay the original possibility.

Then I said I would like to visit a class in political science at the University of North Korea… Maybe even give a lecture … say, on democracy and freedom.

That too was okayed. So I offered the big one.

"And how about a day accompanying the Great Leader, just to see what he does. From all the publicity and stuff, he seems like a nice enough person."

All of these ideas came bouncing out of my ingenuous, naïve little head, and were duly written down by the assistant manager of the Talented Dragon Investment Corporation. He nodded enthusiastically.

All that I requested, he implied, would bear fruit. None of it (it goes without saying) came anywhere near to fruition. What actually happened was for another story, another time, another place.

So I had time to dream about my North Korea. It would have white sandy beaches and clean frosty winters. A fabulous concert season (Vladimir Ashkenazy would join the Pyongyang Philharmonic for a series of Beethoven and Stravinsky). The Japanese karaoke bars would have singalong Schubert.

As for food, Pyongyang–my Pyongyang–would be one of the noble secrets of Asia. Besides New York delicatessens brimming over with brisket and corned beef, sour pickles, and fresh coleslaw, Pyongyang would have the spiciest Szechuan duck, very haute French lamb chops, fiery Thai curries, and a host of Lebanese mezze tavernas, with vats of hummus and anise-filled raki.

Well, the music and beaches were mere dreams. But the food was exactly as I imagined. Oh, perhaps not a hundred percent. Actually, it was only the Jewish delicatessens. All right, ya got me. Just the coleslaw part was true.

Or rather, the cabbage part of the coleslaw. That was true.

But hey, cabbage is a beginning. As well (I found out) as the end. To be absolutely honest, if you liked cabbage, North Korea was paradise – the Elysian fields of cabbage.

Now very few visitors went to the People's Paradise for gourmet dining. They went for the statues of Kim Il-sung, statues that made Augustinian Rome seem unassumingly barren. The statues turned Pyongyang (which means in Korean, "flat basin") into a kingdom somewhere between Xanadu and Gilbert and Sullivan.

Dining was limited to (a) smuggled Chivas Regal by the cadres, and (b) cabbage.

The Chivas has been well documented. The government made its money not through the untiring hard work of the masses but by smuggling whisky and cigarettes from around the world. Only tourists drank the incendiary local soju spirit. The real Koreans –that is, the apparatchiks of the endless bureaucracy–drank XO brandy and Mouton Rothschild. By the gallon!

The cabbage is not so well documented. But cabbage they had. Cabbage hot, cabbage cold, cabbage in the pot ten days old. Or longer.

For it takes months and months to make the national dish, kimchi. But where South Korea (known to its North Korean friends as the Capitalist Slave Dogs of the Yankee Imperialists) adds kimchi to main dishes, the North has always been purist, taking their kimchi as the main dish itself.

I learned about this because Kim, my official translator, shared a love of Humphrey Bogart with me. He was charming, eloquent, and politically correct.

"Yes," he would admit, "the south has more cars. But they are made with Western technology. We have more roads. We have built them ourselves. We do not need cars if we build roads ourselves."

Or: "Yes, you in the West have elections – but only one time a year. In November, I believe. But we in the People's Democratic Republic of Korea have democracy three hundred and sixty-five days a year. That is where we are superior, and why the rest of the world respects us."

Politics is mother's milk in Korea. Curdled, perhaps, but still milk.

Western films are not permitted, of course. But Kim had made one exception. While studying in Beijing, he had seen a single American film. That movie was Casablanca.

"A faultless choice," I told him. "You don't have to see anything more. You have, in fact, hit the Blessed Jackpot of the Silver Screen."

"Do you," asked Kim, "know the music?"

"I know it, sing it, play it…"

Kim almost fainted. "That is wonderful, Harry. We will have dinner tonight. The hotel has a pre-colonialist piano. We will sing together how a kiss is not a kiss…"

I won't go into the details of that day, how time went by (as the old song goes), but Kim couldn't wait. Instead of eating plain cabbage that night, Kim and his friends and I ate spicy kimchi cabbage. He bragged to them in Korean how he would sing a Western song for them. Then he bragged to me about how North Korean kimchi beat the very socks off that decadent South Korean "imperialist" kimchi. (He didn't use that adjective, but I know he felt it.)

After dinner, we approached the battered honky-tonk excuse of a piano. The three of us made a great combination. I am a player who is enthusiastic and digitally spastic. The piano had eighty-eight keys, but thirty-seven could be pushed down, and even these were clangy and bangy. Kim was vigorous and energetic, but could only sing a single note.

Without any of the boisterous details (except that a Russian trade group shouted out to us to "Stop in the name of the Peace of the World"), we continued singing and playing, and Kim insisted on me playing more songs "of that same old period."

I agreed. But we had to make a deal. I would play, but only if I could have an introduction to meet Pyongyang's number one chef.

Kim, a mere translator, looked downcast. My request was apparently beyond state policy. Besides, I wouldn't have time to see the number one chef. I already had an appointment to see, first, the official Kim Il-sung painters (for lack of copying machines, they had individual artists copying the face of the Great Leader) and second, a visit to a hospital for an authentic Korean tonsillectomy.

Well, said I, no chef, no songs. The fact was, though, that I relented and we played. And Kim pulled some strings. So while I never saw an authentic Korean tonsillectomy, I did meet some honored chefs, and we talked kimchi for a few hours.

The most fascinating fact I found here? Kimchi and the American Declaration of Independence had the same origin. Really.

"In 1776," Kim translated, "the greatest cook of all time, Yu Joong-in, wrote the greatest book of recipes in the history of the world, Cheung Bo Sam Rim Kyongle. This was where he wrote out the rules of kimchi. And this we what we follow to this day."

Frankly, I was amazed. The books on the "official" North Korean list were virtually all written by the Great Leader and his son, the Dear Leader. Ancient venerable chef Yu Joong-in would have been known as a running dog. Or, if not exactly called that, he would at least have used running dogs in his recipes.

Still, the chefs praised the aforementioned "Encyclopedia of Korean Cookery" with its hundreds upon hundreds of official recipes for kimchi. I had tasted most in the South, where each home and village had its own, and I was anxious to taste more in Pyongyang.

But it was no go. For in the North, there were only four official kimchi recipes. So said the chef.

Kim stopped him there. Like Scheherazade, who kept her sultan waiting in suspense, I would have to wait for the next day to discover the four official recipes. Before I could get them, I would have to teach Kim some more songs of the 1930s. Due to limitations of player, piano and singer, we limited them to slow songs. Bewitched, Bothered and Bewildered was a hit. There's a Small Hotel was not so popular, since in North Korea hotels have at least six hundred rooms, most of them empty. The idea of a "small hotel" was not easily grasped.

After the lesson, we went back to drinking: the Koreans on Black Label, me slurping down soju.

The next day was a lesson for me. I learned about the quartet of official kimchi: radish, salty fish, cucumber or red peppers. Or for grand occasions, a combination of all four.

Kim and the chef had a whisper together before Kim reluctantly told me more. "They say, Harry, that up in the mountains are a people who…well, who don't follow the official kimchi recipes. But I cannot say anything more about them."

Security unbreached, but my curiosity somewhat slaked, I bade my farewell to the chef (whose name, I believe, was Mr. Kim). We had to get to the War Heroes Museum, the War Heroes Cemetery, and the War Heroes Frieze.

That night was the final one for music. It turned out that Kim could sing Over the Rainbow with heartbreaking noises. I taught him other songs, and when he wanted one "like Mickey Mouse," I taught him that fine old classic from Snow White and the Seven Dwarfs. Kim loved Whistle While You Work, which seemed quite appropriate for the People's Paradise.

Before leaving, Kim called me away from the others. The chef had liked me and allowed the secrets of mountain kimchi to be mine. Ingredients there included mushrooms, vines and wild vegetables, as well as sprouts, leaves, and roots.

Those, I fear, are what are used today. We had had no news of a famine, and only now are the harsh facts revealed.

I had to leave the next day. Kim, though, had promised me a gift, which turned out to be a parchment with part of an eighteenth-century poem pleading for women "to wash my back, prepare the bean curd, and serve the spiciest kimchi."

I in turn mailed Kim a record of Frank Sinatra singing his best sellers. I knew he would enjoy them. But I never heard from Kim again, and communication was stopped even as the Talented Dragon Investment Corporation became an ordinary corporation for smuggling cigarettes and whisky.

As for the Sinatra, I doubt if Kim received it. The People's Republic can get more than a little paranoid when they hear of Strangers in the Night.

POSTSCRIPT: Recently surfing the Web, I found the official North Korean site. Under the heading "Delicious Dishes" was found the following, recorded without comment:

"Gasoline-baked clams can be found only in North Korea. I gave an outdoors party for my North Korean staff members. Huge clams were laid on a gravel pit covered with pine leaves. My driver poured gasoline from a beer bottle over the pit. He then lighted the fuel. To my surprise the baked clams had no trace of the gasoline and were extremely tasty."

Recipe:
Pukpuui T'ongbaech'u Kimch'i
(Northern Style Kimchi)

This was the kimchi all the Northerners ate before the present regime. At this time, ingredients are severely limited, so the kimchi is simpler. But here is the whole shebang – with a very explosive BANG! This recipe is from the authoritative book, *Kimchi: A Natural Health Food*, by Florence C. Lee and Helen C. Lee, published by Hollym.

> 5 celery cabbage heads
> 7 radishes
> ½ watercress cut in 2-inch strips
> Indian mustard leaves
> Green thread onions, about half a bundle
> Dried forest mushrooms, soaked and cut into julienne strips
> 4 dried stone mushrooms, soaked in hot water, cleaned, and cut into strips
> 2 Korean pears (like green Bartlett pears), cut into strips
> 10 chestnuts, cut into slivers
> 5 garlic bulbs
> 3 ginger roots, peeled and crushed
> 3 c. of red pepper powder
> ½ c. salt fish, pickled baby squid, 1 small octopus, each cut into strips
> 1½ lbs. beef brisket, boiled in beef broth
> Coarse table salt and sugar

Preliminaries

First, add the red pepper to water, and knead with the hands to make a paste.

Now trim the cabbage by cutting each head into 4 sections, after trimming the tough outer leaves. But save those outer leaves.

Preparation

1. Soak cabbage sections and radishes in brine prepared with 3 c. salt and 4 qts. water for 4 hours. Rinse with cold water.
2. Halve the radishes, reserving 2 and making slit cuts of the length of the bottom.
3. Cut the pears into thin julienne strips.
4. Cut the pickled fish and squid into narrow strips.
5. Cut the radishes into thin julienne. Mix the radish strips with red pepper paste. Add all the remaining vegetables mushrooms, and chestnuts with the fish. Mix well.
6. Now toss this mixture with oysters and pear strips and season with salt.
7. Pack this mixture between the layers of the old tough cabbage leaves. Fill the slit cuts in the radishes. Stack the stuffed cabbage and radishes in a crock. Cover with the salted outer leaves. After 3 days, add a mixture of salt, salt-fish juice, shrimp juice, and beef broth, enough to cover. Leave in a covered barrel.

Chapter Thirty-One

A Buffet of Haiku
Recipe:
Raw Japanese Eggplant Salad

I never spent much time in Japan. It was, and is, too beautiful, too sensitive. I always had the feeling that one footstep in the snow would destroy the entire environment. We aren't speaking cities here, which, for non-speakers of Japanese, are as boring as sandpaper. But the countryside. In winter.

For my first extended trip, I took a trip from south to north on January 2 through the snow. All I could think of through the countryside on the almost empty train, where skiers might get on at an isolate station and get off at the next tone, was that old legendary abstract painting "White On White."

In Japan, though, we had ten different "whites" upon white. The ground was white with endless snow to the snowy mountains. The sky was white, and the snowflakes were (yes) white. But the white poplars were even whiter with snow. Now, on the bare white tree-branches of the white poplars, the snow was gently gathering in diagonal channels. On the joints where the branches met the tree, the snow was gently piling in oblong balls. As the snow would begin to be too heavy, the streams of snow would fall to the ground, while the snow in the joints of the trees would fall in oblong balls.

All was white upon white upon white. The music was, of course, from that Japan-loving Frenchman, Claude Debussy, whose Footsteps in the Snow was that of a white piano. But the snow spoke for itself.

I had a memory of a junior high school class, where we would compose haiku and ask Zen koans, the best getting a round of applause. Since this was inevitably the sound of one hand clapping, we never figured out the winners. Zen does have its limits. These haiku are written for the book. They are (surprise!) about food.

> The Minestrone Haiku
> Fresh vegetables
> Mate in the bubbling water.
> Quick consommé-tion!

> The Egg Haiku
> "Do you like your eggs
> Ova-done or underdone?"
> "Raw," clucked Miss Chicken.

> The Egg Haiku (variation)
> Chicken rebellion!!!!
> "Resist the baby snatchers!!!
> We shall ova-come!!!"

The Music Haiku I
"Bagels," said Wagner,
"Are worthy of four operas:
Ring of the Nibbling!"

The Celibacy Haiku
Can abstinence be
More comical when poured from
Salt-peter-sellers?

The Escargot Haiku
Boiled for too long
Escargots become bitter
Sometimes hard-as-snails.

The Escargot Haiku (variation)
Escargots not fresh?
You can't fly, rail, or ship them:
They're sent by snail-mail!

The Chopsticks Haiku
The unkindest cut-
lery of all. Wood kills trees,
Plastic poisons worlds.

The Waltz Haiku
In Vienna, they
Waltzed, polka'ed, and sucked red wine
Through Johann Strauss-Straws.

The Islamic Wine Haiku I
Alcohol drinks are
Out, except in palaces of
Radical Sheiks.

The Islamic Wine Haiku II
Iraqi wine's banned
Unless you quaff it from a
Cárafe of Baghdad.

The McDonald's Haiku
"Gimme one Big Mac,
Two apple pies, and a huge
Order of franchise."

The Elizabethan Haiku
If Shakespeare'd written
"Much Ado About Muttons,"
We'd be reading Lamb's Tales.

The Lamb Haiku
Sheepish stewards asked,
"Want some garnish with your chops?"
"No thanks." (They mint well.)

The Cranberry Haiku
She was too juiced up
To offer me her cranberries.
So we talked turkey.

The Cassoulet Haiku
What? Rough-and-ready
Terrine incognito? Huh?
Behold mystery herbs.

The Chili Haiku
The rule of chilies:
Big are pussycats. Tiny
Are pepper tigers!

The Baltimore Crabcake Haiku
Lost in the harbor,
Looking for welcome moorings.
"Jump on my table!"

The Soya Haiku
Plain beans are boring.
So mash, crash, smash, and boil them:
The sauce of good health.

The Eel Haiku I
Crisp Kyoto eels:
"Oh Tempura! Oh morays!"
(Maxim from Japan)

The Eel Haiku II
Battered, not beaten,
Prepared with great care in the
House of Eel Repute.

The Music Haiku II
Rossini changed beef
To tournedos, making
A stormy chef d'oeuvre.

The Brisket Haiku
Ravishing rump roast,
Bite the last gristle. "Meat's
Neat. Bone appetite."

The Legume Haiku
"No pistachios,
Filberts or almonds for me."
(Is this peanuts envy?)

The Grub Haiku
The Queen bee waits
As we gulp down her babies.
"Oh, wasp, where is thy sting?"

The Rattler Haiku
Sultan of crawlers:
A light snake before dinner?
Sheikh Rattle-on-Roll!

The Italian Haiku
The Bridge of Sighs and
Rememb'rance of things pasta:
Breaths in Venice.

The Italian Haiku II
Pungent, fragrant scents
Come…go. Arrivederci,
Aroma. Farewell.

The Italian Haiku III
Gelato koan:
Tiber, Tiber, shining bright,
Dark and chocolate delight!

The Music Haiku III
Mozart loved Mozart
Tarts. "Because I treat myself
From soup to notes."

The Salad Haiku
Hares hopping in leaves,
Hope to gobble the garden.
Please, leave leaves for me.

The Curry Haiku
Waiting to enter
An Indian restaurant, I
Hear, "Please cumin, sir."

The Peking Duck Haiku
Could Manet produce
Such golden skin, tempting meat?
Quelle canard! Slice! Eat!

The Music Haiku IV
Schubert's "Trout" Quintet
Preceded by his "Trout" Song:
Playing Follow the Lieder.

The Minced Onion Haiku
"Stop! Do not chop me!"
The melodrama, ended,
Brought tears to my eyes.

The Apple Haiku
Tasty Apple Crumble
Can't hold together. But Pie
Has esprit de cores.

The God Haiku
He has fed His Flock
With four mild commandments:
"Stay. Eat. Drink. Be good."

Recipe:
Raw Japanese Eggplant Salad

The world knows that they have a healthy penchant for raw dishes in Japan, but raw eggplant, which I experienced once in a bar while pushing away the live lobster, is perhaps new to some. It is not to everyone's taste, but is certainly simple to prepare with the right ingredients.

> 1 lb. eggplant, unpeeled, about ½ inch thick
> This is cut into thin strips, lightly salted, and ready for the marinade, which is made as follows:

Mix together ½ c. soy sauce, 1 tbsp. sake, 1 tsp. sugar, and about 4 knobs of ginger root finely minced. You can substitute dry sherry for the sake, but the taste will be too strong.

Take the eggplant mixture and press it together, extracting all the moisture. Put it in the bowl with the marinade and thoroughly mix/toss/throw it so everything is combined well. Let it stand for at least 2 hours to let the marinade unite with the vegetable. It will serve 4, and the tastes inevitably excite curiosity and delight.

CHAPTER THIRTY-TWO

RHAPSODY IN BALUT
Recipe:
Pearl's Affritada

I was never a Pacific traveller. The islands were far from each other (if you can't go by subway, bus, or train, I figure, you shouldn't go at all). I don't spear-fish, cannot shake my waistline, and find the food uninteresting. Hawaii had been visited when I was in the Merchant Marine, and a Fiji trip was in the offing. But the only Pacific islands I could call my own were the Philippines, which I had visited countless times for stories. They were cultural, architectural, sometimes political.

Never culinary. Neither Spanish-style paella in the northern Iberian town of Vigan nor beef spine and rice with the Moro Liberation League in the deep south island of Jolo has excited me. Manila restaurants try enticing with bangus fish and adobo, to no avail. Oh, and the local gin and rum. While attempting to write "unforgettable nights" with these brews, this would be a lie. By the next morning, I can remember absolutely nothing.

Balut, though, is the exception. Balut has aroused me, disgusted me, I have craved it moonlit nights in Manila, and sometimes long for it in New York. But such desires are considered perverse by more knowledgable gourmets. Balut also, one fateful weekend, turned me into a Saint. A true canonized Saint.

Let me explain.

Of all the Asian dishes usually repugnant to Western tastes—fried fox-bile, steamed sea cucumber, live wasp-larva, puréed python skin, live bat blood in Chinese rice wine—no dish less deserves its pariah status than the balut. Yes, I can understand negative attitudes to questionable friends of the field and forest. But the balut's odious reputation is unmerited.

Balut is rare in the West, so a word for those unfamiliar with this Filipino food. Balut is the egg of a duck, but with a major difference. Fresh duck egg is ready for eating in a duck egg omelet. Twenty-eight days is the incubation period for hatching a duck egg. Balut lies almost exactly in the middle, an eighteen-day fowl still in its egg, yet still close to birth.

At the age of eighteen days, the duck eggs are picked up from the balutan incubators and sold to poor merchants who go out at about midnight and hawk them (so to speak) to balut lovers in the cities.

Therein lies the repugnance for some, the delicacy for us others. After eighteen days, one has more than elementary egg yolk and egg white with which to deal. The embryo is so well established that a biology student could make out the duck's budding bill, thorax, and spiked little claws. Consequently, to most foreigners and a few queasy Western-educated Filipinos, eating balut is odious.

Yet, to speak of a Filipino duck right-to-life movement would be a canard. The balut, after all, is a national treasure. And unlike most national treasures (which are mainly quack icons), the balut is actually delicious. That will be described later.

On one bus journey to the lovely beaches of La Union provinc, I again fell in love with the balut. The six-hour journey from Manila to the northwest had three rest stops, and at each one I ate a couple of balut, which cost about a quarter apiece. I noticed, though, that other bus passengers were staring at me.

I should have ignored them. Except that I was staring at them. Rather, I was staring at what they were eating. Their food of choice was what we once called weenies. In the Philippines, they went under the brand name "Famous Hot Dog." Famous Hot Dogs are a staple of bus stops throughout the islands. I dare not even guess what goofy meats, roots, paper, demulcents, pencil-tips, crayons and, yes, staples might be stuffed into the questionable skin of Famous Hot Dogs. Nor was I impolite to note that the gluey pink pigment that glowed on the sausage was the exact replica of the toenail polish usually applied to the digits of Manila streetwalkers.

In the meantime, I was the object of their eyes on this bus. Especially the Manilan who was my seat-mate on the long journey.

"I have seen many foreigners before," said Joel. "But you are the first one to eat the balut. Why do you like it? Does it make you strong?" (Virility is the inevitable reason Filipinos give for eating balut, though scientists who claim this are probably the same scientists who concoct Famous Hot Dogs.)

"Because," I told Joel, "the balut is a complete gourmet dinner. Balut is soup, appetizer, and main course, wrapped into one healthy calcium shell." Joel looked puzzled.

So in a fit of poetry to "odefy" him, I reminisced about the sensual experience each midnight on the streets of the darkened towns watching the flame-heated bamboo basket. How the balut-seller tenderly removes the egg from under a napkin. Then how he gently makes a tiny crack in the tip of the egg..."Like delicately making love to a virgin," I told Joel.

Then, how the balut lover turns the egg upside-down in the mouth and tongues the thin membrane, letting the warm melting juices run down the throat like the juice of a tiny Irish oyster...

But in this case, the juice has the earthy taste of a rich double-boiled duck consommé.

"Tell me," said Joel, a good Catholic, "about the Virgin again. About making love with the Mother of God."

It was a theological concept broached by an Antichrist, so I told him to ignore that particular metaphor.

I then explained about the opening nourishing duck soup, a soup of which any Jewish mama would approve. Then it's the messy part, the embryo. The salty, hard white meat popping out in a chunk. Yellow bits and pieces are nudged into the mouth. The bits of beak or feather are circumspectly spat to the sidewalk.

"The effort, though, is worth the prize. In this case, the prize of duck giblets and duck liver together. A fine pâté, a mildly salty sauce, a delicacy of health and vitamins and natural ingredients untainted by the hand of man."

Joel was impressed. (With such eloquence on a Manila bus, I should damned well hope so.) I hadn't realized, though, how my discourse had affected the other listeners. They listened with varying comprehension, but were fascinated that a foreign visitor should find poetic solace in a national dish.

That, I thought, was the end of the incident. But in the Philippines, anything quickly becomes the stuff of legend. Replacing eating, I could have uttered a paragraph, a word, a mere semi-colon, and if it struck the humor of the people, I would soon be immortalized. And this is exactly what happened.

A few days later, friends at the resort at which I was staying on China Beach told me that I could purchase, a mere five miles away in the town of San Fernando, about twenty-five fresh oysters for the equivalent of a dollar. This treat was too good to miss, so I jumped on an inter-city jeepney (the chugging little buses of the islands) and headed for the big city, something like Oliver Twist.

Sitting on the bus, I didn't notice that a fellow traveler was looking strangely at me and then telling others in Tagalog, the official Filipino language, something both amusing and exotic. Soon I realized that I was the amusing and exotic one, for others in the bus started looking appreciatively at me. The first storyteller approached me and said, "I was explaining to them that you were the balut eater we were gossiping about after church last night."

"Um…uh, church?" I asked. Not knowing whether I was saint or sinner, I thanked him for gossiping about me, showing all the correct appreciation. But upon disembarking in the San Fernando town square, I found that The Word had preceded me, and began to understand the religious significance soon enough.

The town square is far from the market, but is set around a massive church, and older people sitting on the steps of the church began to approach me, smiling. One touched my hand; others followed.

Next came the children, who stared at me goggle-eyed before going off to play. Much of San Fernando is out of work. (Though this is not politically correct: They are all "on standby.") So they followed me around the street, with shopkeepers coming out of their empty stores to shake my hand. I heard the word "balut" mentioned dozens of times. When I told one lady my name, the words "Harry-Balut" were spoken like a new mantra.

Mind you, everybody was courteous, even respectful. But when this Pied Piper horde of people came to a man who actually sold the balut (a rare sight, since most balut is sold by children at night), I was stopped. Would I (they queried me in mime and words) actually swallow a balut? Or maybe even a pugo, their hard-boiled quail egg?

Before I agreed, they were vying on who would pay for both eggs. But I grandly pulled out a few pesos to show how I would pay for my own.

Then, to the usual oohs and aahs, I not only ate two balut but had a couple of pugos to wash them down.

And by the time I reached Pancita, a lovely oyster merchant in the sprawling riverside market, even the market people knew of my balut prowess. Pancita insisted on giving me a discount on her oysters, but with my newly-acquired noblesse oblige, I nobly obliged her with the correct market price, strolled back to the jeepney, waved to my followers, and took oysters, gin, and myself back to China Beach for a grand feast that night.

The moral? For myself, I had experienced the Warhol equivalent of fifteen minutes of fame, and didn't mind it at all. For the citizens of San Fernando, happiness comes from the tiniest events. Putting us together with a balut, one never can feel even a duckish down-in-the-mouth. For hope, as Ms. Dickinson said in an America once as innocent as the Philippines, is indeed a thing with feathers.

Spice Chronicles: *Exotic Tales of a Hungry Traveler*

Recipe:
Pearl's Affritada

This delectable rarity is the gift of a Luzon friend married to a noted New York State editor, Carl Strock. He and I once edited Asian Golf Digest, although neither of us knew a bogey from a caddie. Anyway, much thanks to both, for cuisine and friendship.

    8 ea. chicken legs and thighs
    8 potatoes, cut into quarters
    3 red bell peppers, cut into strips
    2 med. onions, cut into quarters, lengthwise
    3 cloves garlic, crushed
    2 cans (15 oz.) tomato sauce
    2 tbsp. Canola oil
    2 tsp. sherry wine
    2 bay leaves
    2 bay leaves
    Salt and pepper to taste

1. Heat the oil in a large cooking pan. Add garlic and onion and fry until the onion is transparent.
2. Add chicken and cook for 10 minutes.
3. Add tomato sauce, bay leaves, salt, and pepper.
4. Cover and cook another 10 minutes.
5. Add potatoes and red peppers and cook until the potatoes go soft. Serve with steamed rice.

Chapter Thirty-Three

"Malone Dines" by Samuel Bake-It
Recipe: Mocha Tart

As always in the Philippines, the slightest task turns into a Herculean labor. Typical is the domestic airport where hundreds of signs point to over seven thousand islands. All the signs are handwritten, scribbled, erased, written again, scrawled out, sometimes even legible. One poster, though, is not handwritten at all. In letters that seem to have been carved out by twelfth-century monks, illuminated, beautifully engraved upon an expensive oaken board, are the words: "We regret that our computers are temporarily out of order." Art is not yet dead.

Samuel Becket never came here, since he rarely ventured a few feet from Paris, Dublin, or the world of his own mind. Had he ventured to the Philippines, he might have written "Malone Dines."

While shopping in the Spanish-style town of Vigan in the northern Philippines, I am encouraged to write the Northern Filipino Novel, which I name "Malone Dines." The novel is quite long, but it involves a single incident. Here is a brief summary of that one incident.

The protagonist, who was baptized Malone, is in the town of Vigan and his sweet tooth is bothering him. He loves sweets of every kind, from stirred fudge to Vermont maple syrup to manufactured Hershey bars, Three Musketeers, and birthday cake icing.

In this case, he has strolled past a bakery in Vigan called The Vigan Bakery. His eyes are attracted to a handwritten sign in the bakery. Penned in blue ballpoint ink, it reads: "Delecius Cake! Bun! Cookie! All flavors good!"

Below this is another handwritten sign, this in red ballpoint ink. It reads: "Wanted Another (attractive) Girl Counter."

Speculating that the management wishes to employ a person who would tally up attractive women, for reason or reasons unknown, Malone instead is attracted by the pastries advertised therein.

More than a little hungry, his sweet tooth now raging for sustenance, Malone parts the bamboo strips that serve as a door and spots an appealing box under the title "Creamy Raisin Cookies." This is in a glass case. He waits ten minutes while the lady who apparently runs the shop chats with a friend. Malone is happy to wait, since the aromas of the pastries waft him into a dream land. And this is the Philippines, where the tempo of life is the tempo of a long, sleepy, happy dream.

Then the lady turns and sees Malone. She smiles that wide and shy and nougat-sweet smile of the island of Luzon and calls over an "(attractive) girl person counter" to help him. The (attractive) counter person is about fifteen years old. The older woman disappears and will not come back again. She will have gone to the hairdresser to look even more beautiful.

The (attractive) counter person has eyes the size of peppermint patties and teeth like stalks of laughing vanilla. She is carrying her baby brother, and she puts him in a corner, where he continues sleeping.

"What do you want, sirrr?" she asks. This sounds abrupt, but her first language is Tagalog and she is now facing a person from another country. She is attempting to communicate with the few words she knows from the other country, but the word "sirrr" is given a typical Tagalog burr.

Malone smiles sweetly himself, although his face is like fudge that has been melting in the sun and his mouth resembles brown coconut skin with flecks of white.

"A creamy raisin cookie, please."

"Do you want a cookie?" asks the (attractive) counter person.

"Yes, please," beams Malone. "Or, to be more specific, one creamy raisin cookie. The creamy raisin cookie in the glass case."

"Oh," beams the girl counter person. "What kind of cookie do you want, sirrr?"

"A creamy raisin cookie," says Malone. "Only one, please."

"All right, sirrr. How many cookies do you want?"

"A single cookie. One cookie."

"Thank you, sirrr," laughs the (attractive) counter person. "Would you like a creamy raisin cookie?"

Now, to continue this syrupy colloquy would try the patience of a Trappist monk. But it persists for about twenty minutes. When the (attractive) counter person grasps the need – oh hell, the desire, the obsession, the passion – for a single creamy raisin cookie – she reacts with alacrity. Or, to be more precise, she reacts slowly and languorously.

She must find, first, the key to the glass case wherein the cookies reside. Cautiously, she opens up some drawers in a corner of the room. She carefully moves her baby brother, because the key might be under his blanket. But it is not there. Then she has an idea. She goes to the back of the bakery and looks under a pile of tee-shirts neatly piled in a corner. The key is here, and she returns with that laughing vanilla smile to the front.

Now, with a gesture she has practiced for months, she dexterously slips the key into the lock and opens it. The hinges make a rusty squeal of surprise, but the cookies are clean and fresh. She looks for and finds a cookie and pulls it out from the box. The cookie is a coconut ginger cookie. She offers it to Malone. She is not jubilant. She is modest about her actions. So the coconut ginger cookie rests in her hand, a prize of war in a crinkled brown piece of paper. And she holds the cookie out to Malone.

Malone, though, realizes that a mistake has been made. Ordinarily, he would politely seize upon the erroneous coconut ginger cookie. But in this case, he has his heart set on a creamy raisin cookie. He points the correct box out to the girl. Shyly, the (attractive) girl admits her error with momentarily sad eyes. She returns the coconut ginger cookie back to the glass case prudently. Or, in this case, gingerly.

The coconut ginger cookie has been lying, actually half-wrapped, on and in the delicate brown paper. It is certainly a sanitary disc, and Malone imagines the creamy raisin cookie will be produced from the same kind of paper.

But at this point the story takes a dramatic pretzel-like twist, with a quiet confession from the girl.

"Sirrr," she says to Malone, "I am so sorry. There is no paper to put the creamy raisin cookie on."

A charitable grammarian, as well as a famished one, Malone ignores the preposition ending the statement. He motions that he will accept the cookie in any form.

"From your dainty fingers," he says, his words forming a Walter Raleigh cloak above her hand. "I will be delighted to caress this gift directly from your waving palm."

She, however, must follow the rules of the Philippines Department of Health.

"No," she replies. "No…that will not be possible. I will make a paper."

Some twenty-five minutes later, Malone is standing before the glass case. His feelings are spread out like sweet tarts in a bakery. On the lowest shelf, he is naturally hungry, although he has had lunch. This, though, is intended to be his dessert. Higher, he is a wee bit disturbed that a single transaction, which is still not completed, can take such a long time. Yet his feelings are hardly disapproving. After all, he has nothing else to do in Vigan, and if the transaction is even vaguely efficient, he will have something to do in Vigan.

His alternative had been to sit in the park, reading. Or perhaps wander up to Vigan's eighteenth-century bulbous cathedral, which will be locked anyhow, since the priest is visiting his sister in a nearby town and will not be back before midnight Mass later that week. So waiting for his cookie is actually a refreshing way to spend an afternoon. Not an oppressive burden at all.

The (attractive) girl now walks out from a back room. She is unable to find a sheet of cookie paper. But she has found a page from a newspaper. She takes a pair of scissors, cuts it, and brushes off remnants of cookie flour. Looking more closely, she realizes that newspaper is not suitable for her visitor. Instead, she deftly cuts a square of cardboard from an empty carton of cookies. She brings this square to the outer room. Here, she removes the creamy raisin cookie from its original casket in the glass case. She places it upon the cardboard square and submits it to Malone. Malone takes the square with the cookie, which has been placed in the heart of the square.

At this point, Malone considers the enjoyment of popping the cookie into his mouth, wolfishly crunching it, gulping down the residue of the cookie and patting his stomach with a yum-yum-yum, his usual noises of appreciation.

But that would hardly be dignified after forty-five minutes of waiting. Instead, Malone takes his creamy raisin cookie from the girl with dignity. He looks at it, smiles, slowly lifts his hand to face the (attractive) girl, whispers a soundless "thank you," and quietly takes a bite. He chews it, smiles at her, and wipes a single crumb from his chin. She smiles at him. Then he takes another bite.

At this point, half of the cookie sits on the cardboard. Malone is ashamed to eat it. She is poor, and Malone, being a foreigner, obviously has more money. Thus, he offers the cookie to her. Would she like the remainder of the cookie? She smiles and shakes her head. Would her baby brother still sleeping in the corner like part of the cookie? She repeats the smile and shakes her head. Her baby brother is taking his afternoon nap, and she will not wake him.

Malone finishes the cookie half and her eyes look at him in appreciation at his (Malone's) own appreciation.

It is time for payment. A paper is handwritten in the glass. It says: "Cookie: One peso."

This is about one American nickel, which is certainly reasonable. Malone, though, does not have a one-peso note. Instead, he takes out a five-peso note and offers it to the girl.

Now the smile on the girl turns first into a frown and then into something approaching consternation, since these large notes are not easy to change. In fact, while she has one key that fits the glass case where the cookies are kept, she was never given the key to the drawer that holds the money. The woman who is having her hair done has the only key. Not only is the cash register locked and the key gone, but even inside they know that four pesos of change is not available, since The Vigan Bakery has had no business that day.

"Please, sirrr," offers the (attractive) girl tentatively, "please, because I don't have four pesos. Why don't you eat four more creamy raisin cookies?"

Malone does not have a watch, but the sun is now falling (along with his hopes), so he agrees. He will buy four more creamy raisin cookies.

"Thank you, sirrr," says the girl-person. "Would you like creamy raisin cookies?"

Malone sighs. Yes, he would certainly enjoy four more creamy raisin cookies. She apologizes that she has no paper on which to place them. But if he will wait a minute, she will go to the back room. There she will find the suitable paper or cardboard. Malone excuses her. He meditates upon his situation, and is inspired to write a drama about his condition. The Vigan Condition. The Human Condition. He takes out a pen and begins to write…"Waiting For Oreo"….

Spice Chronicles: *Exotic Tales of a Hungry Traveler*

Recipe:
Mocha Tart

Any cookie shop would sacrifice all their goods and chattels for this delicious recipe. It was developed not in the Philippines but at the Melitta Coffee Company in Germany, for my Complete Book of Coffee, commissioned by that company.

Sponge

    4 egg yolks
    5½ oz. sugar
    4 egg whites
    3½ oz. flour
    1 oz. cornstarch
    1 tsp. baking powder
    1 oz. vanilla sugar
    2-3 tsp. warm water
    2 tbsp. fresh-brewed coffee

1. Whip the egg yolks and water, add 3-1/2 oz. sugar and vanilla sugar, and beat until foaming.
2. Beat the egg whites and 1-3/4 oz. sugar until stiff.
3. Bring yolks and whites together, fold in remaining sponge ingredients, and mix well.
4. Line a baking tin with baking paper, add the mixture, and bake in an oven preheated to 200 degrees for about 40 minutes.
5. Take out of the tin and leave to cool, ready for the filling.

Filling

    9 oz. butter
    7 oz. dark chocolate
    5 egg yolks
    5½ oz. icing sugar
    2 glasses brandy
    2 tbsp. strong filtered coffee
    1 bag mocha beans

1. Whip the butter until creamy.
2. Melt the chocolate in a double boiler, add egg yolks, sugar, and coffee.
3. Blend well and leave to cool.
4. Add butter and mix well, folding in the brandy, then set a small amount aside.

Final Preparation

1. Slice the sponge into 3 layers of equal thickness.
2. Spread filling thickly on first layer, add second layer and repeat, then add third layer.
3. Decorate top with remaining filling and several mocha beans.
4. Decorate the side with 1 tbsp. coffee powder.

Chapter Thirty-Four

Cannibalism II: The Secular Experience
Recipe: Kokoda

Some chapters ago, I offered a taste of cannibalism in the desert. That, I believed, was my first and last encounter with the subject. But cannibalism seemed to dog me, and two more brushes became part of my life.

One was purely literary. At a street-market in Pnom Phen, I picked up two remarkable items. One was a First Edition of a rare work by the Hungarian composer Belá Bartók, a transcription he had made of sonatas by Scarlatti. That cost me a dollar. The other was an English translation of essays by Montaigne, one of which dealt with cannibalism. For the sixteenth century, that was astounding, but equally so were his sympathies. One quote from an extremely long detailed interview he had with a cannibal will suffice.

"I think there is nothing barbarous and savage in that nation, from what I have been told, except that each man calls barbarism whatever is not his own. There is always the perfect religion, the perfect government, the perfect and accomplished manners in all things. Those people are wild, just as we call wild the fruits that Nature has produced by herself and in her normal course; where really it is those that we have changed artificially, led astray from the common order, that we should rather call wild. The former retain vigorous properties, which we have debased to gratify our corrupted taste. Yet the delicacy of uncultivated fruits from these countries is quite as excellent. 'All things,' says Plato, 'are produced by nature, by fortune, or by art; the greatest and most beautiful by one or the other of the first two, the least and most imperfect by the last.'"

My second meeting with cannibalism was a trip to Fiji, which I discovered, was the Holy Grail, the golden sterlet caviar, the Chateauneuf de Pape of anthropophagity. Nor had Fiji reckoned that I would be exploring its darker past. One of the advantages of being an all-purpose writer is that public relations folks believe they can control you, which they usually do. But when I was commissioned to fly to Fiji to write about the resorts, beaches, and golf courses, I quickly took care of that assignment and the main island to explore the famed man-eating customs of these Pacific isles.

The first thing I learned was that when one takes lunch in Fiji, it is a serious breach of etiquette to tell cannibal jokes. As devoted members of the Commonwealth and as faithful Methodists, Fijians shy away from their people-eating past.

Until recently ("recently" being relative, as you will see), Fijians were the most feared cannibals in the South Seas. First, they were feared for their well-deserved ferocity, which can still be perceived at rugby tournaments. Second, this ferocity was teamed up with enthusiasm. For among the international cannibal community, they were the only people who actually loved the taste of a good man – or woman.

The wimps of the cannibal world – Nigeria, Colombia, Brazil, New Guinea, disappearing Bedu tribes (see aforesaid story) – would "ingest the spirit" or "please the gods" or "sacrifice for future prosperity." They simply refuse to accept human flesh on its own terms.

The Fijians weren't cannibal wimps. They were gourmets.

Fijians themselves are reserved about their past. Gaggles of Anglican and Methodist missionaries have taught them that eating people was a very bad thing. Today's Fijians go to church and play sports and remind you that they are the only people who celebrate Prince Charles's birthday as a national holiday.

"And talking of the Prince of Wales," I told an Australian hotel manager near the chaotic sailor-ridden capital, Suva, "Herman Melville used to sail around these places. In fact, Moby Dick was set near Fiji. I bet I can find quite a few prints of whales in the archives."

"Not in Suva," he said. "Suva is the new capital, only a century old. This is the place for tourists. If you want history, you go to Levuka island. Levuka was the traditional capital until 1880. That's where the whales were and still are. That's where the archives are. And the cannibals, too."

"Cannibals? That was last century, right?"

I had been avoiding the subject of cannibals, since my assignment in Fiji had been to do travel pieces for mild, middle-class magazines. But the Aussie assured me that, once you get Fijians talking outside of church, they aren't so reticent about their past.

"Take a trip to Levuka," he said. "Talk to the mayor. He's actually half-American, but his feelings are Fijian. He'll tell you stories…"

Two days later, I was on a motorboat to Levuka. And yes, on the way, through the sprays, I saw my first pod of whales in the wild. So rare today, so plentiful when the seas were swarming with harpooning ships from around the world.

Herman Melville isn't buried in Levuka, but the headstones in the cemetery tell many a tale about unfortunate whalers of the time. One had been "slaughtered in the Great Massacre." Others had "unfortunate deaths and their bodies never discovered."

All of these epitaphs, I learned later, were euphemisms for cannibalism.

When I visited, Levuka consisted of a single beach main street, with a Japanese cannery on one side, the cemetery, a few clapboard houses, and mostly empty shops. It is also eerily quiet. What one sees above all – literally – are the hills beyond the town. Behind these towns lived the most ferocious cannibals in Fiji's history.

The seventy-five-year-old mayor was an exception to the ghost town atmosphere. An ebullient man whose grandfather had come from Michigan during our civil war, he went into the cotton trade, though later went broke during the South Sea Bubble.

"He began planting cotton here, right on this spot," said the mayor. "Then he died. Killed. By them." He pointed to the hills.

"And ate him, I suppose," I said indiscreetly.

"Yes," he sighed. "My grandmother tried to save him by burying him on one of the outlying islands. But they loved white meat and they came after him in their log boats. They dug up his body and devoured him."

Toward the back of Levuka was an old barn with the "archives." The place was filled with hornets and scurrying with rats, but I managed to get an old monograph, which gave the history of Charlie Savage, a nineteenth-century brigand. He had come off a ship in 1808, introducing firearms to the Levukans. He also killed whenever he wanted to, like an old gunslinger. Apparently, he murdered hundreds with his companions who were "profligate and reckless, their depravity amazing even to the Fijian natives." So said this old pamphlet.

Charlie Savage got his inevitable reward, of course. The mayor explained it more graphically than the official story.

"They loved the meat, they did. Usually when Fijians killed, they waited until the bodies were clubbed to death. Then they would patiently take the meat and throw it into the fire and wait until it was roasted.

"But Charles Savage was different. He was seized and made to dig his own roasting hole. His veins were cut, the blood ran down, and the Fijians lapped up his blood. Fishhooks were put into his tongue; his arms and legs were torn off and roasted. The meat was scorched over a fire; the hair and skin were scraped off with shells. These bivalve shells right here on the beach.

"The bones were put to use as well. You know how we drink kava? Well, they ground up his bones and mixed them with the kava root.

"From behind the hills, where they came from, older people still say that kava doesn't really taste delicious until you have bones mixed in it.

"But I personally don't know about those things."

"Oh," he finished. "Savage had taught them how to make fishing nets. So then, as a sign of…I don't know, maybe respect, they used his finger bones as needles. I've never seen them, but I heard they were used."

That was the last I saw of the mayor, who obviously relished the story. Fijians always relish a good story.

Fiji was always known as the Cannibal Islands. The stalwart Captain James Cook gave them that name in 1773, and he studiously avoided the islands. He was not only a great seaman, he was very prudent. Later, when Fijians had momentary control of the nearby island of Tonga, they tried to persuade the Tonganese how good human flesh was, but in Tonga they resisted this treat, and have never indulged.

At the Fiji Museum in Suva, all the lithographs and household goods have captions in Fijian and English. But the cannibal section – daguerreotypes of slaughtered missionaries, cooking pots, throwing clubs – have no Fijian explanation at all.

Later, on the island of Taveuni, I asked a New Zealand sugar planter if this was out of embarrassment.

"In theory, yes," he said. "But the people who work for me are hardly shy about their past, and they can give actual recipes of the old days. Now you write about food, so you might be interested, though I must tell you that Fijians are Christians and they don't eat humans anymore."

"Come on," I insisted. "Let's have the recipe."

"Okay, now my theory is that the Fijians loved meat because they had no indigenous animals on the land. So they were very careful in their preparations.

"When they clubbed the victims – sometimes sailors, sometimes tribes from a different island, because they were always invading each other – they tried not to kill them. To keep them fresh. Then they would dig these pits where today they roast pigs. The pits would always be slow-burning with wood.

"Now if they had time, they would skin the victims. But according to one of my workers, the old women simply couldn't wait, and they would dig in and eat the flesh raw. They were allowed to because of respect for age.

"After that, they had two methods. One was the quick-grill method. They would chop up the bodies and put them in clay cooking pots and stick them on the log fire. Here, I'll show you. I have some of these pots in my garden…

"But the real gourmets, the big chiefs who had plenty of meat, took the bodies and wrapped them in taro leaves. Then they would leave them to slow-burn in the pits. It took about eight hours, and they would sit and drink kava until sundown and then have the big meal."

Several days later, I had taken a dinghy to another of Fiji's three hundred-odd islands, where I was invited to a kava session that night. Kava, by the way, has all the punch, pungency, and efficacy of mild novocaine. After an hour you might feel a bit of tingling in the gums, but little else.

What it does, though, is open up the memories for endless talk. All night they drink and talk, so I asked the head guy, the one who filled up the cup from the barrel, about whether his grandparents had indulged in anthropophagy. This was about twenty years ago, and the headman was about seventy then, and he had asked me not to tell people, but it's probably okay now.

"Hey," he said in almost Filipino English, "it don't matter what my grandfather he done. The Japs came here during the war, and first they was winning. Then the English come and the Japs start losing. And when they start losing, then the English gave us the prisoners."

"'For what?' I ask them. But they don't say nothin'. They just leave the Japs with us. So we sit down with 'em, maybe six or seven of 'em, and they sit there grinnin' at us. And I don't speak Japanese, but I hear 'em talk about the crazy Fiji people and laughin' at us crazy Fiji people.

"So then we lock the door and go out and have some kava and come back, and I take out my knife and tell this little tiny Jap to take down his trousers, which he does, and I quick slit down his leg with my knife and he faints, and the others, I think, they gonna throw up.

"So then I take a piece of that leg and let the blood run out, and my friend and me, we eat it. Didn't taste of nothin'. We just decide to do it. Not for any reason, just 'cause we didn't like them Japs sayin' we're crazy people."

The others were nodding at the story, whispering to each other so I wouldn't hear.

"What happened to the other prisoners?" I asked.

The head guy doesn't bother to answer. He just laughs and fills my kava bowl and then his own, and for some reason he gets on to the subject of the tall buildings in New York. Kava does that sort of thing.

I returned to Taveuni and told the story to the Kiwi, feeling part Robert Louis Stevenson, part James Beard.

"Look," I said, "everybody likes the Fijians. They're smart, savvy, they love a good time, they're great sportsmen. Is all this cannibal stuff history? Bull?"

We were standing by those cooking pots in his flower-filled garden, and he wasn't sure of the answer.

"Look, it's hard to say the truth. But we show video cassettes here at night. And last week I put on that movie called Alive, where these kids in a plane crash in the Andes eat each other to survive.

"Well, the planters here were shocked, really shocked. Then they asked me to repeat the film the next night. Just to express how really shocked they were. I guess I've shown it about six times. Each time, the planters bring their families and say how upset they are at that scene."

The New Zealander walked me back to his verandah. "I honestly believe they were shocked," he said. "I feel perfectly safe in Fiji."

We gazed at Taveuni's silver waters lapping at his garden, and at that moment I honestly believed him.

Recipe: Kokoda

Fear not, Kokoda is not what the preceding piece would imply. In fact, it was my very first dish in Fiji. This is actually Fijian sashimi: raw fish which is tart, juicy, and – if not kept too long – one of the most delicious plates imaginable. (Kept in the fridge for 24 hours, it coagulates.)

> 4 large pieces fresh white fish, filleted
> 3 large limes
> 1 c. fresh coconut cream
> (canned coconut cream simply won't do)
> 1 large Vidalia onion
> Minced chili or other hot sauce
> 2 medium tomatoes
> One bell pepper minced
> Salt and pepper

1. Cut the fish into bite-size pieces.
2. Take the limes and salt and make a marinade. Dunk the fish into the marinade and leave it overnight. The lime will actually chemically work on the fish to give it a kind of "cold cooking."
3. Before serving, add the coconut cream and chopped onion with as much chili as your guests would like. (It will be rather sour anyway.)
4. Put this into a large bowl with the tomatoes and bell pepper for decoration. It should serve 6-8 people.

Chapter Thirty-Five

Miss Emily Dickinson: "The KFC Poems"
Recipe:
Fruit Compote

The problem with visitors abroad is that they inevitably (and understandably) compare everything to their homeland instead of trying to exist, even momentarily, in this bubble called Foreign Land. Korea was the exception. It was such a mythical experience, such a universe, which wasn't even parallel but simply lopsided, that New York, America, everything Western, simply evaporated.

The shock came when we arrived back by train from Pyongyang to Beijing—and it was Thanksgiving Day!!! Yes, a shock, and I decided to immerse myself in that shock by going to an All-American Thanksigivng Day Dinner at the All-American Beijing Hilton Hotel.

That night, rather than napkin scribbles, I dreamed the following.

In the year 1867, three gentlemen visiting Amherst, Massachusetts, approached the neat stately house of a reclusive lady and gingerly knocked at her neat wooden door. At first she refused to answer, but as they insisted, she peered out of her shuttered windows and asked them their station in life.

"We are," said the eldest gentleman, "representing the most esteemed company known as KFC."

The reclusive lady was puzzled for a moment, but asked their purpose.

"We have heard," said this gentleman, "that you are a most productive and inspired writer, and we wish you to pen some verses for KFC to inspire the world."

The reclusive lady, dressed in white, had a revelation (as was her wont). The gentlemen, whose demeanor and dialect were obviously from the Deep South, were perhaps not as schooled as they should be. KFC, thus, probably meant, in their patois, "Kwayker Friends Cooperative," and the lady did have sympathy for their cause, so she immediately agreed, after which she penned some quatrains extolling peace and the quiet life.

Only later did she realize that her poetry had not satisfied the gentlemen, that they wished some verses about poultry, not pacifism. She sighed, but keeping to her promise, penned the following verses, which were recently discovered in a barn outside Amherst, Massachusetts:

A Pentameter of Poems
By One Who is Too Modest to Sign Her Name
(albeit with the pinch of a hint in the last line)

I.
Quail is a thing with feathers.
But I keep it under glass.
It would fly upon the heathers
So I give it the coup de grâce.
A design for toasting my wholewheat bread
Upon which mustard is spread.
Finally my quail, to its fate is wed
To lie upon its nuptial bed.
The world too is bound with dreams unfulfilled.
With day-old yeast never raising.
Let us make our home on a (four-burner) range,
Where hopes, like feathers, are braising.

II.
Because I could not stop, my breath
Had smelled of garlic, so I feared
That all who met me thought of death.
But I had thought of blue cheese shmeered
Upon croissants, upon a roll,
Upon a light and fluffy loaf,
As on my tongue, so in my soul,
So in this ill-bread strophe.

III.
A recipe unwritten
With ingredients unseen
With guests who are unbidden
Sipping Ovaltine.

An uneaten strawberry sundae,
A poppy-cake unseeded,
"Dona eis peccata mundi,"
Says the Father, words unheeded.
Yet 'tis written in my verse
That I'm unheeded too.
Like the bite of chocolate in my purse,
I bid thee sweet adieu.

IV.
Remember the quail? Grilled and basted
Covered with sauce that was canned.
Like life, he was prepared, then tasted,
Flying away, like a bird in the hand.

V.
Inside an egg, I am inside a womb,
Peckings for birth swiftly quicken.
Unheeded I enter the sisterhood's room:
Mis-gendered on earth: Family Chícken's Son.

Recipe:
Fruit Compote

I have little doubt that Ms. Dickinson would have enjoyed this fruity recipe, especially with local maple syrup taken from the trees around her Amherst home. This recipe is taken from a book, the mid-nineteenth-century Handbook of Practical Cookery for Ladies and Profe‑‑‑‑‑‑‑¹ Cooks. Nothing of the original delightful wordage has been chan

    1 pt. basket small or medium-sized ripe strawberries
    1 pt. fresh raspberries
    1 c. maple syrup
    1 c. redcurrant jelly
    Green leaves for garnish

1. Quickly wash the strawberries under running tepid water in a colander. Move your spread-out fingers above them so the water does not hit the berries but dribbles through your fingers.
2. Gently pat the side of the colander and spread the berries on a kitchen towel.
3. Repeat the same procedure with the raspberries, drying them as gently as possible to avoid bruising them.
4. Hull all the strawberries except 1 or 2 that have the greenest top parts and the longest, freshest stems. Set these aside for decoration.
5. Arrange the berries on a serving dish and chill.

Chapter Thirty-Six

Babani's Pants and the Conversion of Saint Paul
Recipe:
The Trousers of the Sheikh

I was not surprised to discover a Burmese restaurant a few blocks from my Greenwich Village East home in New York. Nor is it awesome that a tiny coffee shop I had passed, walking with my dog dozens of times, turns out to be a café with seriously delicious Syrian and Moroccan food. The fact that the most delicious filo pastry I have ever had comes from an Afghan restaurant in New York's theatre district, seems par for the course. Nor is it more than worth a yawn that the best south Thai curry I've ever had is in the borough of Queens.

This all seems appropriate. Returning to my native land after several decades abroad, I discovered that Americans were as aware of World Food the way they had embraced World Music.

True, most of the food is based for American tastes. But that is only natural.

I once dined with a famous ethnic-food writer here, who took perverse pride that he had never been to the countries about which he was writing. "I write for New Yorkers," he said. "If I knew what was authentic, I'd lose my job."

And in that Burmese restaurant, I took an expert on that cuisine, who asked that a certain dish be prepared with the style of the country. They took it from the kitchen, and I asked how I could get the same dish next time.

"It is simple," said the manager. "Ask to have your dish Burmese style."

That is part of the fun of dining in New York. But when I came upon a restaurant serving Kurdish food in the heartland of America, in St. Paul, Minnesotta…well, at that point, I realized how America really had changed its tastes and style.

Back in New York, I feared to tell friends about my find, since everybody in Manhattan is an expert. In fact, the only time I left a crowd of New Yorkers dumbfounded was a particularly innocent comment I made at a dinner party. There had been a lull in the conversation between a heated discussion about steak Tartare ("But would Genghis Khan have even recognized it at La Vendome?") and the best place to get a good slice of Nova salmon ("Certainly not Nova Scotia!" they laughed.).

So in that eating entr'acte, while the cubes tinkled in the Chivas Regal, I broke the ice.

"I guess one thing we'd all have to admit," I said, "is that Rodwan Nakshabandi is the best darned Kurdish chef in the whole friggin' state of Minnesota."

The silence was an abyss as deep as the Grand Canyon. I hadn't realized that New Yorkers enjoy arguing, but they hate to be faced with a fact about which they have no knowledge. So I continued, "Did you know that if you peel an eggplant and cut it up into strips and add some lemon, it resembles a pair of striped Kurdish trousers?"

And that, as I learned, is how to end a party. In four seconds, the room was as empty as nighttime in a village nestling in the arid mountains of Kurdistan itself.

I'm not saying that expressing opinions in New York about Kurdish cooking in Minnesota is the best way to empty a dinner party quickly. But it's certainly an option. The room soon clears, and within forty-eight hours a flyer is pushed through your door asking if you'd like to stay for a while at Father Damien's leper colony.

Two truths, though, which not even New Yorkers know. One is that the Kurds really do have a cuisine all their own, as well as vast areas, tough people, and a history that predates the Bible. Second is that Minnesota, wet, foggy, literate and lake-filled, is the opposite of Kurdistan, which is hot, sparse, mountainous, and Spartan.

The fact that the Kurds live in Minnesota is just part of the perversity of this very perverse people. And discovering them there brought back memories of my own from Kurdistan.

I had been in eastern Turkey, engaged in the filthy pastime of hitchhiking. It was filthy, because the only traffic on the roads consisted of (a) Turkish army jeeps moving down the road in order to blow up Kurdish villages, (b) Kurdish trucks moving down the road to smuggle guns into Iraq to blow up Turkish villages across the border, and (c) trucks carrying sheep. Choosing the latter was safe, but standing all day and all night among sheep bound for slaughter under the fierce Turkish sun was not exactly a holiday.

And then the mind drifted to a journey many years ago in eastern Turkey, to the stronghold of Kurdish society in Diyarbakir. I had been impressed with Kurdish strength, humor, and guts in the face of almost universal animosity. Since biblical times, Kurds had been reviled by all. The Old Testament referred to them as "raiders without a home." Later, Arabs had a saying: "If you have a choice of being stung by hornets or welcomed into a Kurdish home, choose the hornets."

Kurds have never had their own homeland (partly because they argue among themselves as much as with others), but they are certainly a separate people. Their language and customs are rarely studied, but they remain fiercely independent and couldn't care less. They are like a People of the Book themselves – about eighty-five percent Moslem, twelve percent Christian, with a few Kurdish Jews thrown in for good measure – but no one has ever accepted them as countrymen.

And as possibly the strongest, hardiest people of the whole Middle East, everyone has defecated on them. The CIA gave them help in rebelling against Iraq, until the CIA became friends with Iraq and took the funding back. Saddam Hussein tried to gas them out of existence, and the Turks are still trying to destroy them.

Not that the Kurds themselves are always heroes. Their own internecine squabbles make them almost perfect victims for others. They are, in fact, the carrion on which the vultures of legitimate national countries eagerly feed.

Still, I had received hospitality from them after a week in a prison in Diyarbakir in eastern Turkey. I had hitched in on a sheep truck, sat down for some tea and cakes, when the police had approached me. I told them I was American, but they didn't believe me.

"You do not look like American," they said, and put me in a little cell where I learned to smoke cigarettes and survive. A week later I was released, left the town and stayed in a Kurdish village, where the headman, who had fought in Korea, spoke excellent English.

We played with the goats; we ate buns filled with goat cheese, and went for long walks in the hills, where I learned about Kurdish history. Mainly raiding and being raided. But the memories remained bright in my mind, even after the Turks told me that "Kurds are like what dogs extract after a meal."

Sudden segue to Minnesota, in particular, a hallucinatory sign on a restaurant in the middle of St. Paul, the capital. I had been on a triple assignment, to write about the incredible St. Paul Orchestra, to see where F. Scott Fitzgerald had lived, and possibly to get an interview with Governor Jesse Ventura for a Hungarian economics magazine.

But all of that faded into the background as I walked along St Peter Street, just a five minute walk from the capital, and – like another St. Paul – I felt a divine light shining upon me.

The light was not really divine, however. It was fluorescent. And the words were hardly biblical: they read, "Babani's Kurdish Restaurant," and they seemed far more out of place than the heavenly words felt by Paul of Tarsus on his road to Damascus.

My reaction was immediate disbelief. A Thai or Chinese restaurant, yes. But Kurdistan from the Middle East plunked down in the Midwest was hallucinatory.

The results make this one of the more enchanting restaurants in a most unlikely place.

Babani's Kurdish Restaurant does indeed sell real Kurdish food, and is the only Kurdish restaurant in the whole United States. (Some Kurds do own Turkish restaurants, but are warned not to use the name "Kurd.") I love the restaurant for two reasons, food being the second.

The first is that of a very unusual American success story. Tanya Fuad, the founder-owner of Babani's, was born in northern Iraq, part of the Babani tribe, named after Sheikh Babani, whose famous trousers later became an eggplant.

Tanya was on a trip to Liberia when I went to the restaurant. The reason she was there was typical of her personality. When she came to America in 1974 to live in Minnesota, where she had a few relatives, she studied agricultural engineering and joined the Peace Corps. After training, she was sent to Samoyea, a village in Liberia, and she returns every few years to check on its progress.

Later, she joined a non-government organization and was sent to a Kurdish refugee camp as an interpreter. It was there that, after a wonderful but simple meal, she discovered Rodwan Nakshabandi, who today is the best Kurdish chef in all of St. Paul.

"Rodwan," she told me, "could take the simplest ingredients – like the lowly cucumber – and add onions and lemons and make the most wonderful Kurdish salad. So I decided, after eating, that I would love to have a Kurdish restaurant. In St Paul, right in the American heartland.

"America had been so good to me that I decided to return the favor."

Not that she forgot about her Kurdish ancestry when her restaurant became a success. The walls here are filled with photographs she has taken on many trips back to Kurdistan. They are beautiful, grainy, tragic, disturbing, personal. The portraits of women in their homes are shadowy, dark, sometimes startling in their use of shafts of light. The pictures of village life evoke paintings by Bruegel.

Most startling of all, though, are the shots from Diyarbakir, the ancient "capital" of Turkish Kurdistan, with its thick Roman-built walls going back to AD 297. She has caught them with somber magnificence.

The real sadness, though, isn't in the pictures. Tanya has written a still unpublished book about Kurdish women. She sent me a copy of a chapter, and I began to cry. It is a book of a people to be pitied, yet not a word in it asks for pity.

Especially not the cuisine, about which she is an expert. With a population of Kurds extending over seventy-nine thousand square miles, going into Iraq, Turkey, Armenia, Iran, and Syria, the food still has its own character, albeit with Turkish characteristics.

And American characteristics. Lamb, the staple of Kurdistan, has been changed to beef. "American lamb is too strong. Our lamb is sweeter," says Tanya with a rich Midwestern accent. "So we have extra-lean beef. But we still get our old herbs and spices. We have atra, a mountain herb with the aroma of thyme. We have a Syrian spice mix, which combines so many sweet-smelling spices. And, of course, black and red peppers.

"And chicory, another staple of Kurdish cuisine."

Rodwan interrupts to explain the major difference. "In Kurdistan, we used cracked rice. Nobody else does. We use it to make special dumplings, like Chinese dumplings but with many more herbs and spices."

So they make a dish called Kubay Sawar: an oblong dumpling, where the wheat is first soaked, then fried. After that, lean ground beef, walnuts, that Syrian mix and parsley, along with peppers and cardamom, are mixed together. Then boiled and served.

The result is like a texture of phyllo pastry, smooth and thin.

The aforesaid Sheikh Babani starts with eggplant, which is cored and peeled in decorative stripes. Around the stripes are strips of beef mixed with parsley and other spices. Sheikh Babani, one of the founders of Tanya's tribe, who wore these trousers, would have been proud – perhaps – that his pants had helped in the conversion of St. Paul to his own food.

He wouldn't have been so happy if he'd known that Babani's was now serving beer and wine, which certainly is not part of traditional Kurdish culture – though the Kurds are hardly fundamentalists.

"We drink arak," says Tanya. "It tastes like Greek ouzo, anise/licorice-tasting. I wish we had some here … but we'll stick with beer and wine."

One slight caveat for Babani's. The menu describes the Babani tribe with less than political correctness. The men, it says, "are renowned for their fierce fighting habits and their sexual prowess." The women are "kind, forgiving, and excellent cooks."

Tanya, while totally American, has no intention of changing it.

"I was sick and tired of people saying, 'Oh, you poor Kurds, I feel so sorry for you.' So I decided that – whether people liked it or not – I would show we were a real people with real traditions.

"And real home-cooked food, too."

Recipe:
The Trousers of the Sheikh

Kurdish dishes are mainly of Turkish origin (though Kurds would say the opposite was true), but this is one dish, named after a legendary Sheikh of the Babani tribe. The authentic recipe is supplied by Tanya Fuad from a recipe of her chef, Rodwan.

I offer the exact words of Ms. Fuad.

Ingredients (when no measurements, test for taste)
  3 eggplants
  Olive oil
  Lean ground beef
  Green pepper
  Red pepper
  Tomato sauce

1. Use longer eggplant (if it is not a shame to discuss such matters).
2. Stripe the eggplant in design of distinguished man's fine trousers (use your imagination for various styles).
3. Cut the pants into 2 even pieces and core them. Save the core for later use.
4. Salt and sauté cored/stripped eggplant in hot pure olive oil until it softens and looks eatable. Set aside.

5. Brown lean ground beef with salt, lots of black pepper, and red pepper to taste.
6. If you are as impractical as the Kurds, blend before stuffing into the eggplant. Set aside.
7. To make the red sauce, mince eggplant cores, green pepper, and red hot pepper together. Then sauté in pure olive oil.
8. Add tomato sauce and a flavored base. Stir on high for 10 minutes.
9. Place the stripped eggplant into the sauce and heat together before serving.

Chapter Thirty-Seven

Mozart and "The Magic Fruit"
Recipe:
Turkish Keshkul

The problem with editing a classical music magazine from Bangkok (my present position) is that nobody reads it. Outside of that, and outside of 2006 being a Mozart Bicentenary-and-a-half year, it is indeed a cushy job. But back to Mozart. The problem there is that, while his music says everything (usually in a few measures!), writers try to find something new. I decided that, since Mozart loved good sweets and good times, and good dancing and good letters to his father, that he would have loved Thailand in the mid-eighteenth century. So I penned the letters which Wolfgang would have written, had he taken that one wrong footpath in the Vienna woods…

February 30, 1766

My dearest father,

 A tale stranger than the silliest opera scenario do I have to relate now. Roaming through Schönbrunn Forest one afternoon, merrily whistling my latest string quintet, and sipping a dark chocolate with apricot, I was overcome with passion. Was it the aphrodisiac brew? Was it from a delicate crescendo in the first movement? I know not. Yet, in my delirium, dear father, when taking a wrong turn, I was delighted to arrive at a riverside resplendent with orchids and palm trees. Lo, whilst balancing a lotus seed on my tongue, a passing boatman entreated me to embark. To sweeten his imprecations, he presented me with a tiny banana, which was as rich as the low register of a clarinet. For this river was no River Styx (it was called, I later learned, the Mekhong River), nor was this a demonic rower (he was a Siamese boatman). Soon, I was transported over a vast body of water so inspiring that I immediately composed my Sea Major Symphony, and disembarked at this bustling port.

 It was quite a merry adventure, Father, so do not worry. Now I must sleep. I shall write to you in two days.

Your Wolfgang

March 3, 1766

Father,

 This morning, I was wakened and brought to the palace of a Siamese nobleman who had heard my piano performance before the Empress of Austria some years back. Thrilled to meet me, he first gave me a breakfast treat of broth made with delicate rice. But then, he unveiled for me a soft violet fruit, which I sucked ravenously, for this, the Thai mangosteen, was both sweet and juicy. (The juice did stain my Siamese garb, much to the amusement of the servants.)

Then he took my hands and led me to his kraal, filled with two-dozen of his majestic elephants. Next thing I knew, he threw me onto the back of one of these giants, and off we went on a jungle adventure. Oh, it was such a jolly experience that, even whilst bouncing on the back of this huge but kindly pachyderm, I took out my writing paper and quill, ardently inspired to jot down a few hundred bars. Alas, when I alit, my derriere sore but my heart exalted, I could hardly read the notes of my composition (such were the spirited steps of the elephant). Soon, though, my memory overcame my ragged handwriting. Thus, this afternoon I was able to produce my opus, the world's first "Minuet For Elephants."

It is a most delicious work, which incorporates the five-tone scale of the Siamese orchestra, but is in good minuet rhythm, and requires the following forces: three drums, two flutes, seven gongs, and two-dozen elephants, all of which were supplied to me by my new nobleman friend.

The elephants follow me around like they are small dogs! And I have taught them to bow, step forward, then step backward again, as if doing a real minuet in the Salzburg Palace.

And oh, last evening, the Siamese aristocrats and their ladies came to see me, accompanied by their servants carrying large flambeaux, and oh, how they laughed and clapped when they saw "my" elephants dance to this sweet music. "A sweet for a sweet for a suite," laughed my nobleman friend, offering me Thai sweets of glutinous rice topped with leaf-thin slivers of mangos.

A glorious night, dear Father.

Your happy Wolfie

March 6, 1766

Dear Father,

What a lovely few days! The children of Ayutthaya and I have been exchanging lessons!!! They teach me their own scales, which are like ours, but each note divided into three parts! Then they teach me of the pi phat orchestra with gongs, drums, even an oboe. It does sound much like the Turkish music we sometimes make in Salzburg, but has its own rhythm.

When I sang them some of my own arias, they clapped with joy and offered me, as a gift, a plate of rambutans. The hairs outside this fruit looked frightening—though not as frightening as the spears on the jackfruit. With this came a crisp rose-apple fruit. Eating together, the meat inside the joyful trilling of two sopranos singing a duet of love between themselves.

Oh, what am I saying! Anyhow, I now bid you an equally sweet good night.

Your gloriously happy and somewhat silly son,

"Mr. Woof"

March 9, 1766

Khun Paw (or Dear Father):

I am learning a little bit of Siamese, which is inspiring my composition. Also, I was treated to a Thai banquet tonight, and each food prompted musical reflections. They have a soup of vegetables called gaeng liang, which tasted like a string orchestra. (With this they served some cashews, so I was prompted to compose "A Little Nut Music" for my edible string orchestra!)

The gaeng ki is a chicken curry, the chicken as "soloist" amidst an "orchestra" of peppers, lemon grass, corianders, and other herbs and spices, all on a bed of rice. Obviously, this is a piano concerto. When the fried shrimp came sizzling in a pan, covered with a spicy sauce made of fish and garlic, I almost jumped to the bamboo ceiling with surprise. Yet it possessed the scintillating brassy flavor of a military march. I picture a well-disciplined squad of soldiers trying to march in step, yet each soldier bouncing up when swallowing his dish.

We ended with a bouquet of fresh fruits, the taste of which, dear Father, you could not imagine. It is like a majestic septet. The flute is the sweet lychee, the papaya has the mellow grace of a clarinet, the tart pineapple is like an oboe, and the mango, when not oversweet, has the lyric melody of a violin adagio. On the side was a fruit called a durian, which makes lovely tones once you learn to "play it" correctly. The durian is our gustatory bassoon. I know it sounds absurd, but perhaps in the future I will compose an opera on these delicacies.

With this repast, we drank many a tumbler of wine made of rice!!! What a wonderful invention. No music is worthy of this drink, but I was animated enough, after a few drinks, to stand up and sing each voice of the final quintet of Don Giovanni—simultaneously. (And no, I have no idea how it was done. My memory has disappeared like the waves of a pianissimo cymbal.)

Your inebriated but inanely happy,

Woozy Woofy

March 11, 1766

Dearest Father,

    As you know, I am expected to perform in Paris in a few weeks, so have given myself only three more days before leaving here. When I told this to my patron, he immediately made me a proposition.

    "Wolfgang," he said, "before you leave, we would love to have an opera from your pen. I myself am a writer of sorts. And while hardly in the class of your Lorenzo da Ponte, my poetry is well esteemed so perhaps you may turn out something."

    I told him that it would depend upon the libretto—and that I would love to write an opera like a bouquet of magic, love, the river, and Siamese dishes.

    "And what would you call this opera?" he asked.

    So I thought of my ethereal days and nights here, the architecture, my beloved elephants, the mangos and thirty-two different bananas, the sweet lychees, the tart guava, and then thought of the one fruit I loved better than all.

    "What about," I said, "an opera called 'The Coronation of Papaya'?"

    My nobleman friend said, "I'm afraid, Khun Wolfgang, that a century before you, this opera was written by Claudio Monteverdi. May I suggest, instead, that you venerate all your delicious sweet dishes, and call your opera 'The Magic Fruits'?"

    I was entranced; he began to write, I to compose, the children began to sing, and three nights later…well, you know the rest. The world believes that The Magic Fruits was premiered in Prague twenty-five years later. But you and I know that it was born in Ayutthaya.

                          Your Magical Son

March 14, 1766

Dear Father,

This is my final letter, for I have reached your shores. But last night, we performed The Magic Fruits outside, not on a stage, but on the various islands. Each scene, each act was a different island, the stage lit by great torches, the audience following us on our journey. And at the end, when all is reconciled, all at peace, it was midnight, and I had returned to the river-pier from whence I started.

Here, too, was the same mysterious boatman…and after I had made farewells to hundreds of new friends, and been given great gifts of lotuses and sweets and kisses, we rowed silently through the night, disembarking back in Schönbrunn Forest.

Now I am listening to the sparrows chirping and thinking of my Siamese parrot squawking to wake me up. I watch the branches of the pine trees shaking and think of the green bamboo trees reflected in the lagoons, quivering like gentle cello vibrations. Soon I will see you, but in my heart I—like all visitors—will remain in the Kingdom.

Your resounding-sounding sunny scion of the Siamese sun,

Woozy Woofy "Singing-For-The-Love-Of-God" Mozart

Recipe:
Turkish Keshkul

The great Viennese Sacher torte was created after Mozart's death, but he certainly knew his Turkish sweets well, and may have enjoyed this simple but delectable recipe. He could have substituted chunks of papaya for the pomengranate, might have used Thai rice and Thai coconut, and could have replaced the clotted cream with coconut cream.

1 c. sugar
2 c. single cream
1 c. ground sweet almonds
1/2 c. pomegranates
1/4 c. pine kernels
2 c. milk
2 tbsp. ground rice
1/2 c. grated fresh coconut
1/8 tbsp. salt
1-1/2 c. clotted cream

1. Pour 1 c. cream over half the ground almonds, stir, pass through a sieve, and then put aside.
2. Boil the rest of the cream with the milk, add salt, and stir frequently so the cream doesn't stick.
3. Mix the ground rice with a little milk and pour into the saucepan. Boil gently for 5 minutes, stirring constantly.
4. Add sugar and the sieved cream-almond mixture and boil until thick.

5. Remove from the heat and pour into a wetted tube mold, chilling for 2 hours.
6. Now take this from the mold and fill center with the rest of the almonds, mixed with coconut and pine kernels, and top with   fruit.
7. Sprinkle with icing sugar and finish off with cream.

Chapter Thirty-Eight

L'envoi: How Do I Love Thee?"
Recipe:
Tea with Lavender
Attributed to Elizabeth Barrett Brewing

How do I drink thee? Let me count the ways.
I drink thee for the soft caressing touch
On which my tongue delights. Yet oh so much
That time itself improves thy fine bouquets.
The memories of lemony nights and days
Are pure solace; if by myself, a toast
Cheers silent lover, confidant, and host.
With friends, small rooms are blossom-filled cafes.
With lavender, the world and history are unconfined:
To Hangzhou isles, from cups of azure-blue,
Where Mandarin sages sat and supped and wined,
Inhaling flowers, admiring thy flaxen hue,
So sweet, so tart, with scents so interlaced
That every element embraces one exquisite taste.

Recipe:
Tea with Lavender

This was given me by a chef from Louisville, Kentucky, who produced perhaps the first recipe ever made in Louisville without using Kentucky Bourbon. No statue has been erected to her yet in that lovely town.

    1 gal. spring water
    ¼ c. lavender buds
    2½ c. of sugar
    2 c. freshly squeezed lemon juice

1. Boil about 4 c. of the water.
2. Pour over the lavender buds, stir in the sugar, and allow to dissolve.
3. Cool completely.
4. Add the rest of the water and lemon juice. Strain into a pitcher. Keep chilled.
5. Sit in an Edwardian garden and sip your tea while your spaniel raises his snout to sniff the wisteria trees, and bluebirds flutter above your head.

Recipe Index

Abruzzo: Pizza rustica . . .

Albania: Patellxhane . . .

Beijing: Peking duck . . .

Burma: Ginger mixture . . .

China: Congee . . .

Egypt: Labna . . .

England (Merrie olde): Venison stew . . .

Fertile Crescent: Baklava . . .

Fiji: Kokodo . . .

Germany: Glazed peaches and coffee . . .

Germany: Mocha tart . . .

Greece: Selinosalata . . .

Guangdong: Hung Yan Dou Fu–Almond-Flavored Bean Curd . .

Inner Mongolia/Baltimore: Lamb in the Forbidden City . . .

Italy: Peppers stuffed with pasta . . .

Japan: Raw eggplant salad . . .

Java: Ayam rica rica . . .

Kentucky: Blasted brownies . . .

Kurdistan: Babani's trousers . . .

Laos: Kai yang – Laotian grilled chicken . . .

Macao: Prawn pie . . .

Malaysia: Satay . . .

Malaysia: Terengganu laksa . . .

Mauritius: Fried wasp grub . . .

Mauritius: Octopus vindaye . . .

New England: Cold compote . . .

New Orleans: Sweet potato buns . . .

North Korea: Kimchi . . .

Pattaya: Seafood soup . . .

Pennsylvania: Greens and beans . . .

Philippines: Pearl's affitrada . . .

Poochville: Smaller collar diet bone . . .

Russia: Caviar . . .

Sarawak: Spicy stuffed eggplant . . .

Scotland: Honey mead . . .

Sicily: Cassata gelata alla Siciliana . . .

South Carolina: Lobster with Vidalia onions . . .

South China: Almond-flavored "bean curd" . . .

Spain: Spanish omelet . . .

Spanielia: Howl wheat . . .

Sumatra: Rendang beef . . .

Thailand: Jungle curries . . .

Thailand: Mee grob . . .

Turkey: Chocolate marshmallow . . .

United Kingdom: Tea with lavender . . .

Yemen: Farouk's bamia . . .